"Brendan Byrne's commentary on Mark is a wonderfully lucid, succinct, and well-written study of the second gospel. Its approach is theological and contemporary, yet without shirking the difficult exegetical questions of the ancient text. The writer is one of those rare people who, while being an experienced scholar and theologian, knows how to communicate that scholarship in a lively and engaging way to those outside the academic world. This is a beautiful and useful book: for clergy, for preachers and teachers, and for all who are concerned with the meaning of the Bible today."

Revd. Dr. Dorothy Lee
Frank Woods Distinguished Lecturer in Biblical Studies
Trinity College
Melbourne, Australia

"Brendan Byrne's presentation of the Gospel of Mark brings to a close a series on the Synoptic Gospels that has generated a literary form in itself. In all three volumes Byrne has achieved a remarkable marriage between a serious and accurate reading of the text, highlighted by a close familiarity with contemporary scholarship. But this reading never moves away from the impact the message of each gospel can make upon contemporary Christians. In *A Costly Freedom* the difficult text of Mark is consistently presented to a contemporary reader as the portrayal of a conflict between good and evil (Jesus and the demonic) that can only be resolved in the fragile disciple's journey into the future with the risen Lord."

Francis J. Moloney, SDB
Salesians of Don Bosco
Australia–Pacific Province

A Costly Freedom

A Theological Reading
of Mark's Gospel

Brendan Byrne, SJ

LITURGICAL PRESS

Collegeville, Minnesota

www.litpress.org

Cover design by David Manahan, OSB. Icon of "Christ Healing the Blind Man." Courtesy and permission of Uncut Mountain Supply, http://www.uncutmountainsupply.com.

1   2   3   4   5   6   7   8   9

Library of Congress Cataloging-in-Publication Data

Byrne, Brendan (Brendan J.)
    A costly freedom : a theological reading of Mark's gospel / Brendan Byrne.
        p.   cm.
    "A Michael Glazier book."
    Includes bibliographical references and indexes.
    ISBN 978-0-8146-1856-1
  1. Bible. N.T. Mark—Commentaries.   I. Title.
    BS2585.53.B97 2008
    226.3'07—dc22   2007049602

For Morna D. Hooker,
with much gratitude, affection, and respect.

Contents

Introduction

This book on Mark is a companion to my earlier studies of Luke (*The Hospitality of God*) and Matthew (*Lifting the Burden*), and so completes a trilogy on the Synoptic Gospels.[1] Like those earlier volumes, it is offered as a contemporary interpretation of the gospel[2] for students and preachers. I also hope it will be a resource for reflection and spiritual reading. Specialists may find interest in the overall interpretation (the "Three Stories"; see below), as well as in what I have to say about particular passages.

Though the shortest of the canonical gospels, Mark is perhaps the most challenging of the four. For centuries it shared the fate of Cinderella in the well-known German folktale. As Cinderella languished in the kitchen until rescued by her prince, Mark suffered almost total eclipse in Christian awareness by its three longer fellows (Matthew, Luke, and John). A century and a half ago interest in the Second Gospel underwent a revival, in scholarly circles at least. Mark, it was widely agreed, was the earliest written gospel, the source for much of Matthew and Luke, and the account that takes us closest to the voice and actions of Jesus.

The verdict that Mark offered factual history was soon revised, but along with that revision came acknowledgment of the theological richness of the evangelist and, more recently, appreciation of the narrative as a literary composition of no little sophistication and skill.

While scholars may have warmed to Mark in recent years, the gospel has taken rather longer to reestablish itself in wider Christian usage. True, Mark now has his "year" (Year B) in the revised Sunday Lectionary of the

1. *The Hospitality of God: A Reading of Luke's Gospel* (Collegeville, MN: Liturgical Press, 2000); *Lifting the Burden: Reading Matthew's Gospel in the Church Today* (Collegeville, MN: Liturgical Press, 2004).

2. In general, throughout this work I shall follow the convention of writing "gospel" when referring to one or other of the *documents* attributed to the four evangelists in Christian tradition and "Gospel" when referring to the basic *message* proclaimed in those documents and in other New Testament writings such as the letters of Paul.

Roman Catholic Church, which has served as a model for the lectionaries used in other traditions. But there is still some way to go if Mark's voice is to be heard and recognized among the gospel quartet.

This work aims to encourage that process. In form it is a commentary in the sense that it accompanies a reading and study of the gospel from beginning to end. However, what it presents is a personal reading and appreciation of the gospel derived from many years of teaching and also of considering how this scariest and in some ways most demanding of the four gospels might best be interpreted for believers today.

I say "scariest" because even a casual glance at Mark takes the reader into a world inhabited by demons and malign forces with which Jesus is constantly in conflict. Hostility, misunderstanding, and betrayal dog Jesus right up to the unrelieved starkness of his death. Though his resurrection is not in doubt, Mark's gospel (at least in its original form, without the appendix making up vv. 9-20 of chap. 16) never offers us the comfort of a vision of the risen Lord. We are simply left with an empty tomb, the promise of an appearance in Galilee, and three women too paralyzed with fear to spread the good news (16:1-8).

There is very little in Mark that is not repeated in Matthew and Luke, and much of the detail that is particular to Mark is puzzling and obscure (e.g., the parable of the Seed Growing Secretly [4:26-29]; the flight of the naked young man [14:51-52]). Mark also lacks content appearing in the other two gospels that has become distinctive of the Christian faith: the Beatitudes (Matt 5:3-12; Luke 6:20-23), the Lord's Prayer (Matt 6:9-13; Luke 11:2-4), the parables of the Good Samaritan (Luke 10:29-37) and the Lost Son (Luke 15:11-32), the evocation of the great judgment (Matt 25:31-46). Without these Christianity would surely be something else; without Mark it might not have been very different at all—unless we acknowledge, as I think we should, that without Mark's likely "invention" of the gospel genre[3]

---

3. By "genre" I understand a distinct artistic form such as a letter, a novel, a biography, a play, etc. By speaking of Mark's "invention" of the gospel genre I do not mean to suggest that Mark created something lacking all similarity to other literary genres in existence at the time, such as, e.g., that of the "life" (*bios*) of a famous individual. The extent to which the gospels represent a distinct literary genre is a matter of considerable scholarly discussion; see further Christopher M. Tuckett, "Introduction to the Gospels," in James D. G. Dunn and John W. Rogerson, eds., *Eerdmans Commentary on the Bible* (Grand Rapids, MI and Cambridge, UK: Eerdmans, 2003) 989–99, especially 990–92; Raymond E. Brown, *An Introduction to the New Testament* (New York: Doubleday, 1997) 102–7. If, as most scholars hold, Mark composed the earliest gospel, then he was the first to cast the proclamation of the basic "Gospel" (the "good news" about Jesus Christ [cf. Rom 1:3-4]) in the form of a quasi-biographical literary narrative incorporating traditions hitherto circulating in oral form.

we would probably not have the gospels of Matthew and Luke, to say nothing of John.

But why not leave it to scholars to consider this historical debt owed to Mark? What advantage is there for the church in dusting down this neglected gospel, which in many ways has been "improved upon" by Matthew and Luke?

In the first place there is the strictly theological point that the Spirit guided the early church to include this gospel among the four canonically recognized as giving authentic presentations of Jesus. Without Mark the portrait would not be complete. That, presumably, is the reason for the much more frequent appearance of readings from the Second Gospel in the revised lectionaries.

Second, despite the repetition of so much Markan content in Matthew and Luke, Mark has a distinctive voice and message that the church and the world are perhaps more open to hear now than in times past. It is not so much the content but the way Mark tells the story and traces out the path of Christian living that is distinctive, and that seems particularly attuned to address the darkness of unbelief and despair afflicting many human lives today. Differently from Matthew and Luke, Mark opens up the possibility of a fruitful and deeply human *via negativa* in Christianity—a readiness to confront absence and, in some sense, chaos, something that comes across to many people as a distinct gift.[4]

Third, the widespread failure of institutional Christianity on many fronts has led disillusionment to enter into the hearts of believers within once-vibrant but now deeply wounded Christian communities. While not exactly a "gospel of the church" in the sense that readily applies to Matthew, Mark seems particularly designed to address failure in community leadership, and the wider disillusionment and hopelessness to which that failure can give rise. John also does this, I think, but in a very different way. Without being anything like an expert in Markan studies, I have the feeling that this preparedness to confront absence and, in some sense, chaos is Mark's gift.

Finally, I believe that Mark's presentation of Jesus as the Stronger One (1:7; 3:27) who sets human beings free from demonic control, while troubling for the contemporary mind, is also a promising aspect of the gospel as regards interpretation: troubling because it takes us into a world where we, as inheritors of Enlightenment rationality, are loath to follow; promising because if a way can be found to relate the demonic motif to contemporary human life, then a reading of Mark can be a powerful force for liberation.

---

4. I owe this observation to my friend and colleague, Dr. Anne Elvey.

I shall say more about the demonic in the next chapter, which is devoted to the worldview presupposed by the gospel, but it may be helpful to state here at the outset what I believe to be its essential meaning. In essence the demonic has to do with control. People in the ancient world generally and the biblical world in particular spoke of demonic possession when they felt themselves held captive from within by forces and compulsions over which they had no control—transpersonal forces that robbed them of freedom of choice, stunted their human growth, and alienated them from God, from life in community, and from their own individual humanity. This sense that the world, including Israel, has fallen under demonic control is pervasive in the horizon of discourse presupposed in Mark's gospel. Its prominence invites interpreters of Mark to relate the liberating activity of Jesus to all the various "captivities"—personal, social, and economic—under which people of our time labor and which they seem powerless to control or escape. The multiple forms of addiction that burden us as individuals and as societies—huge, transpersonal forces that control us and make us their slaves—can be seen as manifestations of the demonic.

Of course, handling the demonic element in the gospels calls for discernment and skill. A healthy spirituality will acknowledge the reality of spiritual forces opposed to God and to life. But to take the gospel material as an invitation to see manifestations of the demonic or the Devil everywhere is dangerous. Most of us are familiar with a certain type of religious pathology far more preoccupied with evil, with the bizarre and the occult, than with the effects of God's grace and the Spirit. So there are risks and pitfalls in this area. But the encounters with the demonic in Mark's gospel challenge us to look at our own society and consider the supraindividual, societal, and global forces exercising a dehumanizing control over people's lives today.

A Theological Reading

In the title of this book I have qualified "freedom" by the adjective "costly," and added a subtitle to the effect that what I propose is a "theological reading" of Mark's gospel. Let me take these two points in reverse order. By "theological reading" I do not mean to imply that other commentaries have not been theological—at least in a general sense. What I have in mind is "*theo*logical" in the strict sense of communicating a vision of God—and, specifically, a vision of God as the communion of divine love described in Christian tradition as the Trinity. While the overt focus of Mark's gospel is on the person of Jesus, I have come to see that the narrative is equally a revelation of the Father for whom Jesus is the "Beloved Son" in whom the

Father is well pleased (1:11; cf. 9:7) and whose whole mission is impelled and energized by the Spirit sent from the Father (1:10). The rending of the heavens as Jesus emerges from baptism at the hands of John, the descent of the Spirit and the assurance of the Father's love that he hears (1:9-11) initiate a trinitarian involvement in all the subsequent events of his mission.

This divine involvement may be more explicit in moments of overt heavenly revelation, such as those that follow Jesus' baptism (1:11) and transfiguration (9:7). In fact, it runs constantly through the story, reaching a climax when the curtain of the Temple is rent in two immediately after Jesus' obedient death on the cross (15:38). In this sense the Markan narrative depicts the life of Jesus as a playing out on earth, for the benefit of humanity, of the communion of love that is the Trinity. In the person and actions of Jesus the triune God breaks the captivity of the human race to the demonic, setting it free to become truly human in relationship to that communion of love. This repair of divine-human relationship is the essence of the "Rule of God" ("the Kingdom") proclaimed and enacted by Jesus (1:15). In the person of the Son, the Godhead has become vulnerable to the hostility of the demonic in its various manifestations, a vulnerability that comes to a climax when Jesus dies on the cross, to all appearances abandoned not only by his disciples but also by the One he called "Father" (15:34; cf. 14:36). God's raising of Jesus on the third day, which Mark proclaims (16:6-7) but does not depict, assures the reader that the divine love, though vulnerable to the onslaught of evil, is destined to have the last word. It will extend its sway across the world when Jesus returns as Son of Man in glory to establish definitively the rule of God (13:24-27; cf. 14:62).

A Costly Freedom

In connection with the aspect of vulnerability it very soon becomes clear as the gospel gets underway that the freedom proclaimed here will not come about without cost: a cost to Jesus, a cost to the Father, and a cost to those called to associate themselves with his life and mission. Jesus' proclamation of the "good news" of freedom associated with the onset of God's Rule (1:15) and his enactment of this freedom through his teaching and powerful works bring on hostility and grave threat to his life (3:6a; cf. 2:20). The fate of John the Baptist (6:17-29) points to what lies in store for Jesus according to a pattern that begins to emerge in the gospel: "You preach and you get delivered up." John preaches and is "delivered up" (1:9). At the turning point of the gospel Jesus begins to make clear to his disciples that he also, having preached, is going to be "delivered up" (9:31; 10:33), a process described at length in the account of his suffering and death (14:10-11, 18, 21, 41-44: 15:1, 10, 15). Nothing brings home more powerfully the cost to Jesus personally of being "delivered up" than the scene in the Garden of Gethsemane on the eve of his death, when he shrinks from the "cup" of suffering that lies immediately before him and, over and over, begs that it be removed (14:32-42).

Jesus, then, is the primary bearer of the cost of the liberation proclaimed in the gospel. Because he is and remains to the end God's beloved Son, the cost of the liberation he works for humankind is also borne by the Father. It is, I believe, counter to the understanding of the gospel to separate Jesus and the Father in the Passion—depicting Jesus as sole agent bearing the cost of the sin of humankind over against the demand and wrath of the Father. The separation of Father and Son in the work of redemption has been prominent in some traditional understandings of that doctrine, with unfortunate consequences for the image of God communicated to believers. In Mark—as also in Matthew and Luke, and Paul and John—behind the vulnerable love of the Son stands the equally vulnerable love of the Father who sent him on his mission of liberation.

Finally, as Jesus also makes clear from the midpoint of the gospel onward, the cost is one that those who follow him will have to share (8:34-38). These are, in the first instance, the disciples he has called. Like John the Baptist, like Jesus himself, they too will preach and be "delivered up" (13:9-12). A major focus of the second part of the gospel, coming to a climax in the Passion, lies on the failure of the disciples, particularly the male disciples, to come to terms with the costly aspect of Jesus' messianic role and their association with it (8:31-33 [Peter]; 9:30-32; 10:32-34; 14:66-72 [Peter]). As Jesus goes to his death, the cost of following him becomes too much for the disciples; they desert him (14:50), though a number of women witness his death and burial "from afar" (15:40-41, 47). Jesus also foresees similar failure and betrayal in the later community when persecution intensifies the costly aspect of following him (13:12-13). What the gospel also makes clear, however, especially in the words of the (angelic) young man at Jesus' empty tomb, is that failure before the cost does not have the last word. The disciples, forgiven and reassured, are to go back to Galilee (16:7) to see the once-crucified Jesus now raised from the dead and to begin again—and perhaps again and again—to learn and accept what following him and his mission entails.[5]

5. This sense of the faithfulness of God overcoming human failure and fragility, both that of the original disciples and of the subsequent communities of faith for whom the gospel

"A . . . Reading . . ."

The remaining element in the subtitle of this work—"A . . . Reading of Mark's Gospel"—is meant to signal that it offers simply one interpretation among many to which the gospel is open. I believe it to be a valid interpretation, well-founded in the text. However, I shall for the most part simply allow its own developing logic to commend it, without detailed argumentation or constant discussion with other scholarly points of view. Technical details and disputed points requiring further treatment I relegate to the notes. The work is similar to a commentary in that I move through the gospel continuously from beginning to end. It is unlike a commentary in that I do not feel obliged to comment upon everything in detail. My constant aim will be to assist preachers and reasonably educated readers to find theological and spiritual meaning in particular episodes and scenes, as well as in the Gospel of Mark as a whole.

To keep the book within reasonable size and expense I have not, except in a very few places, set out the text of the gospel in English translation. The translation to which I adhere most closely is that of the New Revised Standard Version. I would urge readers to have this by them as they consult or work their way through the book. Of great assistance to more serious students will be a synopsis of the three Synoptic Gospels, such as Burton H. Throckmorton's *Gospel Parallels,* the most recent edition of which uses the NRSV.[6] But, of course, the first and most necessary resource is the Old or First Testament, allusion to which, whether overt or implicit, stands behind so much of the text of the gospels.

Some Presuppositions

Before entering on the commentary proper I would like to make clear certain matters I am presupposing with little or no further justification. All can be pursued at greater depth in the introductory sections of more detailed commentaries on the gospel.

First of all, I am taking the gospel in its final canonical form, rarely pausing to identify sources or traditions that might be thought to lie behind it. Reconstruction of such sources is in any case a hazardous matter in the

---

was written, is the major emphasis of the recent commentary of Francis J. Moloney (*The Gospel of Mark: A Commentary* [Peabody, MA: Hendrickson, 2002]); see especially 352–54.

6. *Gospel Parallels: A Comparison of the Synoptic Gospels* (5th ed. Nashville: Nelson, 1992).

case of Mark, generally considered to be the earliest written gospel. Reference, however, to Mark's "final canonical form" raises the issue of the so-called Appendix, a summary of appearances of the risen Jesus to the disciples, making up Mark 16:9-20.[7] This appendix alleviates the strangeness of ending the narrative at 16:8 with a simple report of the women's fear and failure to act on the instructions they received from the young man at the tomb. It is canonical in the sense of being included within the scriptural canon of mainstream Christian traditions. It is, however, lacking in most of the earliest and best manuscripts and seems to have been unknown to early Christian writers such as Clement of Alexandria and Origen. In the judgment of most scholars it represents a later attempt both to overcome the literary and theological abruptness of the ending at 16:8 and to provide Mark with a resurrection story more closely resembling the accounts in the remaining three gospels. While not omitting comment on Mark 16:9-20 in its place, I shall adhere in this study to what is virtually the unanimous judgment of scholars and interpret the Gospel of Mark on the supposition that it ended, albeit paradoxically and mysteriously, at 16:8, with the fear, flight, and silence of the women.

Again along with most scholars, I accept that Mark was the earliest written gospel—indeed, the pioneer of the gospel genre—and as such a forerunner and significant source for Matthew and Luke.[8] As to when the gospel was written, it seems to me indisputable that Jesus' long discourse on the future in Mark 13 presupposes the destruction of the Temple by the Roman armies at the fall of Jerusalem in 70 C.E. and the acute theological anxiety and expectation of the end caused by that event in the hearts of believers. This means that the gospel must have been written while that event remained a recent and disturbing memory. A date shortly after 70 C.E. (within the range 70–73) seems appropriate.

As regards authorship, the document we are considering came to be known, at least by the late second century C.E., as "the Gospel according to

---

7. Besides this "longer ending" (16:9-20), there is also a "shorter ending" of two sentences, comprising the women's report to Peter and the Lord's commissioning of the disciples. This appears in some late manuscripts, usually as a preface to the longer ending.

8. I would also hold that, in addition to drawing from Mark and sources particular to themselves, Matthew and Luke relied on another source, consisting largely of teachings and sayings of Jesus, that scholars reconstruct and call "Q" (from the German *Quelle* [= "source"]). Without being definite about the nature of this source—especially whether it existed in written as well as in oral form—it seems necessary to postulate some such fount of tradition in order to account for the large amount of non-Markan material that Luke and Matthew have in common, and so to embrace the "Two-Source" theory of relationship among the three Synoptic Gospels.

Mark." The historian Eusebius, writing early in the fourth century, cites an earlier tradition, that of the second-century bishop Papias, who records that the "Elder" (John) was wont to speak of Mark as the "interpreter of Peter." This "Petrine" understanding of the gospel's origin became traditional in the church. It fit well with the reference to "my son, Mark" in the greeting at the close of the First Letter of Peter (5:13) and also with the sense of Rome as the place of composition, a view that finds considerable support in the text as well.

The traditional association of Mark's gospel with Peter came under challenge with the rise of the modern critical approach to the gospels in the nineteenth century. The conclusion that the gospel reached its final shape only after a lengthy process during which the traditions about Jesus underwent considerable shaping in the early communities did not sit easily with the view that Mark's gospel in its final form reflected the testimony of someone (Peter) who had been an eyewitness to the events recorded. Later still came the recognition that the author of the gospel was not, as originally thought, a mere recorder or editor, but a writer and theologian of no mean skill, capable of shaping the traditions about Jesus into a powerful narrative presentation of his person and mission.

But these considerations distancing the gospel account from eyewitness testimony about Jesus are not incompatible with an acceptance, in line with the tradition, that the Markan gospel is peculiarly indebted in some way to the witness of Peter. It is hard to account for the authority it enjoyed, an authority that led to its becoming a model and source for the similar compositions of Matthew and Luke, if it were not believed to rest on ancient and notably authoritative apostolic witness.[9] Likewise, in the absence of any other claimants it is perfectly appropriate to respect the ancient attribution of the gospel to a person called Mark, though whether this author is to be identified with the "John Mark" who appears for a time as a companion of Paul and Barnabas in Acts (12:12, 25; 15:37-39) and the "Mark" mentioned in Pauline literature (Col 4:10; Philemon 24 and 2 Tim 4:11) we cannot know. In any case, I shall refer to the author as "Mark" throughout this study.

The traditional view of Rome as place of composition has also come into question. It remains, though, the majority opinion, since it has much to commend it. The gospel seems to emanate from a location removed from the Jewish milieu. Mark feels obliged to explain Jewish customs to non-Jews (see especially 7:3-4), employs Latin loanwords, and betrays a weak knowledge

---

9. For a vigorous defense of the Petrine authority behind Mark see Martin Hengel, *Der unterschätze Petrus: Zwei Studien* (Tübingen: Mohr Siebeck, 2006) 70–78.

of Galilean geography. The only truly correct human perception of the identity of Jesus from the human side comes from the Roman centurion who has supervised his execution (15:39), and in general there is a sense of the Gentile rather than the Jewish world as the primary focus of mission. Above all, the warnings and prophecies Jesus utters in the discourse on the future in Mark 13 resonate uncannily with accounts of the atrocities perpetrated against Christians in Rome in the year 64 C.E., when the emperor Nero made them the scapegoats for the fire unleashed by him that devastated much of the city.[10] The gospel, moreover, both subtly and more overtly betrays a preoccupation with Rome and the Roman *imperium* as a pervasive, oppressive force, hostile to the liberating rule of Jesus.[11]

None of these considerations requires the composition of Mark's gospel strictly and specifically in Rome. The fact that Jerusalem and its fate also bulk large in the narrative may suggest a location closer to Palestine. All that is essentially demanded is a location where both the culture and might of Rome prevailed—and that, of course, was the case throughout the Mediterranean cities of the time.[12]

In any case, exact determination of the place of composition is a matter of scant importance for the kind of interpretation I purpose to undertake here. More important is to recognize that Mark wrote for a community that, while engaged in the spread of the Gospel to the wider world, had very recently experienced a sharp and devastating persecution. Keyed up in expectation of Jesus' imminent return as Son of Man and judge of the world, the community felt dismay and disillusionment at the seemingly endless postponement of that return despite the presence of signs and portents suggesting it to be at hand, notably the fall of Jerusalem to the Roman armies in 70 C.E.

Other features of the Markan community emerge from the gospel. Cut off from synagogue and Temple, they have made their houses the locus of worship, the place where they experience the presence and power of Jesus.

---

10. In reference to this persecution the Roman historian Tacitus, *Annales* xv, 44, describes the Christians as "hated for their abominations" and speaks of an initial arrest followed by the arrest of others on the basis of information obtained from those arrested first. In Mark 13 Jesus speaks of betrayal by family members and being hated by all (vv. 12-13a).

11. For an interpretation of Mark as pervasively reflecting hostility to Rome see Brian J. Incigneri, *The Gospel to the Romans: The Setting and Rhetoric of Mark's Gospel*. Biblical Interpretation 65 (Leiden: Brill, 2003).

12. This discussion of the place and date of composition of Mark's gospel is much indebted to the very balanced survey provided by Moloney, *Gospel of Mark* 11–15, who in the end (p. 15) suggests somewhere in "southern Syria" as the location for the Markan community.

The gospel seems to want to consecrate this sense of domestic church.[13] It also, particularly in the way it presents the male disciples of Jesus, appears to address a situation in which leadership has failed, in which family life, in particular, has been riven by persecution, and in which women have done better than men in coping with the suffering inevitable in the following of Jesus. These features, and others, will emerge as we move through the narrative.

This reading of Mark's gospel, like those I have already undertaken in regard to Luke and Matthew, presupposes the modern sense of the gospels as narratives designed to promote faith in Jesus and involvement in his mission rather than as conveyors of information about his historical life. Critically examined, they do of course convey such information, though not in the sense or to the degree that would be the case in a modern biographical study. For Mark, as for all the gospel writers, Jesus is the risen and exalted Lord, carrying out his messianic mission through the power of the Spirit. Though Mark would seem to have believed that Jesus truly entered upon his messianic status following his resurrection and exaltation to God's right hand, he nonetheless portrays him as already empowered with the Spirit and exercising a messianic ministry during the brief years of his earthly ministry. There is a continuity, then, between the depiction of that ministry and the risen life of the Lord that is unique to the gospels and forms the basis of their being read as living Word in believing communities to this day. The gospels are not simply about "back then" in the sense of communicating information about Jesus. They are about "now" in the sense of inviting readers and hearers to enter into the narrative and identify with the characters so as to come, like them, under the power and challenge of the living Lord.

If Mark is indeed, as most scholars believe, the first of the gospels and the pioneer of that literary genre in Christian circles, then we ought recognize its extraordinary achievement. The evidence of the earliest Christian writer, Paul, suggests that the essence of the "Gospel" for the earliest believers was the simple message that the teacher and master crucified by Pontius Pilate in Jerusalem had been raised from the dead and exalted at God's right hand, to fulfill in a totally unforeseen and transcendent sense the role of Israel's messiah (cf. Rom 1:3-4; 1 Cor 15:3-5, 22-28). He was now continuing this role through the power of the Spirit that energized the life and mission of the community of believers. In all likelihood it was Mark who gave literary expression to the project of expanding this basic core of the Gospel into an

---

13. See Michael F. Trainor, *The Quest for Home: the Household in Mark's Community* (Collegeville, MN: Liturgical Press, 2001).

extended account of the last days of Jesus' life (Passion narrative) and prefaced this by pressing more or less free-floating traditions about Jesus' earlier life and teaching into a narrative framework that became "the beginning of the Gospel" (Mark 1:1). In so doing, Mark—or the community that sponsored him—created an immensely powerful narrative instrument to communicate a sense of the person of Jesus and the call to discipleship that he holds out to believers in every age.

That said, readers of the early twenty-first century cannot simply pick up the Markan narrative and enter it without further ado. Some preliminary understanding of the worldview it presupposes is necessary if we are not only to avoid going astray in interpretation but also to appreciate the full power of the narrative for our time. The titles and roles the gospel employs in regard to its principal character, Jesus, emerge from that worldview—even if, as applied to him, they undergo radical transformation. Hence, before I begin to comment on the gospel passage by passage, I invite the reader in the following chapter to journey with me for a while into that original Markan world, to review the significant features of the worldview presupposed in the gospel and the background to the titles and roles it applies to Jesus. This will prepare the ground for a survey in a final introductory chapter of the distinctive meaning those same titles acquire in the gospel and of the interplay of the roles inscribed in them. This interplay of roles—or "stories about Jesus," as I prefer to call them—creates, in my understanding, the dramatic tension that sustains the narrative. I urge the reader to regard the material in both chapters, along with the schematic outline that completes them, as essential preliminary reading to the study, in whole or part, of the actual text of the gospel.

The Worldview Behind Mark's Gospel

Mark's gospel, like virtually all the rest of the New Testament, reflects the intersection of two worlds: the biblical-Jewish world and the wider Mediterranean world in which Hellenistic culture prevailed under the dominant power of Rome. A fusion of these two worlds had, of course, been under way since the conquests of the Macedonian Greek, Alexander the Great, in the late fourth century. This gave rise to the form of Greek-speaking Judaism known as Hellenistic Judaism, which chiefly prevailed in the Jewish settlements outside Palestine (the Diaspora) but was not without influence in the Land itself. While acknowledging the fusion of these two worlds, it is also possible to point to features of the gospel that reflect one world or the other in a more distinct way. It is not my intention here to provide anything like a comprehensive survey of the worldview behind the gospel, but simply to indicate and describe some aspects I believe to be necessary for an understanding of Mark. In this, without excluding the wider cultural world, I will focus primarily on aspects of Jewish ideas and beliefs presupposed in the gospel.[1] From time to time it will be necessary to stray also into the early Christian usage (in regard, for example, to "gospel") Mark seems to presuppose.

Eschatology and Apocalyptic

Mark's gospel, again in common with early Christianity as a whole, is heir to a distinctive mode of imagining and describing reality dubbed "apocalyptic." Before we go any further down this track—where we shall encounter several other terms liable to daunt and alienate the nonspecialist—let me clarify what I understand by this term and its closely related fellow "eschatology." To take up the second term first: "eschatology" has to do with speculation or

---

1. In what follows I am indebted to the succinct and clear survey of the topic provided by Dennis E. Nineham in the Introduction to his commentary, *The Gospel of Saint Mark* (Harmondsworth, UK: Pelican, 1963) 43–48. Forty years on, it has not been surpassed.

teaching about what is going to happen in the future—not just any time in the future, but the final future (the Greek word *eschatos* means "limit"). Eschatology refers, then, to the last acts or events in the cosmic drama: the end of the present world, or at the very least its radical transformation. Concepts such as resurrection (of the dead), final judgment (by God), postearthly reward (heaven) or punishment (hell) are eschatological because their application lies beyond the limit of present human existence.

"Apocalyptic" is an adjective describing a cast of thinking or mode of literary expression in which or through which some content, usually about the future, is expressed. Strictly speaking, what makes a text "apocalyptic" is the presentation of its content as something received by "revelation" (the Greek word *apokalypsis* means "revelation" or "unveiling"): a privileged figure—a prophet or seer—receives this revelation through interviews with angels or through being taken on a heavenly tour where details of the divine intent for the future are disclosed. Characteristic of apocalyptic discourse is vivid imagery depicting upheavals and calamities on a cosmic scale (earthquakes, stars falling from heaven, moon turning into blood, and so forth). Such discourse sets the conflict between good and evil in starkly dualist mode; there are no shades of gray. A profound pessimism prevails concerning human possibility in the present era. Sin is pervasive; hope for improvement rests entirely on divine intervention and a radical renewal of the world amounting virtually to a redo of the original creation. When something is referred to as "apocalyptic," the reference is usually to this kind of content rather than to the mode (revelation) through which the content has been made known.

The purpose of apocalyptic discourse is to give encouragement to the faithful now suffering the evils of the present age. It does so by imparting privileged and prior information concerning the divine plan and program whereby God or God's agent(s) will soon intervene. A moment of reckoning and judgment will arrive, which will mean exposure and condemnation for the wicked, vindication and reward for the faithful, who will then share the final triumph of God's rule (the "kingdom of God"). It is this sense of a divinely-ordained program of events leading up to a radical, final reckoning that ensures that eschatology plays a large role in apocalyptic discourse.

A New "Exile": Captivity to the Demonic

This apocalyptic way of viewing both the present and the future situation came to particular prominence in Palestinian Judaism in the centuries just prior to the rise of Christianity. Its paradigm literary expression ("apocalypse") appears in the book of Daniel, written in the mid-second century B.C.E., in response to the religious and cultural oppression visited upon Jews by the regime of the Antiochean Seleucid Greek ruler Antiochus IV Epiphanes. Several centuries earlier, Jews had returned from exile in Babylon (587–538 B.C.E.) with the hopeful prophecies found in the latter part of the book of Isaiah (chaps. 40–55) ringing in their ears. The exilic prophet ("Second Isaiah") responsible for these oracles had proclaimed freedom from captivity, a homecoming across the desert attended by miracles surpassing the original Exodus (from Egypt), and a glorious restoration of national life in renewed covenant relationship with God.

Because of their prominence in later Christian discourse it will be helpful to recall a couple of these texts:

> Get you up to a high mountain,
> O Zion, herald of good news;
> lift up your voice with strength,
> O Jerusalem, herald of good news,
> lift it up, do not fear;
> say to the cities of Judah,
> "Here is your God!" (Isa 40:9)

Addressed to the remnant of the people who had remained home in the ruins of Jerusalem, the passage announces the "good news" ("gospel") that, through action on the part of Israel's God, the captives have been set free and are on their way home. A later oracle picks up the same "good news":

> How beautiful upon the mountains
> are the feet of the messenger who announces peace,
> who brings good news,
> who announces salvation,
> who says to Zion, "Your God reigns." (Isa 52:7)

We should note the reference to the "reign" of God in the last line. The liberation has come about because, as oracles elsewhere in this part of Isaiah make clear, Israel's God has broken the rule of the gods of Babylon who, acting through that empire's rulers, had held Israel captive. The expression "tell good news" (Hebrew *mbsr*) emerges from passages such as these (cf. also 41:27; 52:7; 60:6; 61:1; Nah 1:15) as virtually a technical term communicating this sense of freedom from captivity and the establishment of God's (YHWH's) rule ("kingdom"), not only in Israel but on a world scale. The all-important Christian term "gospel" has its biblical (Old Testament) origin in texts such as these.

The reality of life back in Palestine in the centuries that followed hardly lived up to the assurances contained in these oracles of Isaiah. Save for a brief period of independence under the Maccabees in the second century B.C.E., the Jewish people simply exchanged one form of subjection for another, becoming a client state or satellite of whichever power (Persian, Ptolemaic Egyptian, Seleucid Greek) happened to be dominant at the time, before eventually coming under Roman rule in the decades leading up to the New Testament era. Since the prophecies of Isaiah had clearly failed to find literal fulfilment, they came to be read in a new way: not with reference to the return from Babylonian captivity in the late sixth century B.C.E., but in the hope of a divinely wrought liberation from a far more pervasive state of captivity now in place. Within the framework of the apocalyptic cast of thinking outlined above, the captivity in question was human subjection to the demonic world, led by the prince of demons, variously known as "Satan," or "Belial," or "Beelzebul." This sense of enslavement to evil powers operating on a supernatural level did not suppress the sense of more physical captivity under occupying political powers such as Rome. On the contrary, the latter were widely understood to be simply instruments manipulated by demons for their own evil ends.

I said in the Introduction that it is best to think of the demonic as having to do essentially with control. People in the ancient world attributed to demons control of storms and other manifestations of nature out of control and threatening to human life. Demons could also enter into human beings and bring about illness of various kinds—physical (sickness), psychological (madness), and moral (vice, alienation from God, resistance to divine grace). In general the demonic world was held to be "unclean," standing over against the "cleanliness" or "holiness" associated with God and communicated by God to the covenant people, Israel (cf. Exod 19:6: "You shall be for me a priestly kingdom and a holy nation"). How to preserve the covenant "holiness" and avoid contamination with the unclean and destructive force of the demonic world was a major preoccupation of the Jewish religious system around the time of Jesus.

"Gospel"

A text from the Dead Sea Scrolls,[2] the Melchizedek Scroll (11Q13), despite its fragmentary condition, sheds remarkable light on the way in which the Isaiah "gospel" texts such as the two cited above and a later text,

---

2. These texts, found from 1947 onward in caves around Khirbet Qumran on the western shore of the Dead Sea, represent the most significant discovery in biblical archaeology in the

Isa 61:1-2, were being read in apocalyptic Jewish circles as expressions of liberation from the grip of the demonic. This scroll is worth quoting at some length:

> Its interpretation (reference is to the Jubilee year [Lev 25:13]) at the end of days concerns those in exile which . . . he took captive, about whom he said "to proclaim liberty to captives" (Isa 61:1). (Melchizedek) will make them return. He will proclaim liberty for them . . . and make atonement for their sins. . . . And that which he says concerning the end of days by means of Isaiah the prophet who says: "How beautiful upon the mountains are the feet of him who brings good tidings, that publishes peace, that brings good tidings of good, that publishes salvation, that says to Zion: 'Your heavenly one (lit. "your God") is King' (Isa 52:7)" [and they shall be freed from the hands] of Belial and from the hands of all the sp[irits of his lot.] . . . and "He that brings good tidings" is [the ano]inted of the Spirit (Isa 61:1), about whom Daniel spoke . . . as is written about him (Isa 52:7), "Saying to Zion, 'your God rules.'"[3]

We see here two Isaiah "good news" passages (Isa 52:7 and 61:1) being cited together and related to a coming liberation to be brought about through the agency of a high-priestly figure (a latter-day Melchizedek) who will inaugurate a Jubilee year of release, make atonement for sin, and liberate the faithful. The captivity from which they are to be set free is said again and again (as elsewhere in the Qumran literature) to be captivity to "Belial and the spirits of his lot"—that is, the demonic world. It is not clear from the text whether Melchizedek is to be identified with the one "anointed of the Spirit," whose task is to proclaim in terms of Isa 52:7 the rule of God. However, we see joined together here a striking cluster of motifs that reappears in the Gospel of Mark: the Isaiah "good news" ("gospel") texts, freedom from demonic control, atonement for sin brought about by a priestly agent of God, and the proclamation by an "anointed one" (Messiah?) of the rule of God. In short, the text announces the good news of the displacement of demonic rule by that of God.

   This text from Qumran shows that, just before the rise of Christianity, a Jewish apocalyptic sect consciously associated the Isaiah "good news" texts with the awaited eschatological intervention of God. Like the early

---

twentieth century. They shed immense light on the life, religious expression, and hopes of a Jewish apocalyptic sect just prior to the rise of Christianity.

   3. Reconstructions of the text vary greatly. For a more complete reconstruction and translation see Florentino García Martínez, *The Dead Sea Scrolls Translated: the Qumran Texts in English*, tr. W. G. E. Watson (Leiden: Brill, 1994) 139–40.

Christian movement it understood Isaiah's messenger of good news as referring primarily to the salvation it longed for in its own era.[4] The New Testament "gospel" language almost certainly flows within this stream set in
motion by (Second) Isaiah and subsumed within the wider framework of
Jewish apocalyptic eschatology.[5]

Quite lacking, however, in the Jewish background is anything corresponding to the Christian use of the singular noun *euangelion* in the sense
of "gospel." In the wider Greek-speaking world this word (almost always
in the plural form *euangelia*) occurs in formal announcements of birth, marriage, or anniversaries. A distinctive usage appears in connection with the
proclamation of the accession or birthday of rulers, notably the Roman emperor, of which an inscription from Priene in Asia Minor (9 B.C.E.) is the
best known example:

> . . . the birthday of the god (Caesar Augustus) has been for the whole world
> the beginning of the gospel (*euangelia*); concerning him, therefore, let all
> reckon a new era beginning from the date of his birth.

A sacral aura, the sense of a new age dawning, attaches to such usages in a
manner not dissimilar to the claims made by Christians in connection with
God's raising of Jesus and installing him as Messiah and cosmic Lord (Rom
1:3-4; cf. Mark 12:35-37). It is likely, then, that when the message of and
about Jesus came to be proclaimed in Greek-speaking milieus the early
proclaimers of that message found close at hand a Greek term, *euangelion,*
that not only picked up the nuances attaching to "telling good news" in the
biblical (Isaianic) background but brought rich resonances of its own as
well. As regards the background to the Christian use of "gospel," it is probably necessary, then, to reckon both with influence from the biblical Isaianic
tradition and with a certain "inculturation" within the wider Greco-Roman
milieu.

We can set it out diagrammatically as follows:

---

4. A similar use of the Isaiah "good news" text is to be found in psalms emanating from
another Jewish movement: *Psalms of Solomon,* especially Psalm 11; cf. also a further Qumran
text, 4Q521 (The "Messiah of heaven and earth"), where there is reference to a "Messiah" in
connection with the performance of marvelous works described in language from Isaiah.

5. On this see especially the significant study of the influence of Isaiah's "New Exodus"
motif upon Mark by Rikki E. Watts, *Isaiah's New Exodus in Mark* (Grand Rapids: Baker
Academic, 1997) 96–102.

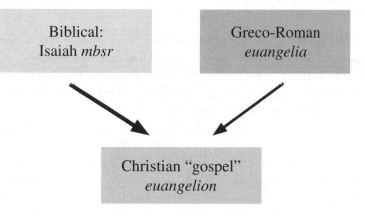

In the earliest Christian writings, those of Paul, "gospel" appears at times in the form "the gospel of God" (1 Thess 2:2, 8, 9; Rom 1:1; 15:16), a phrase that also sums up the content of Jesus' proclamation according to Mark 1:14. The phrase "gospel of God" probably represents the earliest use of "gospel" and very likely goes back to the preaching of Jesus himself. Couched within the Isaianic framework, the "good news" is that the liberating rule of God is close at hand. In early Christian usage, however, the "gospel" proclaimed by Jesus rapidly became the "gospel *about* Jesus"—because of the absolute centrality of his person and destiny in the implementation of the rule of God. Thus more normally for Paul the content of "the gospel" is focused on the death, resurrection, and exaltation of Jesus:

> the gospel concerning his Son:
> who was descended from David according to the flesh
> designated Son of God in power according to the spirit of holiness, by resurrection from the dead,
> Jesus Christ our Lord. (Rom 1:3-4)

It is "the gospel of Jesus Christ" or "about Jesus Christ" in the sense that in raising him from death and establishing him as Messiah and Lord, God has set in place the key instrument for bringing about the downfall of the old era and its captivity to evil powers. The "good news" about his messianic installation is at one and the same time the "good news of God" since that installation is instrumental in bringing about the rule of God, the original intent of the Creator for the world.[6]

6. Paul gives clear expression to this when, albeit working "backward" from "the End," he writes in 1 Corinthians 15: "Then comes the end, when he hands over the kingdom to God

The Rule (or "Kingdom") of God

While central to the preaching of Jesus, the notion of the "kingdom" or "rule of God" is somewhat elusive.[7] I find it helpful to start with the negative: to think first of what it is displacing, namely the opposing "rule" of Satan that holds Israel and the rest of humankind in its dehumanizing grip. Within the apocalyptic Jewish worldview that Mark's gospel shares, the human world, including Israel, has fallen out of the hands of God to languish under the opposing regime of Satan. In this situation the faithful cherish the hope and long for the moment when God, as both creator of the world and covenant partner of Israel, will break this captivity and restore or bring to fruition for the first time the original divine intent for human beings and the world. The rule of God, then, is not something to be established, as it were, on neutral ground. It has to reclaim hostile territory, dislodging the regime of Satan, now currently and ruinously in power. Thus the "good news" about the onset of God's rule that Jesus proclaims (1:15) and the "works of power" by which he expels démons are intimately linked. They are, in effect, opposite sides of the same coin. The exorcisms, healings, even the subjection of destructive natural forces (such as the storm on the lake [4:35-41]), are instances in which God's rule is gaining a foothold in both human affairs and the wider world.

To speak in this way of a foothold already obtained is to move on from the background apocalyptic worldview to the presentation of the Kingdom in the gospel itself. In pre-Christian Jewish expectation the advent of God's rule is still a matter of hope. It lies on the "other side," as it were, of a final struggle with the forces of evil, forces that will not give in before inflicting great suffering and distress upon the faithful. For Mark—and we can say with confidence for Jesus himself—Kingdom eschatology is more complex. The definitive establishment of God's rule may still be a matter of hope, but the contest with evil is already well under way and the power of the Kingdom is already beginning to transform human lives when it finds acceptance through repentance and faith (Mark 1:15). A study of Mark's gospel will

---

the Father, after he has destroyed every ruler and every authority and power. For he must reign until he has put all his enemies under his feet (15:24-25). . . .When all things are subjected to him, then the Son himself will also be subjected to the one who put all things in subjection under him, so that God may be all in all" (v. 28).

7. Strictly speaking the English word "rule," rather than "kingdom," corresponds more exactly to the idea conveyed by the Greek term *basileia,* since what is in view is not a localized political entity but more a regimen or regime. However, because the phrase "kingdom of God" has become established in Christian parlance I shall for the most part speak of "the kingdom."

show that, while Jesus presupposes the conventional understanding of the rule or kingdom of God in the minds of his hearers, a great deal of his instruction is aimed at challenging and transforming that understanding in order to make it conform with his vision of God and the way God is already reaching out in relationship to human beings here and now. The parables, in particular, are designed to address this revisioning of the nature of the Kingdom and the timescale or "program" of its arrival in the world.

Agents of God's Rule (Messiah, Son of God, Son of Man)

While some saw the Kingdom as coming about through direct divine action, more widespread was the view that God would employ intermediary figures as instruments to this end. A variety of views in regard to such figures prevailed. For the purpose of filling in the background to Mark's gospel I shall focus simply on the three roles summed up in the titles "Messiah" (Christ), "Son of God," and "Son of Man."

1. "Messiah"

When Christians approach the topic of messianism they have to be wary of reading back into Jewish literature the developed messianic understanding with respect to the person of Jesus that Christianity simply takes for granted. Messianic expectation in Judaism, where it existed at all, took a variety of forms. "Messiah" in Hebrew simply means "anointed" (hence the Greek translation *christos,* rendered in English as "Christ"). Since anointing with oil was a standard Israelite ritual for installing a person in office, priests and kings (and, figuratively, prophets [cf. Isa 61:1; Ps 105:15) could bear the title "the anointed." In the main, though, the phrase "the Lord's Anointed" became a respectful title for the king (cf. Pss 2:2; 18:50; 84:9; 132:10, 17; etc.). In the centuries following the return from exile in Babylon, disillusionment with the various forms of social and political subjection under which Jews labored led to the hope, in some circles at least, for a restoration of the Davidic dynasty and specifically for the rise of a "son of David" who would set Israel free from foreign control, and rule in righteousness, prosperity, and peace (cf. the late oracle in Jer 33:14-26). As king, this ruler would be "the Anointed One" or "Messiah," but neither the title nor the role envisaged anything more than human status. The expectation, which can now be called "messianic" in the technical sense, was simply for a righteous ruler who would restore in Israel the glories of the Davidic "golden age." While references to such a figure appear most prominently in the Dead

Sea Scrolls,[8] the most complete description is to be found in a few phrases from a collection of (noncanonical) psalms dating from the first century B.C.E., the *Psalms of Solomon:*

> See, Lord, and raise up for them their king,
> the son of David, to rule over your servant Israel . . .
> Undergird him with the strength to destroy the unrighteous rulers, to purge
> Jerusalem from Gentiles who trample her to destruction . . .
> He will gather a holy people whom he will lead in righteousness . . .
> There will be no unrighteousness among them in his days,
> for all shall be holy, and their king shall be the Lord Messiah.[9]

Though renewal in a religious sense is prominent in this description, overtly political and even military aspects are not lacking. What is absent is any sense that carrying out the messianic role will involve suffering and death. It is no surprise, then, to find Jesus in the Gospel of Mark struggling to suppress or combat expectations pinned on him in terms of this conventional view of messiahship—especially in the minds of his disciples.

2. *"Son of God"*

As in the case of "Messiah," the title "Son of God," despite the exalted sense in which the Gospel of Mark applies it to Jesus, does not in and of itself imply divinity. There is a minor though fairly widespread motif running through the Old Testament in which Israel is metaphorically described as God's "son" or "child" (Exod 4:22-23; Hos 1:11; 11:1; Sir 36:17; etc.).[10] Hence all Israelites, unlike members of other nations, can regard themselves as "children of God" (Deut 14:1; cf. Rom 9:4). This privilege was crystallized in the person of the king, who, in a figurative sense, was regarded as "begotten" by God (Ps 2:7; cf. LXX Ps 110[109]:3), and hence as enjoying a filial relationship with God (2 Sam 7:14; Ps 89:26-27). Neither the Old Testament nor later Jewish literature employs "son of God" in a strictly messianic sense, though the circumstantial evidence that the title was so used is very strong.[11] As readers of Mark we have to be aware that when the

---

8. For relevant references to the Qumran evidence see Brendan Byrne, "Jesus as Messiah in the Gospel of Luke: Discerning a Pattern of Correction," *Catholic Biblical Quarterly* 65 (2003) 80–95, especially 80–81.

9. *Pss. Sol.* 17:21-22, 26, 32. Translation by R. B. Wright in James H. Charlesworth, ed., *The Old Testament Pseudepigrapha.* 2 vols. (Garden City, NY: Doubleday, 1985) 2:667.

10. Cf. Brendan Byrne, *"Sons of God"—"Seed of Abraham."* AnBib 83 (Rome: Biblical Institute Press, 1979) 9–78.

11. Cf. ibid., 223.

gospel speaks of Jesus as God's "Son," depending upon who is speaking, a range of understandings is available: from the "merely messianic" in a conventional sense (cf. 14:61) to the full-blown transcendental sense in which Jesus is the "beloved Son" of God (1:11; 9:7; cf. 12:6; 13:32).

3. "Son of Man"

With "Son of Man" we arrive at by far the most controversial description the gospels apply to Jesus. "Son of Man" translates an awkward Greek phrase, *ho huios tou anthrōpou* (lit. "the son of the man"), which occurs throughout the gospels (14 times in Mark), always on the lips of Jesus as a reference to himself (John 12:34 being the only exception). Differently from the instances of "Messiah" ("Christ") or "Son of God," no one *confesses* Jesus as "Son of Man."[12] The phrase seems to be more indicative of a *role* than of a title. The gospel tradition never stops to explain the role designated by the phrase, apparently assuming that the implied audience will understand what it means. The appearance of something so clumsy in the Greek seems to suggest that in this phrase something important from the Aramaic background is being preserved.

In Hebrew idiom "son of . . ." is used to designate membership of a class or guild: "sons of the prophets" = "the prophets." Hence "son of man" (Hebrew *ben ʾadam*) simply indicates a member of the class human = "a human being" (cf. Ps 8:4, where "son of man" stands simply in parallel to "man"). In Ezekiel the prophet is addressed over and over again as "son of man," indicating his mortal, human status over against God.

Most significant is the appearance of the phrase in Dan 7:13-14, where, before the throne of God, dominion, glory, and kingship are bestowed upon "one like a son of man":

> 13. As I watched in the visions of the night,
>   I saw one like a son of man coming with the clouds of heaven.
>   And he came to the Ancient One and was presented before him.
> 14. To him was given dominion and glory and kingship,
>   that all peoples, nations, and languages should serve him.
>   His dominion is an everlasting dominion that shall not pass away,
>   and his kingship is one that shall never be destroyed.

---

12. There is a singular usage in Acts 7:56, where the dying Stephen confesses to a vision of "the Son of Man"; elsewhere the phrase occurs only in two allusions to Dan 7:13 in Revelation (1:13; 14:14).

The prerogatives here bestowed on the "son of man" are later (Dan 7:21-22, 27) conferred upon "the holy ones of the Most High," who many consider to represent the persecuted faithful to whom the book of Daniel as a whole is addressed. The vision is indicating their coming vindication. This would imply that the "son of man" (or "human one," in contrast to the "beasts" who represent various oppressing empires) is a collective symbol for the faithful in Israel—though some scholars see already here in Daniel a reference to an exalted angelic figure, pictured in human form.

Such a development is certainly to be seen in the "Similitudes" section of the (postbiblical) *(First) Book of Enoch* (37–71), where the Danielic son of man has stepped out from purely symbolic status to become a glorious, heavenly figure who reveals mysteries to the elect in the present and who will come at the end of time to execute judgment and usher the elect into the bliss of the eternal kingdom. This view of the Son of Man has clear links with the considerable number of references in the gospel tradition to the Son of Man as an eschatological figure destined to play a very similar role. But whether the gospel tradition presupposes such a development is a matter of controversy, since it is not certain that the section of *1 Enoch* in which it appears (the Similitudes) really antedates the gospels.[13] Many would hold, however, that Jesus and/or the early Christians were familiar with the "Son of Man" concept found in the Similitudes of Enoch even if not precisely with the Similitudes themselves. In other words, the apocalyptic, eschatological expectation, drawn from Daniel 7, of a heavenly Son of Man figure, coming in judgment, was "in the air" at the time, as an expression of hope for the suffering faithful.

The preservation of the phrase "Son of Man" in the gospels, despite its great awkwardness in Greek translation, suggests that its appearance in the tradition goes back to Jesus himself. In what sense, however, might he have used it? Though (with the exception of John 12:34) it always appears as a self-designation of Jesus, some (e.g., Rudolf Bultmann) would argue that originally Jesus spoke of a Son of Man distinct from himself to whose eschatological coming he pointed (cf. Mark 8:38); the identification of the coming Son of Man with Jesus in the gospels would then be the work of early Christian tradition. While Bultmann thought that Jesus used "Son of Man" only with reference to an eschatological figure distinct from himself, others (e.g., Geza Vermes), maintaining that the Aramaic phrase *bar enash* can function as a circumlocution for "I" (cf. the English usage of "one" in this

---

13. Though *1 Enoch* is widely represented in the Qumran [Dead Sea Scroll] literature, the section containing the Similitudes is not.

sense), claim that the "Son of Man" statements referring to present earthly status and suffering (e.g., Mark 2:10, 28; 10:45) go back to Jesus, but without any reference to Daniel. The relevance of the circumlocutory usage to Jesus has, however, been challenged (e.g., by Joseph Fitzmyer).[14]

Whatever may have been Jesus' own usage, "Son of Man" in Mark's gospel clearly has links with Daniel and indeed seems to presuppose the developed Danielic tradition seen in *1 Enoch:* note especially the references to the "coming" of the Son of Man "with clouds" in Mark 13:26 and 14:62; cf. Dan 7:13. The sense emanating from Daniel 7 of vindication and divinely bestowed authority following upon obedient suffering admirably holds together the three categories in which the "Son of Man" sayings appear in Mark: present authority (since the Son of Man gives authoritative rulings [2:10; 2:27]); future coming in judgment (8:38; 9:9; 13:26; 14:62), and especially the sense of present suffering that will find future vindication (8:31; 9:12; 9:31; 10:33-34; 10:45; 14:21 [twice]; 14:41). The role denoted by the phrase would seem to have been particularly appropriate for what Mark wanted to communicate about Jesus and about what discipleship entailed for those called to follow his way. On two key occasions the Markan Jesus responds in terms of "Son of Man" (8:31; 14:62) when others (Peter: 8:29; the High Priest: 14:61) have spoken in terms of "Christ" ("Messiah") or "Son of God" ("Son of the Blessed One" in 14:61). The latter titles are applicable to Jesus but stand in need of "correction" in terms of "Son of Man": Jesus fulfills the function they indicate by obediently undergoing suffering now, with the hope of vindication by God (resurrection and exaltation) and installation as eschatological judge of the world (13:26-31; 14:62).[15] Jesus uses "Son of Man" with reference to himself and in this sense interchangeably with "I," but not simply as equivalent to "I": he uses it self-referentially when hinting at or alluding to a mysterious status or destiny that attends him, which is beyond the present ken of his hearers and which the allusion to Daniel captures best.

In reference to "Son of Man" I have gone beyond the background presupposed in the gospel to discuss the usage of the gospel itself. This is because in the case of this title/role it is so hard—and indeed ultimately impossible—to sift out with certainty what belongs to background, what to the historical Jesus, what to the early tradition, and what to the evangelist

14. For a succinct survey see Moloney, *Gospel of Mark,* 212–13.

15. My understanding of "Son of Man" in this Danielic sense aligns with that of Morna Hooker (*The Gospel according to Saint Mark* [London: Black, 1991] 88–93) and Francis Moloney (*Gospel of Mark,* 212–13).

himself. I hope, though, that the brief discussion of worldview that I have provided in relevant areas will assist understanding of the gospel and, more immediately, will serve as background for the presentation of the Markan drama in terms of "three stories," which I offer in the chapter to follow.

Readers who are still with me following this survey of the apocalyptic background to Mark's gospel will, I trust, now be in a better position to enter the narrative world of the gospel on something like its own terms. I do not minimize the imaginative effort required, but I would hope that words and concepts grown colorless in religious parlance—"gospel," "kingdom of God," "demon," etc.—will have become more concrete and more precisely evocative of the realities to which they refer. In particular I would wish to insist that describing something as "apocalyptic" and/or "eschatological" does not mean that reference is being made to something otherworldly, having little or no connection to present human existence and its concerns. Jewish apocalypticism was and is a symbolic way of referring precisely to the present world and its ills, and of expressing hope for the transformation of this world through the faithful action of God. Partaking of that worldview, while to some extent in dialogue and tension with it, the Gospel of Mark has, I believe, something vital to say to the present and future of our world as we know it.

The Design of Mark:
"Three Stories" about Jesus

Years of studying and teaching Mark's gospel have led me to a view of its unfolding drama that I have found helpful and that I believe to be well grounded in the text. I find in Mark three "stories." They are not really stories in the sense of developed narratives, but it is appropriate to call them "stories" because they are bundles of truths about Jesus—his identity, his fate, and his role—that unfold and interact with each other as the overall story evolves. In regard to each "story" the central question to ask is: Who, at any particular stage, knows the truth about Jesus it enunciates?

Story 1 concerns what is said about Jesus in the opening statement or title line of the gospel: that he is the Messiah, the Son of God (1:1). We, the readers of the text, know this from the start because we have read the title. Jesus knows it, at least as far as the text of the gospel is concerned, from the divine address he—and he alone in Mark—hears as he emerges from the water after his baptism by John: "You are my Son, the beloved; in you I am well pleased" (1:11). The only other parties aware of the truth of Story 1 at this early stage of the narrative are the demons who "feel the heat," so to speak, of his messianic power as, in scene after scene, he wrests human beings from their control. Seeking to control him by naming him, the demons cry out: "I (we) know who you are, the Son of God" (1:24, 34; 3:11; cf. 5:7). But Jesus instantly moves to silence them. His identity and status are not to be made known from this hostile direction.

Meanwhile the disciples, and others who experience Jesus' power, wonder and exclaim about his identity. "Who is this, then," they ask after he has quelled the storm at sea, "whom even the winds and the sea obey?" (4:41; cf. 6:51). His townsfolk at Nazareth cannot account for the powers that one so familiar to them is displaying (6:1-6a), and Herod, also roused to curiosity, satisfies himself that Jesus is John the Baptist risen from the

15

dead (6:14-17). This issue concerning Jesus' identity runs throughout the early part of the gospel as a binding narrative thread.

The disciples begin to approach the truth of Story 1 when, at a turning point in the narrative in the region of Caesarea Philippi, Jesus asks them: "Who do people say I am?" (8:27). After they have reported the various views, he puts the question directly to them: "Who do you think I am?" (8:29a). Peter, speaking for all, at last gets it right: "You are the Christ" (8:29b)—or at least he gets it half right, since in Mark's account (contrast Matt 16:16) there is no addition of "Son of God" (cf. Mark 1:1).

No sooner, however, have the disciples arrived at this awareness of Story 1 than Jesus enjoins on them strict silence concerning it. He then goes on immediately to lay alongside it a new and much more painful story, *Story 2:* that he is destined to suffer many things, go up to Jerusalem to be rejected by the chief priests and scribes, be put to death, and on the third day rise (8:31, repeated in 9:31-32; 10:33-34). A great deal of the drama of the narrative from this point on derives from the tension between these two stories. As we have seen, conventional belief about the Messiah in the Judaism of Jesus' day had no room for suffering and defeat, let alone death and resurrection. The disciples, who plainly share this understanding, struggle and fail to hold the two truths together as, reluctantly and fearfully, they follow Jesus to Jerusalem (9:30–10:52). How could he be Messiah—and indeed God's Son (9:7)—and yet be destined to suffer this fate? The conflict between the two stories comes to a climax at the crucifixion as Jesus is taunted, precisely as pretend Messiah, to come down from the cross so that those who mock may come to believe (15:29-32). Only after Jesus has died, with a cry of abandonment on his lips (15:34), do the two stories come together when the Roman centurion who has supervised the execution, seeing how he has died, exclaims: "Truly this man was the Son of God" (15:39).

Before this climax, however, another truth about Jesus had also begun to emerge, *Story 3:* that he will return at the end of the age as the Son of Man in glory to institute judgment on the world, vindicate the faithful, and complete his messianic work by definitively establishing the rule of God. Jesus had alluded to this ultimate destiny as a conclusion to the instruction on the cost of discipleship in 8:38-39. It forms the climax of the discourse on the future that makes up chapter 13 (13:24-27). Above all, he appeals to it when he stands on trial before the High Priest (Story 2). Interrogated about his identity ("Are you the Christ, the Son of the Blessed One?" [14:61]), he openly acknowledges it (Story 1), but goes on to add: "and you will see the Son of Man seated at the right hand of the Power, and coming with the clouds of heaven" (14:62). The apparent conflict between Story 1 and Story 2, which comes to a climax as God's Son dies on the cross, will find its ultimate reso-lution in the vindication proclaimed in Story 3: the return of the obedient Son of God as Son of Man in glory and as eschatological judge.

One of the reasons, I believe, why Mark's gospel never provides a vision of the risen Lord is that for this evangelist the vindication of Jesus and of the divine cause he served attaches more to this final appearance as Son of Man than to his resurrection, which is essentially a stage on the way to it. The community for whom Mark wrote believed that the crucified One has been raised from the dead and exalted to God's right hand. From here he carries out his messianic task through the Spirit until his final appearance to establish once and for all the rule of God. That is the core of "the Gospel." The "beginning" of the Gospel (1:1) is the anticipation of this messianic rule that Mark describes in his account of Jesus' ministry, from his submission to baptism at the hands of John to his submission to death on the cross (15:37). The three "stories" that interact with one another through the narrative eventually become the single story of Jesus' triumphal accomplishment of the Father's saving design in regard to human beings and the world (cf. Phil 2:6-11).

THE STRUCTURE OF THE GOSPEL

The prominence of the presentation of Jesus as Son of God in Mark's gospel makes it possible to set out what I would call its "macrostructure." The issue of Jesus' identity and the revelation of this in terms of his divine sonship appear at three key moments in the narrative: near the beginning (1:7-11), at the midpoint (8:27–9:8), and toward the end (14:61–15:39). These three moments form what I would call the "pillars" on which the overall framework of the story rests. In light of these three "pillar moments" we can set out its macrostructure in the following schematic way. (My students tell me that it looks like a billiard table seen from the side!)

"SON OF GOD": "PILLARS" OF THE GOSPEL

Baptism	Caesarea Philippi —Transfiguration	Passion
1:7-11	8:27–9:8	14:53–15:39

Baptism	Caesarea Philippi– Transfiguration:	Passion
1:7 (John) pro-claimed, "The One who is more power-ful than I is coming after me; . . . **1:10** And when (Jesus) came up out of the water, immediately he saw the heavens opened and the Spirit descending upon him like a dove; **1:11** and a voice came from heaven, "You are my beloved *Son;* with you I am well pleased."	**8:27** . . . on the way (Jesus) asked his disciples, "Who do people say that I am?" . . . **8:29** And he asked them, "But who do you say that I am?" Peter answered him, "You are the Christ." **9:7** And a cloud over-shadowed them, and a voice came out of the cloud, "This is my beloved *Son;* listen to him."	**14:61** . . . Again the high priest asked him, "Are you the Christ, the *Son of the Blessed One?*" **14:62** And Jesus said, "I am; and you will see the Son of Man seated at the right hand of Power, and coming with the clouds of heaven." **Calvary: 15:32** "Let the Messiah, the King of Israel, come down from the cross now, so that we may see and believe." . . . **15:39** And when the centurion, who stood facing him, saw that he thus breathed his last, he said, "Truly this man was *a son of God.*"

With respect to each "pillar," the issue of Jesus' identity is raised: by John the Baptist (1:7), by Jesus himself (8:27), by the High Priest (14:61), and by those who mock (15:32). In each case a response is given in terms of Jesus' divine sonship: in the first two cases from the Father (1:11; 9:7), and in the third from the centurion who comes to faith (15:39).

LINEAR OUTLINE OF MARK'S GOSPEL

It is impossible to settle on a definitive outline of the content of the gospel. What I propose here would find general agreement in broad terms. Note that sections II, III, and IV begin with a summary followed by a call/ appointment of disciples and end on a note of hostility and/or unbelief.

I. Prologue: 1:1-13:   Title: 1:1
Preaching of John the Baptist: 1:2-8
Baptism of Jesus: 1:9-11; Testing of Jesus: 1:12-13

II. Early Galilean Ministry: 1:14–3:6
Begins with a summary: 1:14-15 and Call of First Disciples: 1:16-20
Ends with plot to "destroy" Jesus: 3:6
Includes: "Day at Capernaum": 1:21-45
Controversy sequence: 2:1–3:6a

III. Later Galilean Ministry: 3:7–6:6a
Begins with a summary: 3:7-12, and appointment of Twelve: 3:13-19
Ends with unbelief at Nazareth: 6:1-6a
Includes: Relatives: 3:20-21; Controversy: 3:22-30; Relatives: 3:31-35;
Parables: 4:1-34; Three Miracles: 4:35–5:43

IV. Jesus Extends his Ministry: 6:6b–8:21
Begins with a summary (6:6b) and mission of Twelve: 6:7-13
Ends with "blindness" of disciples: 8:14-21
Includes: Description of death of John the Baptist: 6:14-29
Two feedings (5000 [6:33-44]; 4000 [8:1-10]), each
followed by a "boat + incomprehension" sequence.
Between the two feedings occurs a shift to the Gentile region,
prepared for by the controversy on clean and unclean: 7:1-23

V. The Messiah on his "Way" to Jerusalem: 8:22–10:52

Begins with the cure of a blind man at Bethsaida: 8:22-26
Ends with the cure of a blind man at Jericho: 10:46-52
Includes: Caesarea Philippi confession: 8:27-30; Transfiguration:
    8:34–9:1
Three Passion Predictions: 8:31-33; 9:30:31; 10:32-34
General theme: the cost of discipleship in various areas

VI. The Messiah in Jerusalem: 11:1–13:37

Part 1: 11:1–12:44
Begins with entry into Jerusalem and the Temple: 11:1-11
Ends with comment on widow's offering to the Temple: 12:41-44
Pervasive theme: the contest for authority in Jerusalem

Part 2: Jesus' Discourse on the Future: 13:1-37

VII. Jesus' Passion and Death: 14:1–15:47

Begins with conspiracy: 14:1-2 and anointing of Jesus by a woman:
    14:3-9
Ends with burial of Jesus and vigil by three women: 15:42-47

VIII. Epilogue: 16:1-8: The Empty Tomb

DYNAMIC NARRATIVE STRUCTURE OF THE GOSPEL

While it is helpful to view the content of Mark's gospel in the linear way set out above, the peculiarly open-ended way in which the narrative ends (at 16:7-8) suggests also a more dynamic approach. The evangelist is prompting the audience to "go back to Galilee" with the disciples to hear or read the story again—and then again. Seen in this way, the gospel calls for a "circular" reading in which the interplay of what I have called the three "stories" about Jesus can be appreciated and appropriated at ever greater depth.[1] Just as the disciples failed, in the first round, to grasp the mystery of Jesus in which they were so intimately involved, so the audience of Mark cannot hope to penetrate that mystery at a single hearing or reading. Like the disciples we have to go back to Galilee where it all began and retrace our steps with Jesus on his costly journey. Once again I attempt to set out in schematic form this dynamic structural aspect of the gospel:

1. While construing the matter somewhat differently, I owe this insight into the circular structure of Mark to Ched Myers, *Binding the Strong Man: A Political Reading of Mark's Story of Jesus* (New York: Maryknoll, 1988) 111–15.

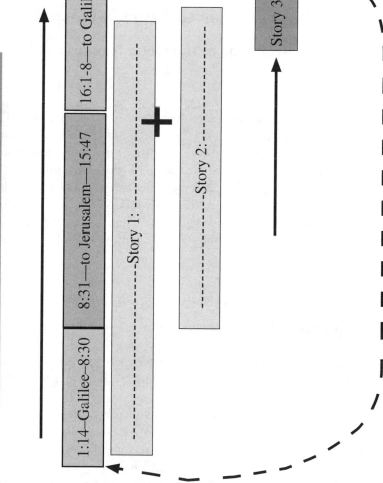

The Prologue to Mark's Gospel

The Beginning of the Good News: 1:1-13

It is easy to slip past the opening sentence of Mark's Gospel: "The beginning of the good news of Jesus Christ [the Son of God]" (1:1). But this simple string of phrases, a kind of title for the gospel, offers key signals for all that is to follow. The title and the scriptural quotation attributed to Isaiah in the following two verses (1:2-3) plunge us immediately into the thought world of the gospel, the chief features of which I have already outlined in an earlier chapter. Unless we bring an understanding of that world to our reading of the text right from the start, much of what Mark has to say will simply pass us by.

"The Beginning of the Good News . . .": 1:1

Within the worldview presupposed by the gospel the opening phrase "beginning of the gospel" (*archē tou euangeliou*) is richly evocative. Let us take "gospel" first. It is one of Mark's favorite terms; he uses it seven times (1:1, 14, 15; 8:35; 10:29; 13:10; 14:9), where the much longer Matthew has it four times, while in Luke and John it is lacking entirely.[1] "Gospel" is so central to Christian religious discourse that it has become devoid of specific meaning. If we are to be grasped by what Mark is signaling to the reader in his opening phrase we need to bring to our reading of "gospel" an awareness of the special meaning it had acquired, from its origins in the texts from (Second) Isaiah proclaiming the "good news" of Israel's liberation from captivity in Babylon (Isa 40:9; 52:7; 61:1; etc.), to its usage with reference to a later form of captivity—to the demonic—in apocalyptic Jewish circles just before the rise of Christianity.

---

1. Luke does have the verbal form, "to proclaim the good news" (*euangelizesthai*) ten times.

22

I shall presuppose rather than repeat here the outline of this development in the introductory survey of the worldview behind Mark's gospel. Let me simply recall four key associations that "gospel" brings with it in view of that development:

1. The "good news" is a message of freedom from captivity, captivity specifically to demonic control;
2. the liberation is being brought about because a new era has dawned in which the rule of Israel's God ("kingdom of God") is usurping and replacing the enslaving regime of Satan and the demonic in general;
3. the announcement of the "good news," and indeed the liberation itself is the work of an agent of God "anointed" ("Messiah") with the Spirit for the task; and
4. the liberation involves reconciliation with God (atonement for sin).

All these motifs will make an early appearance in the narrative that lies before us.

But what does Mark mean by "the beginning (Greek *archē*) of the gospel?"—or, more precisely, how far into the text or into the events it narrates is "beginning" meant to extend? On the one hand, "beginning" could refer to the witness of John (1:2-8), which is the prelude to the appearance of Jesus, the proclaimer and center of the Gospel proper. Or it could refer to the entire prologue, that is, to all that takes place before the beginning of Jesus' public ministry (1:1-13). Or "beginning" could in fact refer to the entire narrative right up to the discovery of the empty tomb and the angel's commissioning of the women (16:7).

Some light is shed on this question if we consider the content of "gospel" as it appears in the letters of the earliest Christian writer, the apostle Paul. At the start of his letter to the Romans Paul announces himself as an apostle "set apart for the gospel of God" (Rom 1:1), and then goes on to quote an early Christian creed giving the content of "the gospel":

> the gospel concerning his Son:
> who was descended from David according to the flesh,
> designated Son of God in power according to the spirit of holiness, by resurrection from the dead,
> Jesus Christ our Lord. (Rom 1:3-4)

While Paul initially speaks of "the gospel of God" (1:1), the focus in the credal statement is entirely on the person of Jesus Christ. In a two-stage statement of his "career," his human descent from David gives him the right credentials to be Messiah, while his resurrection from the dead and endowment with the

Spirit make him Messiah or Son of God in power. Paul does not believe that Jesus only became God's Son at the moment of his resurrection, but it was his resurrection that publicly unveiled—to the resurrection witnesses and subsequent believers—his unique filial status in relation to God, and that inaugurated his messianic campaign to bring about through the Spirit the rule of God. In raising him from the dead and establishing him as Messiah and Lord, God has set in place the key instrument for bringing about the downfall of the old era and its captivity to evil powers. In early Christian parlance, the Gospel can be focused on the person of Jesus as "the good news about Jesus Christ" (Rom 1:3-4; 1 Cor 15:3-5) while remaining also the "good news of God" (1 Thess 2:2, 8, 9; Rom 1:1; 15:16; Mark 1:14) since all that has happened in respect to Jesus is instrumental in bringing about the original intent of the Creator for human beings and the world.[2]

This excursus into Paul's understanding of "Gospel" has placed us in a better position to return to the opening phrases of Mark's gospel and to the question why the *"beginning"* (Greek *archē*) of the Gospel? If, for Paul—and presumably other Christian writers and preachers before Mark—the core content of "the Gospel" was the good news about God's raising of Jesus and the establishment of his messianic reign through the Spirit (Rom 1:3-4), what Mark could be saying, then, at the start of his work is: "You believe the basic good news about Jesus the Crucified One: how God raised him from the dead and revealed him to be Messiah and Son of God. Now I am going to tell you how Jesus anticipated his postresurrection messianic reign in his teaching and activity up to and including his death on the cross. In other words, I am going to tell you how it all *began*." Mark's intent in all this is not simply to communicate information about Jesus but to point out the true way of discipleship that the messianic service of his earthly life models and that alone leads to a share in his risen life (cf. Mark 8:34-38).[3] It is in this sense that the entire Markan narrative (down to 16:8) is "the *beginning* of the good news about Jesus the Messiah, the Son of God."[4] The whole of Jesus' ministry, beginning with his baptism at the hands of John,

---

2. Cf. the divine "program" outlined by Paul in 1 Cor 15:22-28 (cited above, p. xix).

3. Cf. M. Eugene Boring, *Mark: A Commentary.* NTL (Louisville and London: Westminster John Knox, 2006) 31–32, 37–38.

4. The phrase "the Son of God" is absent from some significant early manuscripts (notably Codex Sinaiticus), an omission that is hard to account for if the phrase originally did stand in the text. On balance I think the phrase was missing. However, its inclusion is not inappropriate, since Jesus clearly is the "Son of God" for Mark, as the divine voice following his baptism will shortly attest (1:13). The omission of the title here serves to make that heavenly acknowledgment all the more powerful when it is heard. For discussion see Moloney, *Gospel of Mark,* 29, n. 11.

will anticipate and signal the unique and totally (in conventional Jewish understanding) unforeseen way in which he will be Messiah, not just for Israel but for the benefit of the nations of the world (cf. 13:10).

There is a lot to be said for this understanding of the opening sentence.[5] However, I do not think that referring "beginning . . ." to the entire narrative need exclude a more specific reference also to the ministry of John the Baptist (1:2-8). This is because, as the scriptural quotation in the next two verses shows, the appearance of John in the wilderness and the message he "cries" there (vv. 4-8) is, in fulfillment of Isa 40:3, the "beginning" of the divine intervention, which is what the "good news" is all about.

The Appearance and Witness of John the Baptist: 1:2-8[6]

The fact that Mark does not immediately refer to the appearance of John but—in a way that rather complicates the statement—cites first (vv. 2-3) the scriptural prophecy his appearance will fulfill, shows the immense significance for this evangelist of the reference to Isaiah.[7] So important indeed is this Isaianic background that Mark cobbles together and attributes to Isaiah a composite quotation, the first part of which (v. 2: "Behold, I am sending my messenger ahead of you, who will prepare your way") is not from that prophet at all, but comes from Exod 23:20, with some influence from Mal 3:1.[8]

It is easy to regard this attribution of the whole to Isaiah as due to carelessness or ignorance on Mark's part.[9] Such a judgment is very likely wrong. It fails to recognize two things: first, that composite quotations, attributed to a single biblical author, were not uncommon in literature of the time, including the New Testament (cf., e.g., Matt 27:9-10); second and

5. Cf. Joel Marcus, *Mark 1–8: A New Translation with Introduction and Commentary.* AB 27 (New York: Doubleday, 2000) 146; also Boring, *Mark,* 29.

6. Strictly speaking, Mark refers to him here as "John the baptizer" (also 6:14, 24), but to avoid irritating readers I shall avoid pedantic correctness and retain the traditional appellation (as in Mark 6:25; 8:28).

7. The syntax across vv. 1-4 is by no means clear. I think it is best to see v. 1 as a stand-alone title, and then vv. 2-4 as a single composite sentence, with vv. 2-3 constituting an introductory adverbial clause stressing that the appearance of John (v. 4) is in conformity with the Isaianic promise.

8. The first part of the statement agrees exactly with the LXX of Exod 23:20a; the second part ("who will prepare your way") stands closer to the Hebrew form of Mal 3:1.

9. Matthew and Luke both omit at this point (Matt 3:3; Luke 3:4) the Exod 23:20/Mal 3:1 part of the quotation, beginning immediately and "correctly" with Isa 40:3. The Exod 23:20/Mal 3:1 text, without specific attribution, occurs in another context: Jesus' words about John (Matt 11:10; John 7:27 [= "Q"]).

more importantly, it neglects the significance of Isaiah, specifically Isaiah 40–55, as "carrier" of the hopes for the messianic age. It is not that the scriptural text "serves" the appearance of John. Rather, the evangelist is pointing out that the appearance of John signals the setting in motion of the long-awaited divine intervention described by Isaiah.

The second element of the scriptural quotation (v. 3: "The voice of one crying in the wilderness: 'Prepare the way of the Lord; make straight his paths'") quotes the Greek version (LXX) of Isa 40:3 almost exactly.[10] The text stands, of course, at the very beginning of (Second) Isaiah's message of liberation. Its appearance in the literature of several Jewish movements in the period just prior to the rise of Christianity[11] shows that it was a significant bearer of the hopes for divine intervention cherished across the Jewish tradition at this later time. Within that wider context, its appearance here confirms the sense that Mark sees not only the advent of John but also the entire bundle of events his narrative will describe as the fulfillment at last of all that Isaiah (Isaiah 40–55) promised. In the late sixth century B.C.E. (Second) Isaiah reprised the Exodus tradition that told of YHWH's foundational redemptive act on behalf of Israel to describe a new act of liberation that would reverse the Babylonian exile. Now, in line with a later development of the tradition, Mark portrays the events he is about to describe as the true and final enactment of the "New Exodus" Isaiah proclaimed.[12] This, presumably, is why Mark felt it appropriate to give his whole project the Isaianic designation "gospel."

What binds the composite quotation attributed to Isaiah together is, of course, the term "way" (Greek *hodos*) common to all three texts involved (Exod 20:23; Mal 3:1; Isa 40:3). "Way" will be a very significant term in the gospel.[13] The entire narrative is nothing less than an exposition of the redemptive "way of the Lord" Isaiah foretold—though the "way" as trod by Jesus will take directions totally unforeseen in conventional expectation.

In the original meaning of the texts quoted in verses 2-3 the one for whom the way is to be "prepared" is in the first instance (Exod 20:23) Israel

10. The only difference is that Mark has replaced "the paths of the Lord" with the simple "his paths."

11. Notably in a text from Qumran setting out the basic self-understanding of the community: 1QS (Manual of Discipline) 8:12b-16a; cf. 9:17b-20; also *Psalms of Solomon* 11.

12. Rikki Watts puts it well: "Mark's use of the Isaiah ascription and the 'iconic function' of the Isaiah 40:3 text within various Jewish traditions indicate that the overall conceptual framework for his Gospel is the Isaianic NE [New Exodus], the prophetic transformation of Israel's memory of her founding moment into a model for her future hope" (*Isaiah's New Exodus,* 90).

13. Cf. Mark 2:23; 4:4, 15; 6:8; 8:3, 27; 9:33-34; 10:17, 32, 46, 52; 11:8; 12:14.

(about to enter the promised land), then (Mal 3:1 and Isa 40:3) YHWH, Israel's God. In Mark's composite quotation the "Lord" for whom the way is to be prepared is clearly the one just nominated: "Jesus Christ, the Son of God" (1:1). Already, then, on the threshold of the gospel an exalted christology appears. Jesus is not identified with God, but he is to bear the name "Lord" (Greek *kyrios*) that signifies the presence and power of YHWH (cf. Phil 2:9-11). Moreover, prefacing Isa 40:3 with the text from Exodus makes the entire quotation an address by the Lord (YHWH) to this other "Lord." As YHWH promised, in Exodus 23, to send a "messenger" (angel guardian) ahead of Israel into the promised land, so God makes the same assurance to this Messiah Lord and lays the scriptural ground (v. 3) for identifying John the Baptist as the one who will play that role.

I hope it is now clear how much this complex though brief scriptural introduction (vv. 2-3) tells us about the subject of the narrative that is about to unfold. He is the Messiah (v. 1). He is the "Lord" who will tread the salvific "way" marked out by Isaiah. He is also, through the quotation of Exod 23:20 (v. 2), in some sense replaying the role of Israel: his person will be the foundation of a renewed people of God, destined to enter not the promised land of old (Canaan), but the fullness of salvation associated with the onset of God's rule.

The five verses (4-8) dealing with the appearance and message of John are, then, in strict continuity with the preceding quotation attributed to Isaiah (vv. 2-3). John's "preaching" in the wilderness (v. 4) is the "voice" Isaiah spoke of as "crying (out) in the wilderness" (v. 3). The baptism of repentance he is proclaiming (v. 4) and the large-scale response it attracts (v. 5) constitute the "way" prepared for the Lord. The "way" is not now a physical way in the sense of a smooth road across the desert regions (as in Isaiah). It is a way "made straight" in human hearts: the disposition of repentance and conversion that renders them receptive to the message and ministry of the Lord.

Mark brings all this out by the very careful arrangement of these verses. Verses 4-5 tell of John's preaching (*kēryssein,* v. 4) and the response it attracts (v. 5); verse 6 describes his attire and diet; verses 7-8 (in "inclusive" fashion) tell of a fresh aspect of his preaching (*kēryssein*): his pointing to a coming One who is "stronger" than himself. The description of John's attire and diet seems oddly placed at first sight—something of an afterthought that might have found a more natural location immediately after the mention of John's appearance in verse 4. It actually plays a key role in the transition to the new phase of John's preaching in verses 7-8. John's attire—his being clad in camel hair (presumably a cloak of camel hair) and wearing a leather belt around his waist—evokes the description of the prophet Elijah in 2 Kgs 1:8. Mark requires readers familiar with this biblical episode where the ailing King Ahaziah inquires about the kind of man his messengers had met on the road and, when apprised of his attire ("a hairy man with a leather belt around his waist"), exclaims, "It is Elijah the Tishbite" (v. 8b). Mark wants readers, told of John's attire, to make the same exclamation: "It is Elijah the Tishbite.[14] In other words, the text is signaling that John is to be cast in the role of the returning Elijah, the prophet who did not really die (2 Kgs 2:9-12) and who, on the basis of Mal 4:5-6 (cf. Mal 3:1, alluded to in Mark 1:2) was expected to return before the "day of the Lord" as forerunner of the Messiah.[15]

This awareness that John is to play the role of the returning Elijah (cf. 9:13) leads naturally into the rather different content of the second phase of his message (vv. 7-8). Here John points to the coming after him of "the Stronger One" (*ho ischyroteros*). He makes clear his own radical inferiority to this figure with a striking image: whereas students might carry their teacher's sandals as a mark of respect, to bend down and untie them was a task performed only by slaves. Yet John does not see himself worthy of even this relationship with the One to whose coming he points.

Jesus is "stronger," then, in relation to John. Later in the narrative, in controversy with the scribes over the source of his power to drive out demons, he portrays himself as a burglar able to enter the house of a "strong man" (Satan), bind him and plunder his goods (3:27). We will then understand that Jesus is the "Stronger One" also in relation to the demonic. The "house" of the world has fallen into the grip of the "Strong One," Satan. Jesus is the "Stronger One," come to bind up Satan (through his exorcisms) and "plunder" his "house" in the sense of reclaiming human lives and human society for the freedom of the Kingdom.

Finally, John draws a contrast between himself and the coming one in terms of baptism (v. 8). The baptism he proclaims and performs is a physical

14. It is less easy to fit the details of John's diet (v. 6c) into a recognizable pattern. The fare involved—locusts and wild honey—is typical "desert" food; it reinforces the sense of John as an ascetic prophetic figure who issues his summons to repentance and renewal from that context—"wilderness"—where Israel had its most intense experiences of God.

15. While there is evidence for the expectation of Elijah's return before the "day of the Lord" (Sirach 48; *1 Enoch* 90:31), the association of this expectation with the advent of the Messiah is hard to document in Jewish circles outside Christian literature. The disciples' question in Mark 9:11 ("Why do the scribes say Elijah must come first?") confirms Mark's adherence to this belief, which of course surfaces again just before Jesus dies (15:35-36). See further Watts, *Isaiah's New Exodus,* 74–75.

act—immersion in water—enacting an interior attitude of repentance and change of heart.[16] It is a "baptism of repentance *for the forgiveness of sins*" in that it disposes recipients for the experience of divine forgiveness that the coming Stronger One will authoritatively declare (2:5). This One will "baptize with the Holy Spirit" in the sense of bringing about that total renewal portrayed by the prophet Ezekiel as something to be achieved by divine power in the messianic age:

> I will sprinkle clean water upon you, and you shall be clean from all your uncleannesses, and from all your idols I will cleanse you. A new heart I will give you, and a new spirit I will put within you; and I will remove from your body the heart of stone and give you a heart of flesh. I will put my spirit within you, and make you follow my statutes and be careful to observe my ordinances. (Ezek 36:24-27)

Unlike Matthew and Luke, Mark does not really let us hear any message from John for our conversion (Matt 3:7-10, 12; Luke 3:7-9, 17-18) or moral instruction (cf. Luke 3:10-14). John's sole task in Mark is to point to Jesus and to highlight his unique status and role. What Mark's simpler depiction does underline is the necessity of a repentant heart. That is the only "way" upon which this Messiah can "travel" and bring about the promised salvation. Without repentance, with "hardness of heart" instead, Jesus' liberating teaching will be misunderstood and rejected. The narrative, as it unfolds, will inexorably bear this out.

In these short sentences (vv. 2-8) Mark has identified and fixed John in the scheme of salvation. His appearance and preaching, his preparation of the "way" in the sense described, his being cast in the role of returning Elijah: all fulfill key elements of the Isaianic program heralding the coming of the Lord. They signal that the program is unfolding according to the pre-announced plan (in Scripture) and the conditions have been fulfilled for its central agent, Jesus, to appear. Thanks to the introduction, we already know a great deal about him as he makes his entry upon the Markan stage.

---

16. John's baptizing activity, attested by the Jewish historian Josephus (*Antiquities* 18.5.2; §§116-19), as well as the NT sources, has certain resemblances both to the later practice of proselyte baptism (that is, when non-Jews became Jews) and to the repeated bathing rituals of the Qumran community. It is difficult, however, to find anything closely corresponding to it in the Jewish context, especially in the sense of its being a once-for-all ritual carried out by a single prophetic figure (John) in the context of a summons to renewal in view of imminent judgment. For a full discussion of the likely meaning of John's baptizing activity in historical terms see John P. Meier, *A Marginal Jew.* Volume Two: *Mentor, Message and Miracles* (New York: Doubleday, 1994) 49–56.

Jesus' Baptism and Anointing with the Spirit: 1:9-11

The scene in which Jesus first appears in Mark's gospel is usually entitled "the baptism." But it is what happens immediately after Jesus' baptism by John (vv. 10-11) that renders the episode a "pillar" of the Markan narrative. The voice from heaven makes clear—to Jesus himself and to ourselves as readers—the truth that I have dubbed "Story One": that Jesus is Messiah and God's beloved Son.

Though the main focus lies on this moment of revelation, we should not let overfamiliarity with the story dull us to the striking nature of the event told in verse 9. From the scriptural preparation (vv. 2-3) and the preaching of John (vv. 7-8) we know that the one submitting to baptism is the "Lord" for whom, according to Isaiah, a "way" had to be prepared and that he is also the "Stronger One" for whom the revered prophet John was unworthy to perform even the most menial service. Yet the subject himself emerges from the nondescript town of Nazareth in Galilee simply as one of the mass of repentant Israelites who approach John for baptism. Where Matthew makes explicit the jarring note in Jesus' receiving baptism from John and records a little dialogue between the two to sort it out (Matt 3:14-15), and while Luke does his best to ensure we will hardly notice the event by tucking it away in a subordinate clause (cf. Luke 3:21b), Mark simply leaves the two facts to sit there alongside each other in challenging disharmony: (1) Jesus is the Lord whose saving coming Isaiah promised; (2) he makes his first appearance on the scene in solidarity with thousands of others undergoing a rite of repentance and renewal. Here we see for the first time the pattern of sudden oscillation between the human and the divine that is so striking a feature of Mark's presentation.

The pattern intensifies in the epiphany (revelation of the divine) that follows (vv. 10-11). Precisely[17] as he rises up from the water of the Jordan, Jesus—and he alone in the Markan version—sees the heavens "torn open" (v. 10a) and the Spirit coming down upon him like a dove (v. 10b). The "tearing open" of the heavens (*schizomenous tous ouranous*) responds to the plea recorded in Isa 63:19 (Hebrew 64:1): "O that you would tear open the heavens and come down." The plea stems from a sense that the barrier

---

17. "Precisely" is an attempt to capture the force of the adverb *euthys* (literally, "immediately") that makes here the first of its forty-one appearances in Mark's gospel (out of fifty-one occurrences in the New Testament as a whole). The usage may reflect the origin of the gospel in oral presentation. While awkward at times to translate, it lends the sense of everything proceeding at breathless haste—the unstoppable unfolding of a divine project; cf. Marcus, *Mark 1–8,* 159.

between heaven (the abode of God) and earth has long been impenetrably shut, resulting in a devastating "drought" of divine assistance or communication for Israel. What Jesus now "sees" is a breaching of that barrier to allow the creative power of God, the Spirit, to descend upon him for the renewal of Israel and the world.

Why is the Spirit said to descend "like a dove?" At one level, since the Spirit cannot be seen, the image explains the experience in terms of something Jesus could "see."[18] On a deeper plane the "dove" evokes the hovering of the Spirit over the face of the deep in the original act of creation (Gen 1:2). This lends to the whole scene the aura of a new act of creation. Jesus emerges from the waters of the Jordan as the foundation of a fresh start for humanity, a new "Adam" in whom the Creator's original intent for human beings can at last come true.

Just as he sees something (the Spirit in bodily form), Jesus also hears, through the rent barrier, a divine address. "A voice from heaven" proclaims: "You are my Son, the Beloved; in you I am well pleased" (v. 11). The first phrase echoes the royal—and in this context messianic—Psalm 2 (v. 7). The Father addresses Jesus as Messiah and Son. The addition of "beloved" conveys the sense of a personal relationship going well beyond conventional messianic expectation. It recalls the language of the divine address to Abraham concerning Isaac, the beloved only son, whom he was prepared to sacrifice in obedience to God's command (Gen 22:2, 12, 16).[19] The true force of this allusion will become apparent as Story 2 appears (8:31) and begins to unfold. Though Jesus is God's Son, indeed God's *beloved* Son (cf. also 9:7), this unique status will not exempt him from a destiny to suffer and die. In fact, what God did not in the end require of Abraham, God will, for the rescue of humanity, "require" of Godself, the sacrifice of the beloved Son— something Paul, making the same allusion to Gen 22:16, also saw: "If God is for us, who can be against us? God, who did not spare his own Son but gave him up for us all!" (Rom 8:31-32; cf. John 3:16).[20]

The final phrase, "in you I am well pleased," echoes the opening of the First Song of the Servant in Isa 42:1-9.[21] While it is perhaps premature to read into the present context the full theology of the Isaianic servant songs,

---

18. Cf. Moloney, *Gospel of Mark,* 36–37.

19. Cf. Sharyn Dowd and Elizabeth Struthers Malbon, "The Significance of Jesus' Death in Mark: Narrative Context and Authorial Audience," *Journal of Biblical Literature* 125 (2006) 271–97, especially 273–74.

20. See Brendan Byrne, *Romans.* SP 6 (Collegeville, MN: Liturgical Press, 1996) 275.

21. Cf. Marcus, *Mark 1–8,* 163. The echo is much closer to the Hebrew of Isa 42:1 than to the Greek LXX translation. Appropriately for the context in Mark, the very next phrase of

the gospel will eventually interpret Jesus' death in the language of the Fourth Song (Isa 52:13–53:12) as a "ransom *for many*" (10:45; cf. 14:24). This allusion to the Servant, then, adds a further suggestion that the "way" to be taken by this beloved Son of God will involve the kind of representative suffering that (Second) Isaiah depicted in the figure of the Servant (42:1-9; 49:1-7; 50:4-11; 52:13–53:12).

We should note that the Greek verb expressing the divine pleasure is in the past tense (*eudokēsa*). The tense suggests not simply a timeless divine pleasure in the Son but an approval of the Son in virtue of something just accomplished: Jesus' subjection to baptism at the hands of John and the identification with sinful and repentant crowds that lay behind it. This entrance into solidarity with sinful humanity here at the very beginning of Jesus' ministry anticipates a still more radical entrance into the sinfulness and alienation of the world that he will make in his Passion and death on the cross. At that climactic point Jesus will die bereft of divine comfort and with a cry of dereliction on his lips (15:34). But following immediately upon his death there will be another "rending" (*eschisthē*) of the barrier between heaven and earth.[22] The Temple curtain that walled off the Holy of Holies as divine dwelling-place will be torn in two from top to bottom (15:38) and Jesus' divine sonship will once more be acknowledged, not from heaven this time but from a totally opposite direction: from the Roman centurion who has supervised the execution (15:39). This representative of the Gentile world will become through faith the first beneficiary of the "way" between heaven and earth that Jesus' death has opened up. From this wider perspective Jesus' baptism in the Jordan and the divine response (the rending of the heavens) that follows foreshadows here at the beginning of the gospel ("pillar 1") the more radical "rending" of the barrier between heaven and sinful humanity that the Son's obedient death will bring about ("pillar 3").

We can rightly discern in this scene of Jesus' baptism a Trinitarian moment revelatory of all that lies ahead. The "rending" of the heavens is not going to be reversed. Throughout Jesus' ministry the heavens will stay open (at times explicitly so: e.g., the transfiguration [9:2-8], "pillar 2"). The beloved Son will remain in communion with the Father (cf. 1:35; 6:46) and through the power of the Spirit effect in human lives the liberation from the grip of the demonic that is his mission. What this scene, anticipating the

---

this song reads: "I have put my spirit upon him; he will bring forth justice to the nations" (Isa 42:1).

22. The word "rend" (*schizein*) appears only in these two places (1:11; 15:38) in Mark, thereby forming an "inclusion" linking these two "pillar" moments at beginning and end.

Passion, shows is that the power of the Spirit is nothing other than the divine communion of love played out on the human scene. Divine love renders itself vulnerable to human evil in the person of the Son. It will show itself victorious over evil when the Roman centurion, paradigm and model of all subsequent believers, declares Jesus' true identity as he comes to faith (15:39).

Finally, though perhaps going beyond the immediate ambit of the text, I think it is fair to say that the assurance of divine love addressed to the Son as he emerges from the waters of the Jordan is something he receives on behalf of all humankind. Those who subsequently unite themselves with him through faith and baptism come under the scope of the divine address he received. They can hear addressed to them: "You are my beloved son/ daughter; in you I am well pleased." The doctrine of the Trinity that will gradually emerge in Christian tradition, for all its mystery, is not about the remoteness of God. In the "trinitarian" inauguration of Jesus' ministry we see the heavens "rent" and the Trinity opening its arms, so to speak, to gather up humanity into the divine communion of love that it is the essence of the Kingdom.

The Testing of God's Son: 1:12-13

It is easy to dismiss Mark's brief account of Jesus' testing in the wilderness as a poor relation to the longer accounts in Matthew (4:1-11) and Luke (4:1-13). But in the two sentences devoted to this episode Mark communicates a very great deal. It is best to put Matthew and Luke out of mind and approach Mark's account on its own terms.

First, although the episode is commonly termed the "temptation," this description suits the longer Matthean-Lukan story better than Mark 1:12-13. The same Greek word (*peirazein*) does service for both "tempt" and "test," but we need to distinguish the two meanings. In Matthew and Luke the devil (Satan) puts three outwardly attractive courses of action before Jesus, falsely suggesting he should embrace them in view of his status as Son of God. The bare Markan account simply informs us that Jesus was in the wilderness for forty days *peirazomenos* by Satan. Here it is better to translate "being tested," rather than "being tempted," and to think of biblical precedents where God tests persons called to play a significant role in the story of salvation. The classic instance is God's testing of Abraham by (seemingly at least) requiring of him the sacrifice of his only son Isaac (Genesis 22; cf. Sir 44:20: ". . . and when he [Abraham] was tested he proved faithful"). The entire book of Job places a "testing" framework around God's interaction with its central character and, of course, God "tests" Israel in the wilderness following the

Exodus from Egypt (Deut 8:1-5; 13:3). Such a test may or may not include "temptation"; it certainly did not in the case of Abraham. What it does involve is the placing of a person in a liminal or extreme situation where, in the absence of usual human resources and support, the strength of their adherence to God's calling can be both assessed and refined. Since Israel is God's "son" or "child" (cf. Exod 4:22; Deut 14:1; Hos 11:1; etc.) the biblical tradition describes God's testing of Israel in the wilderness through the image of a father's disciplinary testing or training of a son (Deut 8:5; 32:10 [LXX]).

This, then, is the background to Mark's account. Jesus has just seen the Spirit descend upon him and received assurance of his filial relationship with God. He now relives the experience of Israel in being tested as God's Son and trained for the mission that lies ahead of him. That mission will involve an aggressive conflict with the powers opposed to God and the reassertion of God's rule in the world. Hence the vigor of the language: the Spirit "immediately *drives* him out"[23] into the wilderness to engage for forty days[24] at a personal level the conflict with the demonic he will later pursue on a public and social scale.

In regard to this period of testing Mark adds two details only: Jesus is "with the beasts" and "the angels minister to him" (v. 13c-d). It is not clear how the first should be interpreted. Jesus' being with beasts who apparently did not harm him may evoke the sense of companionship with animals enjoyed by Adam before his fall (Gen 2:18-20), as well as the harmony between the animal and human world that texts such as Isa 11:6-9 ("the wolf shall live with the lamb, etc. . . .") seemed to pledge for the messianic age.[25] In a reference so terse and open-ended this more positive interpretation of Jesus' animal company can hardly be ruled out. However, the detail is more likely to be part of the negative background of Jesus' testing experience.[26]

---

23. The word translated "drive out" here (*ekballein*) is regularly used in the gospel to describe Jesus' expulsion of demons. It appears in the present tense, the first instance of the "historic present" in Mark: describing a past action in the present tense in order to convey vigor and urgency.

24. The "forty days" recalls the experience of Moses on Mount Sinai (Exod 34:28; Deut 9:8, 18) and the forty-day journey of Elijah, who was also fed by an angel (1 Kgs 19:1-8). But otherwise the links with the experiences of these figures are not necessarily close, since in Mark there is no explicit mention that Jesus was fasting and "forty days" is a conventional biblical length of time.

25. Cf. also Isa 65:17-25, especially v. 25; Hos 2:18; *2 Apoc. Bar.* 73:6.

26. Here I am very much indebted to John P. Heil, "Jesus with the Wild Animals in Mark 1:13," *Catholic Biblical Quarterly* 68 (2006) 63–78; cf. also the creative and sensitive discussion of this area of Mark from an ecological perspective by William Loader, "Good News—for the Earth? Reflections on Mark 1:1-15," in Norman C. Habel and Vicki Balabanski,

The wilderness is the habitat of wild and dangerous animals, as well as evil spirits. That Jesus was "with" these adds to the sense of danger, isolation, and distance from human resources that surrounds him. The second detail telling of the "ministry" of angels would then appear as a positive counterpart: the Son of God may be in a highly dangerous situation, bereft of human comfort and exposed to demonic power, but divine care, in the shape of angelic protection, does not cease to attend him.

At this early stage of the gospel the testing of Jesus in the wilderness anticipates and prepares for the supreme test that he as beloved Son will undergo in the Passion, beginning with his anguish in Gethsemane (14:32-41) and concluding with the cry of abandonment on the cross (15:34). The best comment, both on the present test and the one that lies ahead, comes from another early Christian writer:

> In the days of his flesh, Jesus offered up prayers and supplications, with loud cries and tears, to the one who was able to save him from death, and he was heard because of his reverent submission.

> Son though he was, he learned obedience through what he suffered; and having been made perfect, he became the source of eternal salvation for all who obey him. (Heb 5:7-9)

This sense of disciplinary testing is one way in which biblical thought interprets the experience of suffering visited on those who are otherwise devoted to God's cause (cf. Wis 3:1-9). It is not necessarily one that contemporary spirituality or theology finds congenial. What such thinking is trying to express is the sense that the divine care and protection is present and at work even in situations where on the level of experience it seems most utterly absent, where one is simply "with the beasts" in whatsoever shape or form, mental or physical, they may take. Mark's spare portrayal of Jesus in such a situation may give comfort today—as it most certainly would have done in the situations faced by its original readers.[27]

---

eds., *The Earth Story in the New Testament. Earth Bible* 5 (London: Sheffield Academic Press; Cleveland: Pilgrim Press, 2002) 28–43, especially 37–40.

27. Well aware as they were that some of their number had been "condemned to the beasts," that is, thrown to wild animals in the arena, in Nero's pogrom of 64 C.E., the thought that Jesus had faced demonic power in this guise would have been a source of strength for them; cf. Boring, *Mark,* 48.

I
EARLY GALILEAN MINISTRY
1:14–3:6

The Good News of the Coming Rule
of God: 1:14-20

Mark introduces Jesus' own ministry with a summary statement, the first of many such summaries in the gospel:[1]

> [14] Now after John was given up,
> Jesus came to Galilee,
> proclaiming the good news of God,
> [15] and saying, "The time is fulfilled,
> and the rule of God is at hand;
> repent, and believe in the good news."

This programmatic statement locates the ministry in time ("after John was given up" [v. 14a]) and space ("Jesus came to Galilee" [v. 14b]). It presents Jesus as the herald (*kēryssōn*) of the Gospel (v. 14c), spells out (v. 15ab) the content of his message ("the time is fulfilled, the rule of God is at hand"), and indicates (v. 15cd) the required human response ("repent and believe in the good news").

We note first the clear demarcation between the ministry of Jesus now about to begin and that of John the Baptist, which has come to an end with his being "given up." "Given up" (*paredothē*) is an ambiguous term with ominous overtones. While it may refer simply to being "arrested," it can also have the implication "betrayed," "given up to death." The narrative leaves John's fate unclear at this point, but the negative hint will be confirmed when we learn of his execution at the hands of Herod (6:14-29). With respect to "being given up" a chilling pattern emerges: you preach and you get "given up." John has preached and has been given up (1:14); Jesus will preach and will be given up (14:10, 18-21); later (13:9-13) the disciples will be warned that, as a consequence of their preaching, they too will be given up. This

---

1. Besides 1:14-15, cf. 1:28; 1:32-34; 1:39; 1:45; 3:7-12; 4:33-34; 6:6b; 6:53-56.

notice, then, while setting Jesus' ministry apart from that of John, already hints that his task of preaching the good news will not proceed without cost.

What Jesus begins to proclaim in Galilee is "the Gospel of God." In presenting the worldview presupposed by the gospel, and then in connection with the title (1:1), I discussed the resonances "Gospel" evokes within the Isaianic framework that hangs over the narrative. Within that perspective every term in this opening summary has its place. The "time is fulfilled" in the sense that the moment (*kairos*) of deliverance of which (Second) Isaiah spoke has arrived. By the time of Jesus the Isaiah "good news" texts (Isa 40:9; 52:7; 61:1-2, etc.), which originally referred to freedom from Babylonian captivity in the sixth century B.C.E., were being read in apocalyptic circles with reference to the hope of freedom from a more basic captivity: human captivity under the rule of Satan and the demonic world in general. What Jesus is now proclaiming, in the language of the Isaianic herald (cf. Isa 61:1-2), is the "good news" that the time for this captivity has run its course.

It is the "good news of *God,*" first of all, because God is the ultimate agent of the liberation and, second, because the chief factor in the transformation is the replacement of Satan's rule by that of God: the "Kingdom" or "rule of God." The original exile came to an end, as (Second) Isaiah described it, when Israel's God showed the gods of Babylon to be "nought" (cf. Isa 41:21-24; 44:8-20; 45:20-21; etc.), when, that is, the sole rule of Israel's God over the universe was made clear (Isa 52:7: "Your God reigns"). Now Jesus employs the same language to proclaim "the good news" of the imminent displacement of Satan's rule by that of God. Beyond oral proclamation, the exorcisms he will perform will reclaim individual human lives for the coming reign of God.

I say "coming" because, as we see from the language Jesus uses in regard to the Kingdom, it is something that is "at hand" (*ēngiken*) but not fully arrived. The "good news" ("Gospel") is that it is very close, so close as to already begin or at least require the transformation of human lives.

This sense of moral transformation is clearly distinctive of Jesus' proclamation of the Kingdom. Other circles in Judaism of the time may have read the scriptural pledges of the coming reign of God in more political or social terms—especially in relation to achieving freedom and prosperity for God's people in their own state.[2] While such aspects were not necessarily

---

2. For the idea of the kingdom of God in Judaism contemporary with Jesus see Meier, *Marginal Jew* 2:237–88; Norman Perrin, *Jesus and the Language of the Kingdom: Symbol and Metaphor in New Testament Interpretation* (Philadelphia: Fortress Press, 1976) 16–32.

absent from the Kingdom as proclaimed by Jesus, it is clear from the parables and images he employs that renewed relationship with God—or, to be more accurate, acceptance of the renewed relationship God is freely offering—is absolutely central to his understanding of the Kingdom. The Kingdom may not yet have fully arrived in the sense of the transformation of all aspects of life, but the relationship with God pertaining to the Kingdom is available here and now. In terms of this relationship, the Kingdom is in essence already here—even if the physical and social context appropriate for it remains outstanding. In this sense one may speak of the "already—not yet" aspect of the Kingdom: "already" in terms of relationship with God; "not yet" in terms of the physical and social renewal of the world.[3]

If relationship with God is the essence of the Kingdom for Jesus, it is easily understandable that the final element of his proclamation should be the summons: "Repent (*metanoiein*) and believe the good news" (v. 15cd). The Greek verb *metanoiein* implies a change of mind or heart. Behind its usage here may also sound overtones of the Hebrew *shûv,* which not only means "turn around" physically but also has the moral sense of "turn round your life," "be converted."[4] In continuity with John the Baptist (1:4), what Jesus is calling for is, in the first instance, a radical turning away from life under the regime of Satan manifested in personal sin. More positively, he is summoning people to embrace and allow themselves to be claimed by the reality of God's rule now breaking in.[5]

The channel or instrument whereby a person opens himself or herself to that new reality is faith—here specified as belief in the "good news" ("the Gospel of God") Jesus is proclaiming. Faith in this sense is a readiness to accept, in the face of all the evidence to the contrary (the outward signs of the continuance of the old era), that the liberation proclaimed by Isaiah is indeed under way and that one can be drawn into the Kingdom and its coming victory by surrendering to that truth in obedience and trust. Human faith is, in fact, the channel whereby the transformative power of the Kingdom becomes effective in human lives and in the world. As the gospel will show, where faith is lacking that power is checked (Mark 6:1-6a); where faith prevails, transformation—including physical transformation (healing)—can occur. The summons to believe—the final element of Jesus' proclamation—

3. Cf. ibid., 289–306.

4. Cf. Moloney, *Gospel of Mark,* 50.

5. The renewal of baptismal promises during the liturgy of the Easter Vigil reenacts this fundamental response to the Kingdom.

states the essential component on the human side for the advent of the Kingdom.

Founding the Community of the Kingdom:
Jesus Calls his First Disciples: 1:16-20

It might seem fitting at this stage that Jesus would proceed immediately to *enact* his proclamation of the Kingdom (1:14-15) with a frontal assault on the hostile realm. Instead, this is delayed for a moment (until 1:21-28) while he turns aside to call four disciples. The fact that right from the start he builds a community around himself sends a powerful signal that discipleship and life in community will be central to this story.

Reinforcing this impression is the further fact that the four men he calls are two pairs of brothers: Simon and his brother Andrew; James and John, the sons of Zebedee. Calling two pairs of brothers brings the "family" aspect to the fore. For these four men association with Jesus is going to involve leaving behind their natural family and its ties to find themselves members of a new family whose father is God. Put the other way around, in the community of the Kingdom, which Jesus is now beginning to gather, the relationships that will or ought to prevail—with God, with Jesus, and the members with each other—will be familial ones (3:31-35; 10:29-30).[6]

Several details in this call story are worthy of note. Jesus is "passing by"; he is on his "way." To follow him as disciples will not mean a static gathering around a teacher but a journey to a future as yet unclear. Furthermore, he is passing along "by the sea." The sea (actually the inland lake of Gennesaret) will feature prominently in the Galilean ministry of Jesus. It will be a symbol of the world under demonic rule from which people ("fish") must be "caught" for the Kingdom. Hence the significance of the occupation—fishing—the two pairs of brothers are engaged in.[7] Jesus sees four men pursuing their usual occupation as fishers of fish. Beneath and

---

6. In the twofold call it is possible to discern a repeated pattern: Jesus *passes by* (v. 16; v. 19) and *sees* (v. 16; v. 19) *a pair of brothers pursuing their current occupation* (v. 16; v. 19); he *calls* them (v. 17; v. 20a); they *immediately leave* means of livelihood (v. 18)/father and servants (v. 20a) and *follow him* (v. 18b; v. 20b); cf. Marcus, *Mark 1–8*, 182. The call story here is often said to be modeled on Elijah's enlistment of Elisha in 1 Kgs 19:19-21 (so especially, Marcus, ibid., 183), but the verbal links are very sparse and, if anything, Elisha provides a counterexample in that he does not follow immediately but is allowed to go home and say good-bye to his father.

7. John R. Donahue and Daniel J. Harrington, *The Gospel of Mark.* SP 2 (Collegeville, MN: Liturgical Press, 2002) 76, see a difference in status between the two pairs: Simon and Andrew are making a cast in the sea from the shore, using circular casting nets (Greek

beyond this, but in symbolic continuity with it, he sees a deeper vocational possibility: fishers of fish can become fishers of people for the Kingdom.[8] Along with continuity, there will also be a transformation that he will work ("I will make you . . ." [v 17b]). Much of the narrative to follow will show Jesus attempting—initially with very limited success—to transform these fishers of fish into fishers of people.

The alacrity with which each of the pairs responds to the call (v. 18; v. 20) is a first display in this gospel of Jesus' authority (*exousia*). With no hesitation or bargaining, the fishermen simply leave the instruments of their trade and go after him. The first pair, Simon and Andrew, leave the nets they had been casting into the sea; they will need to learn a new form of casting to catch fish for the Kingdom. In the case of the sons of Zebedee the family aspect is more prominent: James and John leave their father and whatever companionship they had with the hired men in the boat. In the new boat—the church—from which they will fish they will have a Father (in heaven) and coworkers who will not be servants, but brothers and sisters in the Lord (cf. 3:33-35; 10:28-30). In calling these four men, Jesus inaugurates a community destined to enjoy with him the familial intimacy with God (cf. 1:11) characteristic of the Kingdom.

---

amphiballein); the family of Zebedee is wealthy enough to have a boat and to employ hired men.

8. The image of "fishing for people" has some verbal precedents in the Old Testament (Jer 16:16-17; Amos 4:2; Ezek 19:4-5) but all are very negative—as is also the comment on Hab 1:14-17 in the Habakkuk Commentary from Qumran: 1QpHab 5:12-14 (cf. also 1QH 5[13]:7-8).

A "Day" at Capernaum: 1:21-45

The preliminaries over, Jesus enters upon his messianic ministry in a sequence of scenes located in or around the lakeside town of Capernaum (1:21-38). Everything takes place within the compass of a single rather long "day" that Mark seems to present as typical of the ministry now getting under way.

A First Victory over the Demonic:
Jesus Teaches in a Synagogue: 1:21-28

In general it can be said with respect to all four gospels that the way each evangelist presents the beginning of Jesus' public ministry is programmatic in the sense of pointing to what will be most significant in the wider story to follow.[1] Mark is no exception to this in beginning the public ministry of Jesus with a scene portraying him as teacher and exorcist.

The structure of the episode places these two roles in close parallel. Verse 21 sets the scene: Jesus goes to Capernaum with the disciples he had just called, enters the synagogue on the Sabbath, and begins to teach. Verse 22 describes the reaction—amazement—that his teaching "with authority" provokes among those present. After the exorcism (vv. 23-26), the episode ends with a similar expression of amazement at his teaching, this time taking account also of the exorcism (v. 27). This arrangement serves to place the exorcism within the frame formed by the two reactions—one at the beginning, one at the end—to Jesus' authoritative teaching.[2] Moreover, for all the drama of the exorcism that has just taken place before their eyes, the con-

1. Matthew begins the public life with Jesus authoritatively reinterpreting the Torah on a mountain (Matt 5:1-3); for Luke he is the prophet who proclaims the Lord's acceptance but himself experiences rejection (4:16-30); John has Jesus reveal his "glory" by remedying the failure of wine at a wedding (John 2:1-12); cf. Marcus, *Mark 1–8,* 190.

2. We have, then, an early instance of the "sandwiching" technique so frequently characteristic of Mark's narrative arrangement.

gregation "keep on asking each other" first (v. 27a) about his teaching with authority; only subsequently (v. 27b) do they comment on his command of the evil spirits. What links the two is the note of authority (*exousia*).

The parallel between exorcism and teaching that emerges from this arrangement goes along with an odd feature of this gospel. Mark, while constantly presenting Jesus in the role of teacher, actually gives us very little of the content of his teaching.[3] Presumably if we asked after the content Mark would respond: "I gave you the essence of it in the opening summary of Jesus' preaching the good news of the Kingdom (1:14-15). That is all you need to know about the content. What I want you to appreciate is that his authoritative teaching is as much part of the onset of the Kingdom as his expulsion of demons." Both are exorcisms, exercises of liberation: lives can be controlled by false images of God, by being anchored in hopes and fears belonging to an age that is passing. Jesus' teaching is "new" (v. 27) with the "newness" of the Kingdom that will bring into being for the first time the Creator's original intent for human beings and the world. It contrasts with the teaching of the regular religious experts, the scribes (v. 22c), because it does not rely, as does theirs, on disputatious interpretation of Scripture. Jesus simply states, with the force of the Spirit, that the "time has come" for the rule of God to be under way.

The intervening exorcism (vv. 23-26), then physically enacts the effect of Jesus' teaching. The demon-possessed individual had presumably sat through Sabbaths of scribal teaching and been left unmoved. As soon as Jesus appears on the scene and begins to teach, the demon feels the "heat" of his presence and accurately owns the threat to demonic control it represents: "What is there between us, Jesus of Nazareth? Have you come to destroy us?" (v. 24)—a question to which the implied answer can only be "Yes indeed!" The demon's last-ditch effort to gain the upper hand by naming Jesus ("the Holy One of God") only succeeds in drawing from him in response a rebuke and a silencing that in its language and effect echoes the divine rebuke of primeval chaos at the dawn of creation (Gen 1:6-10; Job 26:10-12; cf. Mark 4:39). In the person of Jesus one is dealing with the power and presence of God.

The entire episode, then, breaks like a thunderclap over the entrenched rule of Satan. It serves notice that here in this synagogue, where scribal teaching has for years ineffectively chipped away at that rule, a new era has

---

3. One can point to the long parable discourse in 4:1-34, but the purpose of that seems more to deepen mystery than to provide information about content. The instruction in 7:1-23 is polemical and rather pointedly focused on a single issue: "uncleanness." The discourse on the future (13:5-37) is more exhortation than teaching.

dawned. The demon's "rending" of the person as it leaves (v. 26a) unmasks its destructive intent; the accompanying loud cry (*phōne megalē*) is both an acknowledgment of defeat and a protest that the regime of the demonic in this human life has come to an end (v. 26b). We shall hear a loud cry again and see that destructiveness rampant in far more extreme degree as Jesus dies on the cross (Mark 15:37). But that moment of apparent triumph for the demonic will actually be the moment of its defeat, the "exorcism" of the world. In all these ways the episode in the synagogue, a report of which spreads widely throughout Galilee (v. 28), opens up and sets the pattern for the entire ministry of Jesus that has now begun to unfold.

Healings in Capernaum:
Peter's Mother-in-law and the Crowd in the Evening: 1:29-34

Leaving the synagogue, Jesus enters immediately into the house of Simon and Andrew, along with the other pair of brothers, James and John, whom he had just called (1:16-20). In the worldview of the gospel physical illness is no less a mark of the rule of Satan than overt demonic possession. There is, then, continuity between the healing that will occur in the house and the preceding exorcism in the synagogue.[4]

Nonetheless, the transition from synagogue to house is highly symbolic. Right here in the ordinary, everyday house where Simon and Andrew have been living, and in the person of a close family member (Simon's mother-in-law), the disciples who make up the nucleus of Jesus' new "family" are to witness his power to raise up and heal. The scene begins the consecration of the "domestic church" that is so much a feature of this gospel. The locus of worship has begun to move from Temple and synagogue. Gatherings in simple homes will henceforth be the place where the risen Lord will be "at home" in all his power to heal and make alive.

When Jesus enters the house "they" (presumably Simon and Andrew) "tell him about her" (v. 30). There is no reason to suppose that at this point they were hoping for anything extraordinary. More likely their words are an embarrassed explanation of the difficulty of providing hospitality (provision of a meal). The reason is that the member of the household who would normally provide it is lying ill with a fever.[5]

Jesus responds (v. 31) by "approaching" her (the verb is *proselthōn*)— presumably by going to a less public part of the house where she is in bed.

---

4. Cf. Marcus, *Mark 1–8*, 199.

5. Mark's language (*katakeito pyresousa*) suggests a fairly serious health situation; cf. Boring, *Mark*, 66.

In an unmistakable echo of the language of resurrection we are told that he raises her up, grasping her by the hand. In the conventional understanding of holiness such contact with a seriously ill woman carries the risk of incurring ritual impurity and at least temporary exclusion from the life and worship of God's people.[6] In the presence of Jesus the "flow" is exactly the reverse: *he* does not contract uncleanness from her; at his touch *she* "catches" healing and wholeness ("holiness") from him. The fever "flees" like a demon (v. 31b). Jesus' entry into the house has banished "uncleanness," bringing healing and new life. Simon's mother-in-law becomes the first person reclaimed for the physical wholeness associated with the onset of the Kingdom.

As a demonstration of her restoration to health she "begins to serve (*diakonein*) them" (v. 31c). At one level she is now providing the hospitality her illness prevented her offering earlier on. But the Greek verb has deeper resonances in this gospel. In a warning against misplaced ambition and wrong use of power Jesus will employ this same term to sum up his saving mission: "the Son of Man has come not to be served but to serve (*diakonein*) and give his life as a ransom for many" (10:45). Toward the close of the gospel, following his death on the cross, the women who, in contrast to the male disciples, have stayed to the end, are described as those who "had followed him and served (*diekonoun*) him" (15:40-41). The mention of this "service" on the part of women at the beginning and end of the narrative, along with the associations with Jesus' own "service," makes Simon's mother-in-law a paradigm of all, especially women disciples, who are "raised" for the life of the Kingdom and give expression to this new life by sharing in his ministry.[7] This simple incident in Simon's house, so easy to pass over in the flow of the narrative, completes the picture begun in 1:16-20. It provides a place for the ministry of women alongside that of the male disciples.

As news of the healing spreads and when the close of the Sabbath allows,[8] the house where Jesus had performed his first cure becomes a base for healing on a much wider scale (vv. 32-34). The "whole city" gathers at the door, bringing their sick and "those possessed by demons" (v. 33).[9] We

---

6. Cf. especially Moloney, *Gospel of Mark,* 55.

7. Cf. Elaine M. Wainwright, *Women Healing/Healing Women: The Genderization of Healing in Early Christianity* (London, UK; Oakville, CT: Equinox, 2006) 106–12, especially 111.

8. Hence Mark's double time-marker: "That evening, when the sun had gone down . . ." (v. 32).

9. We should perhaps note the distinction made in the text between "all who came" and the "many" who were healed; cf. Moloney, *Gospel of Mark,* 56.

see here a first instance of something that will become a constant factor in the Galilean ministry: the press of the crowd on Jesus in the enthusiasm generated by his healing. But this popularity is not without ambiguity. The demons who bear the brunt of his messianic power are set to betray his identity. As in the synagogue (1:24), Jesus silences them. In the presence of all this enthusiasm, disclosure of his messianic status (Story 1) would create a popular perception of his mission that is counter to its true direction (Story 2).[10] Confronted by the afflicted crowd, Jesus heals and works exorcisms, but this exercise of compassion is not without personal cost to him.

A Moment of Withdrawal and Renewal of Mission: 1:35-39

Presumably to reclaim the true direction of his mission in the face of this threat, Jesus leaves the town very early in the morning[11] and goes to a deserted place to commune with his Father in prayer. This attempt to gain a moment of seclusion is not entirely successful. "Simon and those with him"—who have now become, in modern parlance, his "minders"—"hunt him down" (*katediōxen auton*), and when they find him, exclaim: "Everyone is looking for you" (v. 37). The tension apparent in the previous scene continues: Jesus' healing ministry creates widespread popular enthusiasm—an enthusiasm already beginning to infect his disciples—but he seeks to distance himself from it.[12] He does not return to Capernaum (as presumably they wish), but proposes (v. 38) to continue his preaching elsewhere, in the surrounding towns, adding the enigmatic explanation: "For that is why I came out" (*exēlthon*). "Came out" from where? from Capernaum? from Nazareth? Or, in a more fundamental sense, from a "prior" existence with God (cf. John 16:28)? The christology of the gospel is not necessarily closed to this final suggestion.[13] A concluding summary statement (v. 39) describes Jesus fulfilling this mission from the Father by preaching in synagogues throughout all Galilee "and expelling demons." The summary confirms the impression

10. We have here a first instance of the Markan motif conventionally though not entirely adequately dubbed "the messianic secret": the numerous—and frequently unsuccessful—attempts on Jesus' part in the narrative to suppress belief that he is this Messiah of conventional understanding (Story 1 without Story 2); for a thorough discussion of the motif and critical survey of scholarly theories in its regard see Boring, *Mark,* 264–71.

11. The language communicates a sense of Easter: cf. 16:2: . . . *lian prōi* . . .).

12. Cf. Marcus, *Mark 1–8,* 202. Marcus also (p. 203) sees a nuance here of the friction to come between the disciples and Jesus.

13. *Pace* Moloney, *Gospel of Mark,* 57, n. 51. Cf. Simon J. Gathercole, *The Preexistent Son: Recovering the Christologies of Matthew, Mark, and Luke* (Grand Rapids and London: Eerdmans, 2006) 154–57.

that we should understand the incident in which Jesus expelled a demon while teaching in the synagogue at Capernaum (1:21-28) as archetypal of a wider campaign to loosen the grip of Satan and reclaim human lives for the rule of God.

Breaking the Clean/Unclean Barrier: 1:40-45

The scene in which Jesus cleanses a leper[14] shows him confronting the "uncleanness" associated with demonic control of human life in a most intense degree. Regarded as punished by God, people experiencing severe skin diseases suffered extreme social and religious exclusion as prescribed in Lev 13:45-46:

> The person who has the leprous disease shall wear torn clothes and let the hair of his head be disheveled; and he shall cover his upper lip and cry out, "Unclean, unclean." He shall remain unclean as long as he has the disease; he is unclean. He shall live alone; his dwelling shall be outside the camp.

In defiance of this prescription of the Law the man approaches Jesus, beseeching him. Like other desperate figures later in the story (cf. 5:25-34; 10:46-52) he displays a faith prepared to break through barriers. He believes that Jesus has the power to make him clean—a power the biblical tradition attributes to God alone.[15] The only issue is whether Jesus "wants to" or not (v. 41b).

Jesus' reaction is curious (v. 42). "Becoming angry," we are told, "he stretched out his hand and touched him, and said, 'I do so will: be made clean!'" In regard to Jesus' emotions, most manuscripts and translations provide "overcome with compassion"—an alternative that offers a far more reasonable and comfortable sequence of thought. Precisely for that reason, however, it probably represents an early attempt to ameliorate the reference to anger, which, as the "harder" reading, has better claims to originality.[16]

---

14. The literal translation is "leper," but the Greek word *lepros,* translating the Hebrew *psōraat,* could refer to a variety of skin ailments and not just the disease subsequently classified as "leprosy" or Hansen's disease. The latter did not exist in Old Testament times, though there is some evidence that it began to appear in the Near East and possibly Palestine by the time of Jesus. See further David P. Wright and Richard N. Jones, art. "Leprosy" in David Noel Freedman et al., eds., *Anchor Bible Dictionary.* 6 Vols. (New York: Doubleday, 1992) 4:277–82. The main point is not the precise nature of the disease but the "uncleanness"—ritual impurity—it involved. I retain the traditional designation "leper" because it preserves the sense of social exclusion so central to the biblical prescription that the text presupposes; so also Boring, *Mark,* 70.

15. Cf. Moloney, *Gospel of Mark,* 58, n. 59, citing Num 12:10-16; 2 Kgs 5:1-19.

16. For a full discussion see Meier, *Marginal Jew* 2:748, n. 106.

But why and with whom is Jesus angry? At the man who has dared to approach him contrary to the legal prescription? At the questioning of his willingness to exercise the power at his disposal ("If you want to . . .")? At the manifestation of the demonic hold on humanity displayed in the man's ravaged physical condition?[17] All these explanations are possible. But the anger could be connected with a tension that runs through the scene. Jesus has the power and the willingness to make the man clean. But, as the sequel to the cure (vv. 43-45) makes abundantly clear, he will not do so without cost to himself.[18] Adding this kind of cure, requiring virtually divine power, to those he had already worked could only serve to attract in even greater degree the public enthusiasm that threatens the true direction of his mission—the threat he had attempted to escape by withdrawing to a deserted place after his healing activity in Capernaum (1:35-37).

This would explain why Jesus, after the leprosy has left the man,[19] drives him away with a further display of strong emotion (*embrimēsamenos*),[20] warning him not to say anything to anyone but to show himself to the priest only, in fulfillment of the legal requirements.[21] The warning is ineffective: the man spreads the news everywhere (v. 44a), the crowds come from all sides (v. 45), and Jesus is back in the situation from which he had attempted to escape just before (vv. 35-37). Ironically, *he* ends up unable to enter towns and cities, compelled to live the kind of "outcast" and wilderness existence (v. 44b) from which the now-cleansed man had been set free.

The episode is far more, then, than the record of an isolated act of compassion on the part of Jesus. It anticipates the whole costly "entrance" of the Son of God into the "uncleanness" and alienation of the human situation, an entrance that will come to a climax as he dies on the cross, hanging between two bandits and with a cry of abandonment on his lips. As Jesus

17. So Joachim Gnilka, *Das Evangelium nach Markus.* 2 vols. (Zürich: Benziger; Neukirchen-Vluyn: Neukirchener Verlag, 1978, 1979) 1:93; Hooker, *Saint Mark,* 80; Marcus, *Mark 1–8,* 208.

18. Note that the aftermath (vv. 43-45) takes up far more space in the episode than the cure itself.

19. As in 1:31, the disease, personified, leaves like an expelled demon.

20. The Greek verb includes a note of anger. In the Fourth Gospel it twice describes Jesus' emotions just before his raising of Lazarus (11:33, 38). In that scene the anger of Jesus would seem to proceed from the same tension as in this scene in Mark: compassion leads him to work a stupendous miracle (cleansing a leper/raising the dead), yet the publicity that follows places his own life under threat (cf. John 11:45-54); on John 11 see further Brendan Byrne, *Lazarus: A Contemporary Reading of John 11:1-46* (Collegeville, MN: Liturgical Press, 1991) 57–60.

21. Cf. Lev 13:40; 14:2-4.

"touches" the man in all his dehumanizing disfigurement, so in his Passion he still more radically "touches" the whole human condition. Once again (cf. 1:31), as on the individual so on the universal scale, the cleanness/uncleanness transaction goes contrary to conventional expectation. He does not "catch" uncleanness from this contact; on the contrary, all who, despite feelings of moral or physical disfigurement, approach him in faith "catch" healing and wholeness from him.

The cost to Jesus, then, is not uncleanness. Rather, it lies in the hostility his healings provoke when, as in this case, despite his warnings they are not concealed[22] but instead arouse the enthusiasm that leads to jealousy on the part of those currently in power (cf. 15:10). His will and determination to reach out and touch us in all our uncleanness is clear: "I do so will!" (v. 41). The cost he inevitably incurs in so doing will come to a climax in Gethsemane and on the cross.

---

22. It is interesting that Matthew, ever more favorable to the Torah than Mark (or Luke), omits from the scene the man's failure to follow Jesus' instruction: there is nothing corresponding to v. 45 (or Luke 4:15-16) in the Matthean parallel at Matt 8:2-4.

The First Signs of Opposition: 2:1–3:6

Up to now Jesus' activity of teaching and healing has generated extraordinary enthusiasm among the people—so much so that he has been compelled to live in lonely and deserted places (1:45). There is something about this popularity that threatens the true direction of his mission. Now (2:1) a threat to his proclamation (1:14-15) emerges from a fresh direction. A hint of this had already appeared in an otherwise innocent-sounding observation made by those who heard him teach in the synagogue at Capernaum: "for he taught them as one having authority, and not as the scribes" (1:22). Here already is the seed of a conflict with the religious/legal authorities currently in power. A sequence of conflict stories (2:1–3:6) brings the threat out into the open and indicates its basic cause. Jesus' proclamation of the Kingdom and the renewal of relationship with God it holds out (1:14-15) presents a challenge to prevailing understandings of God's ways and a threat to the religious and legal authorities who guard them. In Jesus' striking image (2:22) the "new wine" of the Kingdom is beginning to burst the "old wineskins" currently in place.

In these scenes of conflict we do not see Jesus in explicit confrontation with the demonic world, but that fundamental conflict is not absent. It is simply more concealed. The demons now counterattack through human forces[1] and under the guise of religion. The telltale destructiveness of the demonic appears in the otherwise surprisingly hostile note on which the sequence ends: "The Pharisees went out and immediately conspired with the Herodians against him, how to destroy him" (3:6).

By the same token this series of scenes showing Jesus in conflict with Jewish religious authorities presents responsible interpreters with the challenge of avoiding anti-Jewish interpretation. It is important to recognize that the hostility represented here reflects not so much the interactions of Jesus'

---

1. Cf. Marcus, *Mark 1–8,* 212.

own time but several decades of growing estrangement between the followers of Jesus, Jewish and non-Jewish alike, and the vast majority of Jews who had not come to faith in him as Messiah. Interpreters should also remember that subsequent Christian history contains countless examples of the repression and persecution of figures who disturb set religious patterns, figures whose challenge and witness often find acceptance long after they have suffered and died. The conflict recorded here is not between Jesus, on the one hand, and Judaism, on the other—as if Jesus were not himself a Jew! The conflict is between the liberating, life-affirming challenge of the Kingdom and the kind of repressive, ingrained, and antihuman legalism to which any form of religion, Christianity included, is prone.[2]

As is now widely recognized, the sequence of conflict stories comes in a carefully arranged block. Enclosing the whole are preceding (1:45) and concluding (3:7-8) summaries describing how Jesus is compelled to withdraw in the face of the great popular enthusiasm he is arousing among the people. Within these outer frames there is a linear flow of themes and topics that serves to "clamp" each scene to the one preceding and the one that follows.[3] The first scene, the healing of the paralytic (2:1-12), features forgiveness of *sin,* which then flows into the call of Levi the tax collector and Jesus' controversial *eating* "with tax collectors and *sinners*" (2:13-17). The *"eating"* motif is a foil to the controversy over fasting (*"not-eating"*) that forms the third or middle element of the sequence (2:18-22), and this same motif continues in the fourth controversy sparked off by the disciples' plucking ears of grain on the Sabbath and *eating* them (2:23 28). The final "clamp" comes in the shape of the "Sabbath" motif common to both this element and the final controversy, Jesus' healing of the man with the withered hand on the Sabbath (3:1-5).

2. For further helpful reflections on this topic see Donahue and Harrington, *Gospel of Mark,* 97–98.

3. See Marcus, *Mark 1–8,* 214.

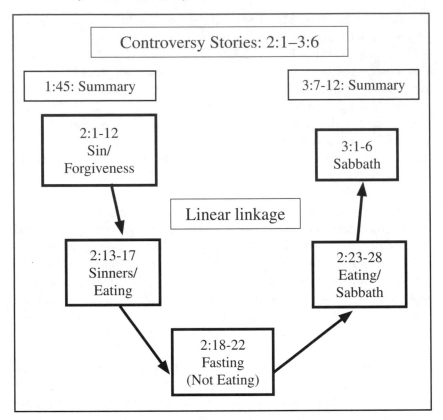

Alongside this linear flow of connection it is also possible to find a circular or chiastic structure: A B X B' A'. Thus the first (A) and the last (A') element both involve a miracle, hostility stemming from the "heart" (2:8; 3:5), and a rising up (2:11-12) or "saving of life" (3:5). The second and second-last (B and B') involve "eating" and human need. This leaves the controversy about fasting as third and central element X (2:18-22), making the mysterious and ominous reference to the "taking away" of the Bridegroom (v. 20) the point of focus and emphasis for the whole. The arrangement can be set out as follows:[4]

---

4. This analysis is indebted to the key study by Joanna Dewey, "The Literary Structure of the Controversy Stories in Mark 2:1–3:6," in William R. Telford, ed., *The Interpretation of Mark* (Philadelphia: Fortress, 1985) 109–18; also eadem, *Markan Public Debate: Literary Technique, Concentric Structure, and Theology in Mark 2:1–3:6.* SBLDS 48 (Chico, CA: Scholars Press, 1980) 65–130; see especially 115–16.

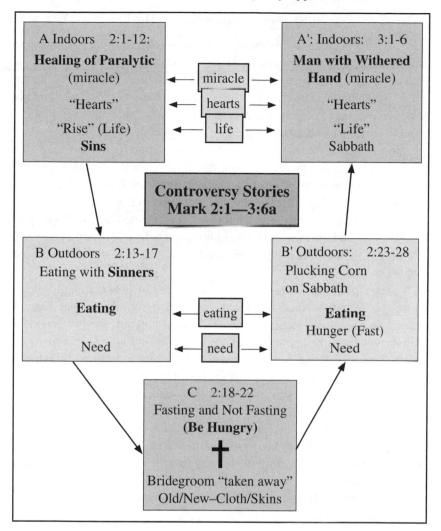

While the analysis of the linear pattern has been widely accepted, fewer interpreters are convinced of the circular or chiastic pattern.[5] Whether or not the latter pattern was in Mark's mind, it seems to me to offer an imaginative and illuminating way of seeing the sequence as a whole.

5. Cf., e.g., Marcus, *Mark 1–8*, 214; but see also Donahue and Harrington, *Mark*, 97.

A Paralyzed Person Receives Forgiveness and Healing: 2:1-12

The first episode in this sequence features a healing miracle wrapped around a controversy concerning Jesus' authority to forgive sin. Jesus is back in Capernaum, living quietly in the same house, presumably, as the one in which he had cured the mother-in-law of Simon (1:29-31). Soon his presence becomes known and draws so large a crowd that there is no longer room in the house and some people are forced to congregate outside around the door. This crowded house then becomes the venue for his speaking "the word" (vv. 1-2): presumably the basic "good news" of the inbreaking of the Kingdom and the summons to respond with repentant faith (1:15).[6]

Jesus' preaching suffers a dramatic interruption (vv. 3-4). Four men, unable to bring in a paralyzed man through the crowded doorway, go up to the roof, make a hole in it,[7] and lower him down before Jesus on a stretcher. Interpreting their efforts as a sign of faith,[8] Jesus offers the man an assurance that his sins are forgiven (v. 5).

The response in terms of forgiveness when physical healing is surely what is being sought comes as a surprise. It is also troubling in that it seems to imply a causal connection between sickness and sin: the paralysis is a punishment for sin; forgiveness of the sin paves the way for recovery of health. The connection is undoubtedly to be found in biblical literature,[9] though there are also passages that contest it—notably John 9:2-3.[10] It is best, however, to place our worries on this account on hold for the time being, until we see how creatively Jesus brings healing and forgiveness together in the end. In any case, what he first confers on the man is the benefit that stands at the center of his proclamation: "Repent and believe the good news" (1:15). Faith, shown by the lengths to which the paralyzed man and his bearers were prepared to go to in order to gain access (vv. 3-4), has become the channel whereby the divine acceptance associated with the Kingdom reaches out and grasps him. In his transformed relationship with God

6. Since by Mark's day "the word" had become a technical expression for the basic Christian proclamation, for the original readers of the gospel the scene in the house would prefigure the risen Lord's proclamation of the word through the preachers and prophets of their own "domestic church"; cf. Boring, *Mark,* 76.

7. Mark's description of the process (contrast Luke [5:19], who speaks of "tiles") seems to presuppose the typical Palestinian village house, the roof of which would be constructed of beams laid across the upright stone walls with thatch or straw filling the space between.

8. By speaking vaguely of "their faith" the text leaves open the possibility that community faith suffices for the power of Jesus to flow to a person in need.

9. See Marcus, *Mark 1–8,* 221 for biblical and postbiblical references.

10. The entire book of Job can be seen as a sustained contestation of the notion that suffering necessarily implies guilt and alienation from God.

this man is already a paradigm of what is being offered to all who hear Jesus' word in faith.

The declaration of forgiveness provokes a hostile, if initially hidden, reaction in the hearts of some scribes who are sitting close by (vv. 6-7). They find Jesus' words blasphemous, since forgiveness of sin is the prerogative of God alone.[11] Knowing with prophetic insight what they are thinking, Jesus brings it into the open (v. 8). Defiantly, he flings back the challenge: which of two things is "easier" to say to the paralyzed man: "your sins are forgiven" or "arise, take up your pallet and walk" (v. 9)? From a human point of view the issue of which is "easier" is otiose. On human lips a declaration of forgiveness is, as they rightly hold, blasphemous, while to command a paralytic to get up and walk is ridiculous, since it lies beyond human capacity to make such a command effective. But in the person of Jesus we are dealing with more than the human: for *him* both sayings are equally "easy." And to demonstrate ("that you may know . . ." [v. 10]) that this is the case, he makes the (physically verifiable) healing the proof of his (inwardly) effective declaration of forgiveness (v. 11). When the paralyzed person gets up, takes up his pallet, and walks out before all (v. 12),[12] the inevitable conclusion must be that he ("the Son of Man") has authority on earth to forgive sins; for him to declare sins forgiven is not blasphemy. On their own terms, therefore, the scribes must confront the question: if, as they rightly hold, only God can forgive sins and sins have here ("on earth") been forgiven, *who* then do we have on our hands? Is it not someone who uniquely brings to this house the power and presence of God?

We can now, I think, better appreciate how effective has been the otherwise troubling conjunction of forgiveness and healing in this scene. Without any *necessary* implication that the man's need to receive forgiveness was the cause of his condition, the narrative has brought the two together in a way that makes the visible physical healing the proof of the more fundamental but hidden gift of forgiveness. Here, in this house, the assembled throng has witnessed an enactment of the "word" Jesus has been speaking: the "good news" of the imminence of the Kingdom and the renewed relationship with God that precedes it. The paralysis that held the man bound is an effective symbol of the captivity under which the entire human world labored prior to the onset of the Kingdom. Jesus' command, "Arise (*egeire*),

11. "God alone" (lit. "one God") has echoes of the *Shema* summons, which stands at the heart of Israel's faith: Deut 6:1-6.

12. The Greek text, with its repetition of the verb *airein* ("carry"), makes the point that the man goes out *carrying* the stretcher on which initially he had *been carried:* cf. Boring, *Mark,* 77–78.

take up your pallet and go home" (v. 11) is the word of life that he, the risen One, addresses to all believers. Forgiveness and the renewal of relationship that goes with it is not raining down from heaven; it is being communicated here "on earth" by One who personally embodies the reconciling presence of God (cf. 2 Cor 5:21).

Jesus Calls a Tax Collector (2:13-14) and Keeps Bad Company (2:15-17)

Having just communicated divine forgiveness and defended his authority to do so (2:1-12), Jesus now enters even more deeply into the issue by calling a "sinner" to be one of his close associates. As he walks along by the sea, accompanied by a large crowd he is teaching (v. 13), he once again (cf. 1:16-20) sees someone pursuing his occupation and issues a call: "Follow me." Like the earlier disciples, who left their means of livelihood (nets and boat), Levi immediately rises from his counting table and follows Jesus (v. 14). The difference is that whereas Peter and his companions had been pursuing a reputable trade, Jesus now sees and deliberately calls one whose occupation makes him an outcast and a "sinner."[13]

But this is not where it ends. Levi throws a banquet in his house for Jesus and his disciples, inviting many of his former associates as well.[14] The upshot is that Jesus and his disciples are to be found sharing a celebratory meal with "many tax collectors and sinners" (v. 15). As in the case of the leper (1:40-45), Jesus has broken through a "clean/unclean" barrier, risking ritual contamination in so doing. The difference is that he is also involving in this behavior the many disciples he has now acquired (v. 15c).[15] But the same pattern prevails: *he* does not acquire uncleanness from association with

---

13. Tax collectors were minor officials who collected the tolls and tariffs, the right to collect which had been farmed out to the highest bidder in a system patently open to extortion and corruption. Because their occupation required contact with Gentiles and also because they had the reputation of being dishonest, they were commonly regarded as outside the pale of the holy people of God in both an ethical and ritual sense. Hence the expression "tax collectors and sinners" (v. 16) likely has the sense "tax collectors and other sinners"; cf. Marcus, *Mark 1–8*, 225–26; Boring, *Mark*, 81–82; Donahue and Harrington, *Mark*, 101–2.

14. The text of v. 15 does not make clear whether Levi or Jesus was host. The fact that the guests "reclined" (*katakeisthai*), implying a feast rather than an ordinary meal, suggests the former (so explicitly Luke 5:29).

15. This is the first time Mark mentions "disciples" as a group, as distinct from the five who have followed Jesus (the four in 1:16-20 plus Levi). In view of Mark's constant portrayal of Jesus as teacher, "disciples" is a particularly appropriate designation for those who "follow" him.

sinners; rather, his company extends acceptance, forgiveness, and inclusion to them. In fact, because one of *them* has just been made a disciple it is not really possible to draw a rigid distinction between disciples and "sinners."[16] To be a disciple is to know two things above all: that one is a sinner and that one is called precisely as such to companionship with Jesus.[17]

Again, Jesus' behavior provokes criticism from the guardians of the present religious order, here described as "the scribes of the Pharisees" (v. 16). The Pharisees make their first appearance in the gospel here. Despite their overall negative presentation in the gospels, they were in many ways the real spiritual leaders of the Jewish people at the time of Jesus.[18] Through their creative interpretation of the Torah and respect for oral as well as written tradition they sought to preserve the identity of Israel as a "holy nation" compelled to live in a multiethnic and multireligious population. Their stress on external observances, especially Sabbath and food laws, clean and unclean, and the like served this aim, extending to the nation as a whole the holiness requirements that the Torah imposed only on priests. In terms of theology Jesus would probably have adhered more closely to them than to any other movement in Judaism. What he disagreed with—the gospels suggest—was their tendency, in the name of their tradition, to draw the "holiness" requirement so tightly as to exclude considerable numbers of the people, including some, such as the tax collector Levi, excluded not so much by his personal way of life as by his very occupation. For Jesus this was at odds with God's reaching out to the very margins of society in view of the inbreaking of the Kingdom. The Kingdom was not a closed door but, for the present at least, an open invitation.

To defend his association with "bad company" Jesus, typically, turns to an image: it is not the well who have need of a physician, but the sick (v. 17a). The image, though simple, is very telling. Healing requires contact. What use would a medical professional be who refused to have anything to do with the sick or to go among them? The image further implies that whereas the critics see sinfulness as something simply to exclude and

16. Cf., again, the ambiguity of the "many" who "follow" at the end of v. 15: is the reference to the disciples, or to the tax collectors and sinners? The ambiguity may be intentional: on the pattern of Levi, all followers of Jesus are repentant sinners who have become disciples.

17. I am echoing here the well-known characterization of a Jesuit according to the description given at the beginning of Decree 2 ("Jesuits Today") of the 32nd General Congregation of the Society of Jesus: "What is it to be a Jesuit? It is to know that one is a sinner, yet called to be a companion of Jesus as Ignatius was" (GC 32; Decree 2, §1).

18. Cf. Donahue and Harrington, *Mark,* 102.

avoid—and certainly to judge and condemn—for Jesus "sinners" are sick people in need of inclusion and healing.

A final pronouncement, "I have not come to call the righteous but sinners" (v. 17b), harks back to the "calling" of Levi (v. 14), making it paradigmatic. Jesus has not come simply to summon people to repentance, but actually to "call" them into the community of the Kingdom. He reaches out to the marginal because they stand, apparently at least, in greatest danger of being lost. But the division in the statement between "righteous" and "sinners" is ironical.[19] The summons of the Gospel: "The time has come; the rule of God is at hand; repent and believe the good news" (1:15) is universal. No one is completely "righteous"; *all* stand in need of the repentance that gives access to the grace of the Kingdom. Jesus' much-criticized celebration with "tax-collectors and sinners" anticipates and prefigures the "banquet" of the Kingdom to which he is now issuing invitations.[20]

The Old and the New: When to Fast and When to Feast: 2:18-22

Feasting with tax collectors and sinners flows naturally into the controversy over fasting that stands at the center of the sequence as a whole. While fasting may be the "presenting issue," the episode develops into a sustained insistence on Jesus' part that there is a radical discontinuity between the old and the new. The flow of thought is not smooth, however. Opening (vv. 18-19) and closing (vv. 21-22) elements, both of which suggest that fasting is not appropriate, enclose a central statement (v. 20) in which Jesus insists that a time is coming when the disciples *will* fast. The overall statement, then, is tension-laden and in several respects more intriguing than may appear at first sight.

The disciples of John the Baptist and the disciples of the Pharisees fast (v. 18a), but the disciples of Jesus—and by implication Jesus himself—do not. This leads to the kind of complaint that the religiously observant are wont to make against people they regard as lax. Once again Jesus meets the charge with an image: wedding guests[21] cannot fast while the bridegroom is present. In Palestine at the time of Jesus, as in rural areas of many countries today, weddings were significant occasions of celebration involving the entire

19. See especially Moloney, *Gospel of Mark,* 65, against Gnilka, *Markus 1–8,* 109.

20. Cf. Boring: "The whole scene has overtones of the inclusive eucharistic celebrations of early Christianity, the proleptic celebration of the messianic banquet in the dawning kingdom of God" (*Mark,* 81).

21. Literally "sons of the bride-chamber." The reference could be more strictly to the attendants of the groom, but it is likely to include all the guests.

local community; to fast at a wedding would be so gravely insulting to the families concerned as to be unthinkable. The implication is that Jesus' disciples do not fast because they know themselves to be guests at a "wedding" in the sense of already belonging to the messianic age, which the biblical tradition typically portrayed in nuptial imagery in texts such as Hos 2:19-23; Isa 54:4-10; 62:4-5; Ezekiel 16 (cf. John 2:1-11; 3:29).

For Jesus, then, the issue is not whether religious practice should be more or less ascetic; it is a matter of eschatology. His practice—or *non*practice—in regard to fasting is of a piece with his basic proclamation of the inbreaking of God's Rule (1:15).[22] The (voluntary) fasting of John's disciples and the Pharisees was in view of the coming of the Kingdom—to prepare for it and in a sense "hasten" its arrival.[23] For Jesus the Kingdom has already dawned, creating a whole new reality with respect to divine-human relations. By continuing to fast, John's disciples and the Pharisees relegate themselves to an era already overtaken by the "good news of God" (1:14).

The two concluding images to which Jesus appeals—the patching of garments and the storing of new wine—reinforce this sense of a new era requiring a completely new mindset. The kingdom has the dynamism and vitality of an unshrunken piece of cloth (v. 21)[24] or of new, unfermented wine (v. 22). The violence of the images—the ripped cloth and the burst skins—reflects the violence that his "new" teaching (1:27) and liberating action have inflicted on the prevailing order. Attempting to contain or grapple with the new reality in old, outworn categories is as futile and destructive as the behavior excluded in the images. A complete "change of heart" ("repentance" [*metanoiein*]) is required (1:15).[25]

What, then, are we to make of the intermediate statement (v. 20) that seems to run counter to all this and undercut its force? Jesus speaks darkly of a time when the "bridegroom" will be "taken away," a time when the disciples will indeed fast. Here the "wedding" image (v. 19) has become an allegory in which the bridegroom is Jesus himself and his "taking away" a

22. Cf. Meier, *A Marginal Jew* 2:448: "While the saying in Mark 2:19a does not explicitly mention the kingdom of God, that is in all likelihood the reality referred to by the imagery of the wedding."

23. For Jews the Law of Moses enjoined fasting only on the Day of Atonement (Lev 16:29). But occasional fasts were proclaimed (cf. Joel 1:14; Isa 58:1-5; etc.) and the Pharisees fasted voluntarily twice weekly (cf. Luke 18:12; also Matt 6:16). On fasting see further Donahue and Harrington, *Mark,* 106.

24. Literally a patch of cloth that has not been subjected by the cloth refiner to the process of thickening and shrinking.

25. The concluding phrase "new wine, new wineskins" sounds almost like a slogan of the Markan community deriving from Jesus' image; cf. Marcus, *Mark 1–8,* 238.

blunt allusion to his violent death. The warning transposes us from the time of Jesus' pre-Passion life to that of the early post-Easter community, still grappling with the death of its Lord and keenly awaiting his return as Son of Man to usher in the Kingdom (13:24-27; 14:62). In *this* sense of waiting for the Lord to complete his messianic work the Markan community—like the subsequent Christian Church—is in the position of those (such as the disciples of John) who fasted and prayed in anticipation of the Kingdom.[26]

The presence of this "counterstatement," then, reflects the complex eschatological situation in which believers find themselves. Through the advent and teaching of Jesus, and in the power of his Spirit, they live now the relationship with God characteristic of the Kingdom. But his death and resurrection have plunged them into a curious interim period in which he both is and is not present and in which each one has to "take up his or her own cross" and follow after him (8:34). In this sense they will continue to "fast" even as they share also the "joy" of the Bridegroom.

The sequence as a whole, then, holds together both the sense of living in a new age in which old categories have been broken through and the memory of the cost (to Jesus) of that breaking through, a cost members of the messianic community will continue to share until the Kingdom is finally in place. In this situation the demonic will be recognizably at work when the categories of the old understanding, in all likelihood cloaked in religious "righteousness," are invoked or appealed to in such a way as to challenge messianic joy, to undermine the relationship with God characteristic of the Kingdom, or to suggest that the sufferings of the present, "in-between" time are signs of separation from the Bridegroom rather than union with him (cf. Rom 8:17-18).[27]

Lord of the Sabbath: 2:23-28

The final two conflict stories bear on the Jewish institution of the Sabbath. The observance of Sabbath is a key marker of Jewish identity. It is the subject

---

26. Whether the statement means that they literally fast or is a general indication of a mourning and longing time (as clearly indicated by the sufferings and persecutions foretold in Mark 13) is not clear.

27. One is put in mind here of the teaching of St. Ignatius Loyola concerning consolation and desolation: ". . . it belongs to the evil spirit to cause anxiety and sadness, and to place obstacles in the way, disquieting the soul by false reasons, so that it makes no further progress; and it belongs to the good spirit to inspire it with courage and strength, to give it consolations, tears, inspirations, and peace, making things easy, and removing every impediment, that it may make progress in good works" (Rules for the Discernment of Spirits, *Spiritual Exercises* §315).

of the most developed item among the Ten Commandments (Exod 20:8-11; Deut 5:12-15) and gave rise in Judaism to an extensive body of legal interpretation regarding what did and did not violate the Sabbath rest.[28] The evidence of the gospels suggests that while Jesus did not reject Sabbath observance as such, he did question interpretations he judged at odds with its original purpose. The two Sabbath controversies that follow, while bearing signs of development in the post-Easter tradition, basically reflect this attitude of Jesus.

The first controversy arises when the disciples, walking with Jesus through fields of standing grain, begin to pluck heads of the ripened grain. The Law allowed travelers to satisfy their hunger in this way, provided they did so in moderation (Deut 23:25). When the Pharisees suddenly appear on the scene[29] what they object to is not the walking through the cornfields or the harvesting of the grain per se, but doing so on the Sabbath.

In defense of the disciples Jesus first (vv. 25-26) appeals to biblical precedent: David's action in entering the house of God, when he and his followers "had need" and were "hungry," to eat "the bread of the presence," which was reserved for the priests (cf. 1 Sam 21:1-7).[30] In several respects the two cases are not parallel. David's action did not take place on the Sabbath, nor did it concern the priest "Abiathar," as Mark records, but his less-well-known father, Ahimelech.[31] The text does not state that David ate the bread or that he gave it to his young men—though the implication is that that was what he had in mind. In short, the appeal to the incident appears to rest on the single point that an exemplary biblical character, faced with his own need (hunger) and that of his followers, violated a legal prescription in order to address it.

More significant, however, is the fact that it was *David* who acted in this way.[32] Despite Mark's overall reserve in regard to davidic Messianism, there is an implied messianic claim in Jesus' appeal to David.[33] What David

28. See Donahue and Harrington, *Mark,* 110–11.

29. Their appearance in the grain fields is one factor suggesting that the episode as narrated may owe a fair bit to the dramatization in the gospel tradition of a controversy originally located elsewhere; cf. Marcus, *Mark 1–8,* 240.

30. According to the prescription in Lev 24:4-9 (cf. Exod 25:30; Num 4:7) the Bread of the Presence referred to twelve loaves placed on a table in the sanctuary every Sabbath as an offering to God; the priests consumed the old loaves when they were replaced by fresh ones on the following Sabbath.

31. Both Matthew and Luke in their parallel accounts do not mention the name of the priest.

32. The "Davidic" aura presumably also accounts for the naming of the priest as Abiathar rather than Ahimelech. Whereas Ahimelech makes a very minor appearance in the biblical story, his much-better-known son Abiathar had a great deal to do with David (2 Sam 15:24-29, 35; 17:15-22).

33. Cf. Hooker, *Saint Mark,* 104; Moloney, *Gospel of Mark,* 69.

could do without blame for the benefit of himself and his followers, a fortiori the Son of David, who a later controversy (cf. 12:35-37) will show to be David's "Lord," can do in the same regard.

Hard upon this implicit christological claim, Jesus takes the defense a step further (v. 27), authoritatively declaring the Sabbath's true purpose: "the Sabbath was made for human beings, not human beings for the Sabbath." The passive construction "was made" refers to the order of creation (Gen 2:2-3), which Jesus is reclaiming in the name of the Kingdom.[34] The statement is, then, more than a general maxim reflecting a humane, anthropocentric view of religious law.[35] As in the previous controversies, Jesus reveals the mind of the Creator and implicitly proclaims the coming of the Kingdom.

A final comment (v. 28) draws a christological conclusion from the ruling just given: "So the Son of Man is Lord of the Sabbath." Just as the Son of Man has authority on earth to declare sin forgiven (Mark 2:10), so the Son of Man has equivalent divine authority to dispose over the Sabbath. As agent and instrument of the Kingdom now dawning, Jesus has authority as Son of Man to institute the original plan of the Creator for human beings and to challenge, with equal authority, all structures, however venerable, holding back the realization of that design. An incident that began with a challenge concerning a fairly trivial infringement of the Sabbath has ended with Jesus authoritatively declaring God's ultimate will for humankind: the enjoyment of an eternal Sabbath "rest" in the Kingdom. Present Sabbath observance should not be a legal straitjacket, but a joyful foretaste of that final outcome.

Enhancing Life on the Sabbath: 3:1-6

The final conflict story grows out of the preceding one (2:23-28) in that it shows Jesus (literally "the Son of Man") to be indeed "Lord" of the Sabbath (2:28). Entering a synagogue "again" (cf. 1:21-28), Jesus moves directly into a fresh conflict with the same religious leaders, the Pharisees, who had criticized his disciples over their eating of the grain. In fact, he seems to

---

34. Exactly as he will do in the case of the ruling on divorce in 10:5-9.

35. While both the Matthean (12:1-8) and Lukan (6:1-5) parallels omit the statement found in Mark 2:27, there are remarkably similar Jewish parallels to Jesus' statement about Sabbath—though attested for a somewhat later period (e.g., "The Sabbath is handed over to you, not you to it" [*Mekilta* on Exod 31:4]; "he (man) was not created for the world but the world for him" [2 *Apoc Bar* 14:18]); see Marcus, *Mark 1–8,* 245.

walk directly into what looks like a "setup."[36] If the Pharisees have not actually introduced the man with the withered hand,[37] they are at least using his presence to place Jesus in the dangerous situation of flouting the Sabbath law.[38] Traditional interpretation of that law allowed for exceptions in matters of life and death.[39] It is the fact that the man's ailment is not life-threatening that places Jesus in a position of testing. He could, after all, ignore the man or at least postpone dealing with his condition until another day. But, discerning what is going on, he confronts the situation directly.[40] Bidding the man to come out in front of all (v. 3), he puts to his adversaries questions that go to the heart of what the Sabbath is all about (v. 4ab): is it about doing good or evil, saving life or destroying it?

With the terms set so starkly the answer is obvious, but, to save face the adversaries will not voice it (v. 4c). Jesus has already taken the issue beyond the limits in which they had set it—Sabbath regulation—to the level of God's salvific will to communicate life to human beings. He "grieves with anger"[41] at "the hardness of heart"[42] that ranges them on the opposing side of death and destruction (v. 5a). Then (v. 5b), as in the case of the cure of the paralytic (2:1-12), the miraculous restoration of the man's limb validates the truth of what Jesus is pronouncing.[43]

---

36. Suggested by the verb *paretēroun*, which has a hostile sense of watching to catch someone out.

37. Literally "a dried up hand." The Greek expression suggests a long-standing paralysis, perhaps from birth; cf. Donahue and Harrington, *Mark,* 115.

38. According to Exod 31:14-15 and Num 15:32-36 breaking the Sabbath was punishable by death, though such penalties were hardly enforced in Jesus' day. Jewish law always allowed for action to preserve life on the Sabbath.

39. Cf. Donahue and Harrington, *Mark,* 115, who point out considerable variety of interpretation of what was and what was not permissible on the Sabbath.

40. One is put in mind of the maxim Blessed Mary MacKillop gave to her sisters: "Never see an evil and do nothing about it." (Mary MacKillop [1842–1909] founded a congregation of Catholic religious sisters in Australia to educate and care for the isolated and disadvantaged. She was beatified in 1995, the first Australian to be set on the path to canonization in the Catholic Church.)

41. As so often, in contrast to the parallel accounts in Matthew (12:9-14) and Luke (6:6-11), Mark highlights the emotions of Jesus.

42. "Hardness of heart," used with reference to the disciples in 6:52 and 8:17, is a biblical usage denoting resistance to the divine will or plan (cf. Ezek 3:7; Acts 28:7; Rom 2:5); and the whole tradition of the hardening of Pharaoh's heart (Exod 4:21; 7:3; etc.) picked up by Paul in Romans (9:18) with reference to the resistance of Israel to the Gospel (11:9, 25).

43. Ironically, the healing involves no breach of the Sabbath. Jesus does not have to "work" to achieve it. He simply tells the man to stretch out his hand and the healing takes place as he does so.

In the person of Jesus the pledge of human wholeness associated with the Kingdom is already becoming effective. To have postponed the cure to another day would be to deny its onset. Thus this healing of a comparatively minor ailment becomes in its own way a further proclamation of the Kingdom and a symbolic rescue of human life from the powers opposed to God's rule—their influence seen here not in overt demonic possession, but in the hardness of heart resistant to life and wholeness.

Jesus' victory in this culminating controversy—and indeed in the four preceding ones—does not come without cost. The episode, and with it the series of conflicts as a whole, ends on a menacing note with the instigation of a plot "to destroy him" (v. 6).[44] This is the first overt suggestion in the narrative of the gospel that Jesus' liberating activity and teaching on behalf of the Kingdom will place him personally in mortal danger. We now know what the "taking away" of the bridegroom (2:20) might mean.

44. The association of Pharisees with a party described as "Herodians" (also 12:13) is puzzling. The latter are probably supporters of Herod Antipas, the ruler of Galilee during the life of Jesus. Mark's point would seem to be that religious authorities have banded together with the secular power in antagonism to Jesus; cf. Moloney, *Gospel of Mark,* 71, n. 126.

II
LATER GALILEAN MINISTRY
3:7–6:6a

The Renewed People of God: 3:7-35

The second phase of Jesus' ministry in Galilee begins, like the first (1:14–3:6), with a summary (3:7-12; cf. 1:14-15) followed by a calling of disciples (3:13-19; cf. 1:16-20), and ends on a note of opposition and unbelief (6:1-6a; cf. 2:1–3:6, especially v. 6). In the first phase we have seen that, along with popular enthusiasm, Jesus' message and ministry of liberation had begun to provoke opposition—not merely from the demonic forces but also from the guardians of the prevailing religious system who find nothing but threat in the new wine of the Kingdom. This conflict intensifies in the scenes that follow. But alongside conflict with the authorities, and to a large degree provoking it, runs Jesus' ever-widening popularity with the mass of the common people (3:7-12). In the context of rejection from the leaders of Israel (2:1–3:6; 3:22-30) and misunderstanding from his own blood family (3:21-22, 31-32) and townsfolk (6:1-6a), Jesus moves to reconstitute the people who are flocking to him as the Israel of the end time by appointing twelve disciples to serve as its symbolic foundation (3:13-19, 33-34). In the midst of the countercurrents of rejection and enthusiasm, the parables sequence (4:1-34) addresses the question whether the opposition and resistance falsify the reality of the rule of God that Jesus proclaims. That this is not so is then validated in a sequence of particularly powerful miracles in which Jesus shows a divine mastery in three key areas: destructive natural forces (calming of the sea: 4:35-41), a "legion" of destructive demons (5:1-20), and death itself (5:21-43). In this way a coherent narrative line emerges from a sequence that might otherwise appear rather disconnected.[1]

---

1. This understanding of the rationale behind the sequence of scenes in 3:7–6:6 is very much indebted to Marcus, *Mark 1–8,* 255.

Summary: The Widespread Popularity of Jesus: 3:7-12

In stark contrast to the hostility of the religious authorities, who have just gone off to plot Jesus' destruction (3:6), Mark provides a summary of his growing popularity with the mass of the people (vv. 7-10) followed by a description of his corresponding impact on the demonic world (vv. 11-12). It is easy to pass over these summaries, but they play an important role in Mark's presentation of Jesus and the impact of his presence.

Jesus "withdraws with his disciples to the sea" (v. 7). The impression is that he is withdrawing from the kind of oppositional dialogue with the authorities shown in the preceding controversy stories. The "sea" will be a constant background in the scenes that follow. It represents the world that can be hostile and threatening and yet remains the sphere from which Jesus and, in time, the disciples must catch "fish" for the Kingdom (1:17).

The narrative stresses the size of the crowds that flock to Jesus,[2] the far-flung regions from which they come, and the reason they do so: their having heard about what he was doing. The localities mentioned cover those areas of Palestine that were inhabited by Jews or at least contained significant Jewish minorities.[3] There is a sense, then, that at the expense of those currently in power Jesus is drawing to himself the allegiance of a great mass of Israel, while mention of non-Jewish regions such as Tyre and Sidon foreshadows the Gospel's later outreach to the Gentile world.

The size and enthusiasm of the crowds is not without an element of menace. Lest he be crushed, Jesus warns the disciples to have a boat ready as a means of escape (3:9). People afflicted in various ways fling themselves down before him in an effort to touch him (v. 10). The overall impression is that of a celebrity being dangerously mobbed by an overenthusiastic and violent crowd.

At the core of this chaotic situation is the demonic world, manifesting itself in the cries of persons possessed by unclean spirits (v. 11). As in 1:23-24 and 34, and later in 5:7, this world feels the effect of Jesus' liberating presence and so recognizes his true identity as Son of God. Their falling

---

2. The Greek phrase *polu plēthos* occurs twice (v. 7b and [in reverse order] v. 8), to form a typical Markan "frame" around the geographical names designating the areas from which people flocked to Jesus.

3. Galilee represents the northern area of Jewish habitation, Jerusalem and Judea the south. Idumea had been conquered a century before by the Jewish Hasmonean dynasty; the region across the Jordan, while no longer under Jewish control, probably contained a Jewish minority, as perhaps did Tyre and Sidon on the Mediterranean coast. Significant omissions from the list are Samaria, which Mark never mentions, and the Decapolis area, which he does (5:20; 7:31).

down before him and acknowledgment of his status may represent an act of submission (cf. Phil 2:10-11),[4] but Jesus, as before (1:34), reduces them to silence. His divine sonship (Story 1) is not to be made known from sources such as this, and certainly not until the revelation of his destiny to suffer, die, and rise again (Story 2) discloses how it is to be rightly understood.

The Reconstitution of God's People: 3:13-19

In response, it would seem, to the flocking of the crowds around him, Jesus "ascends the mountain" (v. 13). The phrase recalls the ascent of Moses up Mount Sinai preparatory to the ratification of the covenant sealing the Israelites as the original people of God (Exod 19:3; 24:1-4). From out of the wider mass Jesus summons "those whom he wanted" (v. 13b), and then from within this select group of disciples he establishes "Twelve" (v. 14).[5] The number inevitably recalls the twelve sons of Jacob, the ancestral figures of the twelve tribes making up the Israel of old.[6]

Like ancient Israel, the members of this renewed, eschatological Israel have to be won from the captivities under which they currently labor. The Twelve will not have a static, merely symbolic role; they are to assist Jesus in his liberating mission. They are to be "with him" in close companionship, and are to be sent out to preach (the Gospel) with authority to expel demons (vv. 14b-15). That they are to be "with him" and also to be "sent out" is not contradictory. Being "with" Jesus in Mark's gospel entails not simply physical presence but living in close companionship as disciples. The capacity to preach effectively and expel demons flows from that companionship and is its essential outreach. We have here the kernel of the missionary vocation of the church: the liberating proclamation of the Word (1:14-15) and the reclaiming of human minds and bodies for the Kingdom through the grace of the sacraments.

The listing of the names of the Twelve (vv. 16b-19) begins as a bestowal of nicknames, first of all on Simon, who becomes "Rock" (v. 16b), and then James and John, who become the "Boanerges," "sons of thunder" (v. 17). The meaning of the latter is obscure: it may refer to the kind of impetuous

---

4. Marcus, *Mark 1–8*, 259.

5. This is to interpret "those whom he wanted" and who "came to him" in v. 13b as a wider group out of whom he further chose (and "appointed") twelve (v. 14a; v. 16). It is also possible to relate both choices to the Twelve, but this seems less likely.

6. Mark's account particularly stresses the "Twelve" by the repetition of the phrase "and he appointed twelve" in v. 16a, thereby setting a characteristic "frame" around the threefold statement of the purposes for which the Twelve were chosen (vv. 14-15a).

character later displayed in the bold request described in 10:35-37. If Simon's nickname also refers to his character, then the designation becomes ironic in view of his later failures, which Mark catalogues at length. More likely, in view of the leadership position that, despite his failure, he undoubtedly has (8:29; 9:5; 10:28; 11:21; 14:37; 16:7),[7] it refers to a foundational role or status within the community conceived of as (holy) building.[8] In any case the three who have received new names form a select group at key moments in the story (5:37; 9:2; 14:33). Apart from Andrew (1:16, 29; 13:3), none of the remaining members of the Twelve receives individual mention—apart of course, from the last named, Judas. The notice of his betrayal (v. 18) intensifies the shadow beginning to gather over the narrative. Even Jesus' inner circle is not immune from demonic infiltration.

False and True Understanding of Jesus and His Works: 3:20-30

After the formal institution of the Twelve on the mountain, Jesus returns to the more characteristic Markan location of a house (v. 20). He returns also to a situation of misunderstanding and misinterpretation that carries forward the conflict now building up around him (2:1–3:6). The misinterpretation stems from two quarters: his natural family and scribes who have come from the center of authority, Jerusalem. In a further example of "sandwiching" technique the evangelist has woven together material dealing with misunderstanding and accusation from both these directions in such a way as to set them in quasi-parallel. The arrangement also makes central (3:27) the image by which Jesus presents himself as the Stronger One, come to bind up and plunder "the house" of Satan. We can set it out schematically as follows:

---

7. Cf. Hooker, *Saint Mark*, 112.

8. The Markan gospel would thus provide a base for the kind of elaboration of Simon Peter's role seen in Matt 16:19-23. Marcus links the new name "rock" with the patriarchal role of Abraham, described in Isa 51:1-2 as the rock out of which Israel is hewn (*Mark 1–8*, 268).

Failure of Jesus' natural family: 3:20-21

Accusation of Scribes:	Beelzebul Charge: v. 22 Divided Kingdom: vv. 23-26 "Binding Strong Man": v. 27 Real Blasphemy: vv. 28-30

Jesus' True Family: 3:31-35

The effect is to create a very negative portrayal of Jesus' immediate family—an issue I shall take up in due course.

The sequence begins with Jesus once again being mobbed by enthusiastic crowds. As in 2:1, he is inside the house but the pressure of the crowd that has gathered outside is sufficient to make it impossible for him even to have a meal. In this situation his family[9] "come out" —presumably from their home town, Nazareth—to get hold of him (v. 21a). Their motive, as expressed in a final tart clause, is their belief that he has gone mad (literally: "is beside himself" [*exestē*]). They appear to regard whatever he is doing to attract such wild enthusiasm as a sign of dangerous derangement. Hence their aim to remove him from his present path and get him back home where he belongs.[10]

In this bid Jesus' relatives may not actually be regarding him as possessed by a demon—though insanity was often attributed to demonic possession in the ancient world (cf. John 10:20). However, the immediate introduction of the "scribes from Jerusalem" with their explicit charge (v. 22) that Jesus was possessed by Beelzebul and expelled demons through the power of this prince of demons[11] clearly appears as a parallel, if more serious, misunderstanding. The accusation is grave because it really amounts to a

9. The Greek expression *hoi par'autou* is best interpreted in this way since this group is distinguished from Jesus' immediate disciples mentioned in the previous verse.

10. This small pericope describing the action of Jesus' relatives (3:20-21) is one of the comparatively rare Markan passages without parallel in Matthew or Luke, both of whom present Jesus' family in more positive light.

11. The parallel between the two accusations in v. 22b clearly establishes Beelzebul as "prince of demons" and hence as another name for Satan. See further Marcus, *Mark 1–8*, 272.

charge of practicing sorcery—a capital offense—and is made by legal authorities who come from the national center of power, Jerusalem.

Jesus rebuts the accusation in two stages. First (vv. 23-26) he appeals to common sense or, rather, to a generally accepted maxim about the survival or fall of regimes and kingdoms. Those that show signs of internal division are bound to fall. Since Jesus' exorcisms threaten Satan's rule, it would be nonsense for Satan to be behind them; it would signal the end of his power. Second (v. 27), Jesus has recourse to an image that provides the authentic interpretation of what his exorcisms are achieving. Just as the goods of a strong man cannot be plundered unless an even stronger one first binds him up, the exorcisms represent a binding of Satan preparatory to the plundering of his house.

Both stages of Jesus' rebuttal presuppose the view, widespread in Jewish apocalyptic thinking, that "the house of the world" has fallen under the dominion of Satan. This rule of Satan is the negative background to the onset of the rule of God proclaimed by Jesus. As already indicated by the Baptist (1:7), he is that "Stronger One" who, with the power of the Spirit (1:10), has come to tie up Satan and plunder his house in the sense of liberating human beings from the captivity associated with his rule. This liberation is the content of the "good news" that Jesus proclaims in his teaching (1:14-15) and which his exorcising and healing activity enacts.

Not content with warding off attack, Jesus goes over to the offensive, pointing out what the scribal accusation implies (vv. 28-30). Since it is through the power of God's Holy Spirit that he expels demons, to accuse him of doing so through the prince of demons (v. 22) is tantamount to identifying the Spirit of God with the unclean spirits of the demonic world. Whereas all other blasphemies may in due course find forgiveness, that is a blasphemy so grave and so placing of a person outside the reach of salvation as to be in effect unforgivable.[12] The thought of an unforgivable sin has been a torment for the delicate Christian conscience. Rather than asking about what species of sin might be open to such extreme characterization it is best to restrict the sense to what is here in view: since the Spirit at work in Jesus (1:10) is the agent of salvation, to persevere in denying the presence of that Spirit or in identifying it with the adversarial power is to effectively place oneself out of the reach of salvation and so of ultimate forgiveness. Moreover, in concentrating on the mention of an "unforgivable sin" in v. 29 we should not pass over the strong assertion of universal forgiveness in the

---

12. For a brief survey of various traditional interpretations see Donahue and Harrington, *Mark*, 134–35.

preceding verse (v. 28). Jesus has come to proclaim and offer the universal forgiveness associated with the onset of the Kingdom (1:15; 2:5). Only those who identify his activity with what is in fact its diametric opposite place themselves beyond the reach of God's saving grace.

Jesus' True Family: 3:31-35

At this point (v. 31) Jesus' natural family—"his mother and his brothers"—reappear in a further bid to make contact with him. They come very much as outsiders. Jesus is in the house, seated with a crowd around him. The family have to send for him through the crowd, who in their turn pass the request on to Jesus (v. 32), adding "your sisters" to the family list. Jesus makes no direct response but instead looks about and, pointing to the group gathered immediately around him, identifies *them* as "my mother and my brothers" (v. 34), before stating more generally that whoever does the will of God is "my brother and sister and mother" (v. 35).

This Markan text clearly ranges the natural family of Jesus, including his mother, on the side of those who misunderstand Jesus and seek to divert him from his mission. At the same time it shows him surrounded by a new family defined as those who do the will of God. Doing God's will means understanding and acting in accordance with God's will for the present time characterized by the inbreaking of the Kingdom. In seeking to recapture and restrain him, Jesus' natural family show themselves to be on the side of the old era that the Kingdom is supplanting. Those who do God's will by giving themselves to the Kingdom find themselves in a new family gathered around Jesus, constituting his brothers and sisters, and even his mother. Notably absent from the list is "my father." The members of the community of the Kingdom share with Jesus one Father: God.

By setting the attempt of Jesus' natural family to get hold of him in quasi-parallel with the "Beelzebul" accusation, Mark shows how the control exercised by the closest human relationships can inhibit full dedication to the Kingdom—can be part of that overall captivity in which the demonic holds human beings bound. That said, the negative rating Jesus' natural family receives here is troubling, especially for the Catholic tradition with its high veneration of Mary and valuing of family life in general. If one is looking for a rich theology of family life in the New Testament, Mark's gospel is hardly the place to begin. Whatever may have been the attitude of Jesus himself, Mark's negative view may reflect the situation of the community for which he wrote, where commitment to the Gospel required heavy sacrifice in the area of family attachment and also perhaps severe lack of support or even betrayal from family members (cf. 10:28-31; 13:12-13).[13] At the same time we should keep in mind that Mark's gospel is only one element in a total New Testament picture. Its particularly keen sense of the present world coming to an end has the effect of relativizing the value of structures and institutions of this world, the conventional family included. New Testament documents reflecting a less pressing eschatology, such as the letters to the Colossians and Ephesians and the Pastoral Letters present family life more positively (Col 3:18-21; Eph 5:21–6:4; cf. 3:14-15; 1 Tim 3:1-5) and fill out the picture. It should also be noted that Luke's very positive portrayal of Mary, especially in the Infancy Story (Luke 1–2), contains moments when she does not understand (2:46-50; cf. 2:33-35) and has to ponder in her heart the mystery of all that is happening (2:19, 51). In this respect Luke stands in some continuity with the Markan picture in which the family of Jesus has difficulty in surrendering him to his mission. More fundamentally, for all his negative portrayal of Jesus' own family Mark reclaims and indeed exalts the notion of family by presenting the community of the Kingdom as the new family of God.

13. See further Marcus, *Mark 1–8,* 280.

Jesus Teaches in Parables: 4:1-34

As we have often noted, Mark continually portrays Jesus as a teacher. His teaching and his exorcising activity go hand in hand, with equally liberating effects on human beings. But so far we have learned very little about the *content* of the teaching. Now the narrative pace slows down and we hear Jesus preaching at some length.

The scene that unfolds describes him teaching in parables. Since parables are colorful, illustrative stories taken from everyday life, this should mean that the teaching Jesus gives here forms one of the most accessible parts of the gospel. But this is not the case. Two of the three parables (the Sowing [vv. 3-9] and the Seed Growing Secretly [vv. 26-29]) are mysterious in themselves, and the parables come interspersed with reflections on why Jesus speaks in parables. These reflections (vv. 10-12, 21-25, 33-34) make the difficult suggestion that he employs parables not to elucidate his message but to confuse and, ultimately, to exclude and condemn those who have taken a stand against him. The upshot is that this is one of the more difficult and puzzling sections of the gospel—making it more than ordinarily necessary to review the structure of the sequence as a whole:

vv. 1-2: The Setting: Jesus preaches to the crowd from a boat

vv. 3-9: The Parable of the Sowing

vv. 10-12: Reflection on Jesus' reason for speaking in parables

vv. 13-20: Explanation of the Parable of the Sowing

vv. 21-25: Reflection on the use of parables

vv. 26-29: Parable of the Seed Growing Secretly

vv. 30-32: Parable of the Mustard Seed

vv. 33-34: Reflection on Jesus' practice of speaking in parables

An additional complication is that with the reflection that begins at v. 10 the scene shifts from a public address to the crowds by the lakeside to instruction given to Jesus' more immediate disciples ("those around him with the Twelve"). They hear the reflection (vv. 10-12) and also the explanation of the parable of the Sowing (vv. 13-20) and the further reflection in vv. 21-25. But the comment at the very end (vv. 33-34a) suggests that the remaining two parables (vv. 26-29 and vv. 30-32) are once again addressed to the people as a whole. This lack of clarity about the audience adds to the difficulty of interpretation—though not insuperably, as I hope to show.

One important matter to keep in mind from the start is that Mark appears to be exploiting the wide sense that "parable" (Greek *parabolē*) has in the biblical tradition. This stems from its origins in the Hebrew word *mashal,* which can refer not only to an illustrative story or image but also to a puzzle, riddle, or enigma. Because of this background, "parable" has a variety of uses and effects. As an illustrative story or image it is a vehicle of communication and learning; as a puzzle or riddle it can just as well tease, mystify, and alienate. That Jesus' preaching was replete with images and parables is certain, and that he used parables chiefly as instruments of communication is also likely. This does not mean, however, that he did not at times exploit the capacity of parabolic language to shock and disarm, to open up new worlds of meaning, especially in connection with the rule of God, the unforeseen nature of which was so central to his message. While many of his hearers found the use of parables illuminating, there were doubtless others whom they mystified and disturbed. The sequence in Mark 4 seems designed to explain the reason for this negative reaction and to hold it up as a warning against "hardness of heart" (cf. 3:5).

Let us remind ourselves of where we are in terms of the wider flow of the story. Conflict has been growing around Jesus from early in his Galilean ministry (2:1–3:6). It has come to a climax with the deadly charge made by the scribes who have come from Jerusalem attributing his power to expel demons to an alliance with Beelzebul, prince of demons (3:22), a charge that has led Jesus in turn to speak in their regard of an unforgivable, eternal sin (3:28-30). In the face of this opposition from leading authorities Jesus has begun to establish the nucleus of a renewed Israel built on the foundation of twelve select disciples (3:13-19) and constituting the new family of God (3:31-35). The hostility, however, means that the rule of God proclaimed and enacted by Jesus (1:14-15) is not establishing itself without a struggle. The opposing rule of Satan is still very much around—something true for the time of Jesus' ministry, for the time when the gospel was written, and indeed for all time until the coming of the Son of Man to definitively establish the Kingdom (13:24-27). The parables sequence addresses this situation, and in particular the dismay and questioning it evokes. Is this really the time of the dawning of the rule of God? Is Satan being deposed, or is he in fact still calling the shots? What does this "coexistence" say about the nature of God's rule and the way and the time in which it may finally be expected to triumph in the world?[1]

The Setting: Jesus Teaches by the Sea: 4:1-2

Mark introduces the scene at considerable length, informing us no less than three times in the space of two verses that Jesus is teaching and that he is doing so "beside the sea," the symbol of the world from which "fish" must be caught for the Kingdom (1:17). The press of the enthusiastic crowd is so great as to lead him to teach sitting in a boat a little way off the shore (cf. 3:7-12).[2] The crowd at this point form something of a third party between Jesus' close disciples ("those around him" in 3:34-35) and the hostile scribes (3:22-30).[3] The crowd is wildly enthusiastic—witness its pressing upon Jesus—but the enthusiasm is not an unalloyed good. The popular idea of what Jesus has to offer is by no means identical with his sense of his mission in the service of the Kingdom. If people are to be won for that cause they must really "hear" his teaching (v. 3; cf. the warning at v. 9) and respond appropriately. The parables both illustrate and address this need.

---

1. Cf. Marcus, *Mark 1–8,* 288.

2. The boat allows Jesus to adopt the posture of a teacher by sitting down. The boat, of course, is a symbol of the church, through which Jesus, as risen Lord, will continue to teach the multitudes.

3. On the identity of this "third" group see the excellent discussion by Watts, *Isaiah's New Exodus,* 199–205.

The Parable of the Sowing: 4:3-9

This parable is traditionally known as "the Sower," but the title is not all that adequate since, once mentioned at the start, the sower fades completely from view. More prominent is the variation in the quality of ground into which the seed cast by the sower falls and the growth that occurs in each case. Hence I think it is best to name the parable simply "the Sowing": Jesus describes what happens when seed is sown according to the agricultural custom of Palestine with which he is familiar.[4]

This first parable is unique in that, though it stands alone (vv. 3-8), it is subsequently supplied with an interpretation (vv. 13-20) given privately by Jesus to his immediate disciples. The interpretation turns the parable into an allegory. (On allegory, see below.) Nonetheless, as the spatial separation between the parable and the allegory in the text of Mark 4 suggests, it is appropriate to consider the parable of the Sowing simply in itself and not to allow awareness of the allegorical explanation to entirely "swamp" the meaning.

As typically in the parables told by Jesus, the parable moves directly from his observation of everyday life. In the Palestine of the day those who sowed crops threw the seed about in a fairly casual way. By no means all of it landed in good soil. Quite a bit could fall in the three situations—on a path, on rocky ground, among thistles[5]—where it might well suffer the various outcomes described. The account of the three losses rises in dramatic intensity as it unfolds: in the first instance birds snatch the seed away before it gets any chance to take root; in the second there is a brief moment of promising growth before the sun burns it away; in the third case, at long last, hope seems secure: the seed takes root and grows for some time, but it too suffers the same fate, choked by the thistles that render it unfruitful. Then, right in the face of this final loss comes the surprise. Balancing the three losses—and vastly compensating for them—

---

4. Some Jewish sources, albeit somewhat later than the time of Jesus, suggest that in Palestine plowing followed sowing; cf. Joachim Jeremias, *The Parables of Jesus,* 3rd ed. (London: SCM, 1972) 11–12. For Jeremias this explains why the sower casts the seed so "carelessly" upon the path (a temporary one made by people crossing the field): it would all be plowed in later. But whatever the order of sowing and plowing, what is important for the parable is the broadcast method of the sowing, resulting in some loss of the seed.

5. "Thistles" seems to be the best rendering of the Greek *akanthai,* a general term for thorny or prickly plants, especially such as grow up unwanted in fields; cf. Vincent Taylor, *The Gospel according to St. Mark: the Greek Text, with Introduction, Notes and Indexes* (London: Macmillan, 1957) 253.

come the three outcomes in which the seed falls on good soil, producing yields thirtyfold, sixtyfold, and—finally and fantastically—one hundredfold.[6]

In this last figure the parable displays the kind of "over the top" exaggerated outcome that is a feature of many of Jesus' parables. If in the end the story seems to leave the world of everyday reality, that is the point: we are not dealing with the reality of ordinary human life but with the power and generosity of God at work in the Kingdom. What conditions the outcome in all four cases is the nature or situation of the soil on which the seed falls. The various types of soil correspond within the story to a variety of human responses to Jesus' preaching. Like the sower, Jesus "sows" the good news of the Kingdom in a way that is similarly casual and "wild." In a great many hearts it suffers the fate of the seed in the three cases of loss. But when it finds a receptive heart and truly strikes home, the way is set for the arrival of the Kingdom in the extraordinary fullness described. The Kingdom presupposes faith and repentance (1:15). Its primary address is to the human heart. That is where the struggle to obtain ascendancy over the opposing rule of the demonic begins, even if it must go out from there to transform communities and social situations.

Understood in this way, the parable addresses and accounts for the mixed response to Jesus' preaching of the kingdom. If it has been only partially successful, if the rule of Satan is still palpably at hand, this does not signal weakness or ultimate defeat. If one were to understand the Kingdom along the lines of earthly regimes such might indeed be the case. But the rule of God establishes its base in the repentant human heart. Where that good "soil" is lacking it suffers check and opposition, but where it does meet positive response the outcome, though not necessarily evident at present, will be so overwhelmingly great as to more than compensate for all the failure and loss.

The parable, then, is basically an expression of hope that God's rule will finally prevail. But, especially in the Markan version, there is also an aspect of warning. Jesus begins with the command "Hear!" (Mark 4:3)[7] and concludes, "Anyone with ears to hear had better listen!" (v. 9). Since the onset of the Kingdom is conditioned by the "soil" that receives it, what is crucial is that it be heard with repentance and faith. The crowd Jesus addresses in this scene may press upon him with great enthusiasm, but unless they truly "hear" what he is teaching in this way they will not be truly won for the Kingdom; they may find themselves aligned with the opposition.

---

6. Cf. Marcus, *Mark 1–8,* 292–93 for references to ancient literature suggesting that the yields involved would have been considered remarkable—as indeed they would be also in agricultural practice today.

7. Some interpreters find here a conscious echo of the beginning of the *Shema* credo ("Hear, O Israel . . .") all Israelites are required to recite daily (Deut 6:4-6).

The Reason for Speaking in Parables: 4:11-12

The scene now changes from the lakeside to a locale where Jesus is alone with his more immediate disciples: "those around him, together with the Twelve." He has already (3:34) indicated "those around him" as his new family. The rather vague phrase offers readers of the gospel an invitation to see themselves as members of this privileged group alongside the Twelve. When they ask Jesus "about the parables" he makes a distinction between them and "those outside" (v. 11). Whereas they (the disciples) are the privileged recipients of the "mystery of the Kingdom of God," for those outside "everything is in parables." This is not so that they may understand. On the contrary, as Jesus goes on to maintain in language taken from Isa 6:9-10, it is to encase them in their blindness and inability to hear, "lest they be converted and find forgiveness" (v. 12).

This is one of the most puzzling and theologically troubling statements in the New Testament. Jesus appears to state unequivocally a divine intention to lock permanently in a state of unresponsiveness, and therefore in exclusion from forgiveness and salvation, those who are described as "outside." What are we to say to it?

First, the distinction between the disciples and "those outside" is best taken in a moral rather than a strictly spatial sense. That is, it does not distinguish between the disciples and the crowd who have just heard Jesus teaching on the lakeshore, but between those who have become disciples through faith and conversion, on the one hand, and those who through failure in this regard have placed themselves or are at risk of placing themselves in a situation of permanent exclusion ("outside") from the Kingdom.[8] To the disciples is given "the mystery of the Kingdom" in the sense of a God-given capacity to grasp its true nature and the mode and time of its arrival, as communicated in the parables (the Sowing and the ones to follow) rightly understood.[9] For "those outside," however, "everything is in parables" in the more

---

8. Cf. Boring, *Mark,* 123.

9. The use of "mystery" here reflects a usage common to the New Testament and other Jewish literature of an apocalyptic nature (especially the literature of Qumran). "Mystery" refers to some unforeseen or strange aspect of the way things will work out at the endtime, according to the plan of God disclosed to privileged ones (seers and prophets) who have access to it through special revelation; cf. Paul's usage in 1 Cor 15:51; Rom 11:25-26. The classic discussion is that of Raymond E. Brown, *The Semitic Background of the Term "Mystery" in the New Testament.* FBBS 21 (Philadelphia: Fortress Press, 1968); cf. also Marcus, *Mark 1–8,* 298. See also Watts: ". . . the mystery of the kingdom (4:11) concerns not only the mystery which is the kingdom, but also the mysterious way in which the kingdom is expressed and revealed in Jesus' mighty deeds, in his powerful words, and ultimately, linked to his identity (*Isaiah's New Exodus,* 228).

negative sense of "parable," where it does not denote an instrument of communication but, on the contrary, a puzzle or riddle. They may "see" in an external sense, but they do not really "see" in the sense of understanding; they may "hear" the words spoken but not "understand" their meaning—as though they were listening to a foreign language they do not understand.

But why should this negative response be something willed and brought about by God?[10] We have to keep in mind the preceding sequence in which Jesus has been accused of driving out demons through the power of Beelzebul.[11] He rebutted the charge with two "parables" (the Divided Kingdom [3:23-26]; the Stronger Man [3: 27]) and went on to speak of those who uttered such blasphemies (against the Holy Spirit at work in Jesus) as guilty of an eternal sin (v. 29). In view are adversaries who appear to have permanently excluded themselves from the Kingdom and are in fact ranged on the side of its opposite. As I have explained above, the parables sequence as a whole is addressing the disturbing fact of this continued resistance to the Kingdom—a resistance not confined to the ministry of Jesus but continuing on into the life of those for whom Mark wrote the gospel. While at one level that resistance was the result of human choice, the gospel seeks to account for it further by having recourse to a biblical pattern of thought in which human resistance is also attributed to the intent and action of God. This pattern of "dual causality" (human and divine) famously appears in the Exodus tradition, where God hardens Pharaoh's heart to make him resist Israel's departure from Egypt (Exod 4:21; 7:3; 9:7, 12, 34; 14:4, 17; cf. Rom 9:17-18). It is also seen in the text setting out the mission of Isaiah (Isa 6:9-10), paraphrased in the present passage in Mark[12] and cited still more explicitly in the Matthean parallel (13:13-15; cf. also [more briefly] Luke

---

10. Despite numerous attempts to explain the language of v. 12 in a less theologically confronting way, it seems inescapable that the Greek conjunction *hina* standing at the beginning has its usual final sense (that is, expressing intent)—something confirmed by the conjunction *mēpote* ("lest") that introduces the concluding phrases in the statement. For a review of possibilities and critical discussion see Taylor, *St. Mark*, 256–57; John R. Donahue, *The Gospel in Parable: Metaphor, Narrative, and Theology in the Synoptic Gospels* (Philadelphia: Fortress Press, 1988) 40–42; Marcus, *Mark 1–8*, 299–300; Watts, *Isaiah's New Exodus*, 187–99 (stressing the influence of Isa 6:9-10 not only on the language but also on the content as formulated by Mark).

11. Cf. especially Watts, *Isaiah's New Exodus*, 185–86.

12. Mark's paraphrase basically follows the language of the LXX of Isa 6:9-10 but, in a way that agrees with the (Aramaic) Targum version as distinct from the LXX and the MT, has the verbs in the third person rather than the second, and speaks at the end of being "forgiven" rather than "healed." Mark differs from all versions by placing the "seeing" couplet before the "hearing" one. Cf. Watts, *Isaiah's New Exodus*, 186–87; Marcus, *Mark 1–8*, 300.

8:10).[13] Although the attribution of such resistance to divine action as well as to human choice creates difficulty for later theology, it represents a way in which biblical authors could place such troubling resistance within a wider framework. The allusion to the Isaiah text shows that resistance to the Kingdom has been foreseen and is in some sense held within God's overall plan of salvation.

While such a biblical understanding is at work here, we may also have in the closing phrases an undertone of ironic lament. "Those outside" may have sealed their fate, but *had* they "turned" (biblical language for conversion) they would have found forgiveness. This may serve as a warning to the "middle group," the multitude for whom it is not yet too late to access the Kingdom through conversion. God's original and abiding intent for human beings is not exclusion from life, but rather that through forgiveness and repentance they may gain access to the Kingdom.[14] Mark 4:12 remains a difficult text, but we should not miss the note of forgiveness on which it concludes and the role it plays as an ultimately *salvific* warning.[15]

The Parable of the Sowing Interpreted: 4:13-20

Jesus finally responds to the disciples' request for an explanation of the parables (v. 10). He prefaces his explanation with an exclamation such as a teacher might make in response to an ill-informed question from dull students: if they cannot understand this parable (that is, the Sowing), how are they to understand "all the parables" (v. 13b)![16] The exclamation suggests that there is something paradigmatic about the parable of the Sowing. Put more positively, it intimates that the allegorical interpretation Jesus now goes on to supply for this parable shows how the disciples are to understand all the parables of the Kingdom—that is, in the allegorical way now to be set forth.[17]

While a parable is an extended image in narrative form making a single point, an allegory, for the purpose of warning, exhortation, or explanation

---

13. The Isaiah text appears elsewhere in the New Testament (Acts 28:26-27; John 12:40; Rom 11:8) in contexts dealing with Israel's seemingly final "no" to the Gospel.

14. Cf. Hooker, *Saint Mark,* 129.

15. Cf. Robert A. Guelich, *Mark 1–8:26.* WBC 34A (Dallas: Word Books, 1989) 214.

16. Mark may see the exclamation justified in the sense that, having been given the mystery of the kingdom of God (v. 11), the disciples ought to have been able to understand the parable. The exclamation foreshadows the theme of the disciples' obtuseness or inability to understand that is to become so prominent in the narrative (4:41; 6:51-52; 8:14-21; 8:31-33; 9:32; 10:32).

17. Cf. Hooker, *Saint Mark,* 131.

relates a range of details in a story or extended image to various aspects of a particular situation. While it is not impossible that Jesus used allegory, where allegory appears in the gospel tradition it seems to reflect the situation of the later church rather than his own historical usage. The early believers, after Jesus' death, and in light of his resurrection and expected return, allegorized his parables in order to make sense of them for its own time and situation, to draw lessons from them and to trace in them a divinely guaranteed guide to the otherwise puzzling story of salvation.[18]

This appears to be the case with the allegory of the Sower, which seems to presuppose a period of time in which commitment to the Gospel has to be lived out amid persecutions and other temptations (the lure of wealth) that hardly reflect the brief moment in time of Jesus' own ministry.[19] The "word" has become a technical term for the message of the Gospel. Here it is identified with the seed sown by the sower. Strangely, the sower himself receives no allegorical identification, leaving open the possibility of finding in this key figure not only the original Sower, Christ, but also missionaries of the later believing communities who took up the spreading of the word in his name. The story, then, is as much about their time—and our time—as it is about Jesus.

In each of the four cases that follow, the word is "heard" but the response differs according to the quality of receptacle (the soil) on which it falls.[20] Of the three negative cases (vv. 15-19), in the first two the problem comes from without. On the hard surface of the path (v. 15) the seed has no chance to germinate at all. Like the birds in the parable, Satan simply snatches it away before it has a chance to sink in at any level. Such is the case when the preached word simply bounces off those who hear it; the Kingdom obtains no purchase in them; they remain captive to the demonic world. In the case of the seed in rocky ground (vv. 16-17), the Kingdom makes a welcome entry and for a time, while conditions are favorable, all is well. But when adherence to the word becomes costly—when persecutions or other trials arise (such as has indeed been the case for the Markan community), the commitment of

18. This process has left its mark particularly in the Gospel of Matthew. The remaining parables in Mark outside chapter 4—the Wicked Tenants (12:1-12); the Doorkeeper (13:33-37)—are both presented as allegories.

19. Boring, *Mark,* 129–30, lists ten considerations suggesting that the allegorical explanation reflects the life of the early church.

20. With respect to the remaining identifications, the logical flow is somewhat awkward since while at the start the seed is "the word," as the interpretation proceeds the seed becomes the recipients of the word, its fate determined by the location or quality of the ground on which it falls. It is best to understand the reiterated refrain, "These are those . . ." in the sense "This is the case with . . . ."

some falls away;[21] the Kingdom has not really taken "root" in them, strengthening their character through solid virtue.

For others (v. 18) the problem is more subtle and comes from within. The summons of the Kingdom has made a firm entry into their lives; the seed has become a "seedling" and grown for some time. But alongside it there have also sprung up other plants ("thistles") the farmer had not removed before sowing. These, growing up vigorously, stifle the continuing attention to the word that is required for the Kingdom to maintain its hold.[22] The allegory, with considerable spiritual subtlety, lists three such "thistles" (v. 19). First are "worldly cares," that is, concerns for matters of the present, passing age that the era of the Kingdom is replacing.[23] Such concerns may be justified in themselves, but they can grow to such an extent that they totally absorb a person's life and stifle the more fundamental orientation to the Kingdom. Second is "the deceit of wealth." Wealth is a "deceit" because it appears to hold out to anxious human beings a security and a promise of happiness that turns out to be illusory; the only truly lasting security is that provided by God.[24] Third and more generally, there enter in all manner of desires for "remaining things," that is, desirable things other than riches. Desires orient a person's life; desires for such things as power and status and luxury can stifle the fundamental desire for God, which the Kingdom fulfills. All these things render the word "unfruitful" (*akarpos* [v. 19]), that is, incapable of bringing about the kind of transformation of life that reflects the grace of the Kingdom.

Finally (v. 20), the seed sown[25] on good soil illustrates the case of those who not only hear the word but welcome it; they bring forth "fruit" (in the sense explained above) in the triple measure outlined in the original parable. The allegorical explanation has dwelt on the three negative cases rather than building to a positive climax as in the original parable. Nonetheless, it preserves the sense of the final, positive response, more than compensating for the three cases where the sowing is unfruitful.

21. Lit. "they are scandalized" *(skandalizontai)*. The Greek verb has the sense of tripping against some large obstacle so as to fall down completely; cf. Taylor, *St. Mark,* 260.

22. The sense is then that the word is something to be heard continually in Christian life.

23. Such concerns are given extended comment by Jesus in the "Q" tradition shared by Matthew (6:25-34) and Luke (12:22-31).

24. This is a very prominent theme in Luke's gospel. Cf. Byrne, *Hospitality of God,* 114–15.

25. The Greek aorist passive *sparentes* (contrast the present passives in the three negative cases) communicates the sense of a process of growth that has been under way for some time.

What are we to make of the allegory of the Sowing taken as a whole? Interpretations go along two main lines. Adhering more closely to the direction of the original parable, one interpretation sees it as offering comfort and reassurance to a community—the Markan community—that has experienced lack of response to its mission, that has had its numbers reduced by persecution and the apostasy of some of its members, or, in more settled times, has seen some fall away from the high demands of the Gospel because of the lure of riches or absorption in other affairs.[26] To such a community the message of the interpreted parable is "Be of good heart! The faithful remnant in which the word continues to be heard and lived out at depth remains a firm beachhead of the Kingdom that will prevail." Alternatively, the allegory, especially the analysis of the causes of the three losses, can be seen as a warning to the community to be aware of the traps and snares that may lead its members away from the path of true discipleship and place them with "those outside" (v. 11b).[27] While this second interpretation has been by far the more common one in Christian history, it is important not to let the former slide from view—especially at a time when institutional Christianity, particularly in Western societies, is suffering such diminution and reduction to a faithful remnant. In the end it is not necessary to choose between the two: the allegory can function with equal validity on several levels: as comfort and warning as well as diagnosis of the traps and snares preventing people from allowing the Kingdom to enter in and transform their lives.

The Lamp, the Measure, and Related Sayings: 4:21-25

Following the interpretation of the Sowing comes a series of images and sayings[28] that Mark seems to have gathered together[29] to reinforce for

26. So especially Marcus, *Mark 1–8,* 312–13; C. H. Dodd, *The Parables of the Kingdom* (rev. ed. London: Fontana, 1961) 135; Nineham, *Saint Mark,* 140.

27. Cf. Gnilka, *Markus* 1:176; Moloney, *Gospel of Mark,* 92–93; Jeremias, *Parables,* 79; Hooker, *Saint Mark,* 132.

28. Marcus describes all four as "parables" (*Mark 1–8,* 314–15). The first statement, the saying about the lamp (v. 21) could be so described if "parable" is understood in the broad sense so that it can refer simply to an image without that being developed into a "story," as in the three "seed" parables in this chapter. The remainder are more in the nature of axioms or wisdom sayings; cf. Gnilka, *Markus* 1:178.

29. The four sayings (v. 21, v. 22, v. 24b, v. 25) are found distributed in different contexts (and meanings) in Matthew and Luke, though Luke has three in the parallel to Mark 4 in Luke 8:16-18 and Mark 4:25 has its parallel in Matt 13:12. For a tabular conspectus see Marcus, *Mark 1–8,* 316–17.

the disciples the message of the Sowing parable and its interpretation.[30] The questions about the lamp (v. 21) appeal to commonsense practice in everyday Palestinian village life on a kind of a fortiori basis: if none of us would light a lamp and then be so stupid as to cover it up by putting it under a bushel measure[31] or under a bed, how foolish to suppose that God would light the "lamp" of the Kingdom in the world only to keep it covered up forever.[32] It may presently be hidden (v. 22) but that is only so that it may all the more powerfully one day be revealed and come into the light of day. Once again the couplet gives reassurance to the disciples in the face of discouragement about the Kingdom.

Following a summons to watchful hearing (vv. 23-24a; cf. v. 3; v. 10), the second couplet (vv. 24b-25) shifts the focus from the Kingdom in itself to the aspect of response or receptivity on the human side. In the human marketplace measures of goods are exchanged in exact proportion to each other (v. 24c). But where God's gift of the Kingdom finds true receptivity (repentance and faith) on the human side, not only is that capacity filled, but more and more will be added as the journey of faith continues (v. 24d). At the same time (v. 25; cf. vv. 11-12), those who have within them no capacity for the Kingdom will not only not receive it but will be deprived of whatever privilege they may have imagined themselves to have. In view here are probably the "outsiders" represented by the religious leaders who have become deadly adversaries of Jesus and the Kingdom.[33]

While the main thrust of the sequence is to give assurance to the disciples (vv. 21-22) in view of the varying responses to the Kingdom (vv. 24c-25), there is also a parallel current of warning (vv. 23-24a).[34] On the journey of faith the disciples must "take heed" of what they listen to (v. 24a); the word of God is not the only word abroad in the world; deceitful Satanic

---

30. The sayings come in an arrangement of two quasi-parallel couplets (v. 21 and v. 22; v. 24b and v. 25), separated by a repeated warning to "hear" (cf. v. 3; v. 10).

31. The bushel measure refers to a metal utensil used for measuring corn. Jeremias (*Parables,* 120) suggests that placing such a vessel over a lamp might well have offered a safe means of extinguishing it, while simply blowing out the flame could have created sparks or filled the house with smoke.

32. The wording of the Greek at the beginning of the image—literally, "Does a lamp come . . ."—could suggest a reference to Christ as "light"; cf. Gnilka, *Markus* 1:180; Boring, *Mark,* 135.

33. The Markan community would probably relate this to the "no" to the Gospel on the part of the bulk of Israel; cf. the discussion of v. 12 above.

34. For Moloney (*Gospel of Mark,* 93–94) this is the main emphasis of the sequence.

words also clamor to be heard (cf. the warnings in 13:5-6, 22-23).[35] There is a constant need for discernment.

The Seed Growing Secretly: 4:26-29

The two remaining "seed" parables relate explicitly to the kingdom of God (v. 26; v. 30).[36] The first, the Seed Growing Secretly, appears only in Mark. It envisages the growth of a harvest in three stages: (1) first, a man casts seed upon the earth (v. 26b); (2) then follows a long interval when the seed sprouts and grows within the earth while the man carries on with other aspects of his life (vv. 27-28); (3) only when the ripened grain appears does the man exert himself again to reap the harvest (v. 29). The point of the parable seems to lie in the contrast between the inactivity of the man in the middle stage and his vigorous resumption of work at the time of harvest.[37] Once the seed is sown, the man simply lets it be, going about his life, confident that the soil will work a growth process he does not understand without any intervention on his part.[38] But[39] when he sees the grain is ripe, he knows it is time to put in the sickle.[40]

Understood in this way, the "story" told in the parable illustrates the present and future situation in regard to the Kingdom. The "seed" of the Kingdom has been "sown"—presumably in the preaching of Jesus. Then follows a long period—the present time—when nothing seems to be happening, at least nothing visible or dramatic, but all the while growth is taking place and a time for the harvest will arrive. In this way the parable confronts those with more dramatic and conventional expectations of the Kingdom. It urges Jesus' hearers to think of God in terms of the person who sowed the seed and then sat back, allowing the growth process to run its

35. Cf. Marcus, *Mark 1–8,* 319.

36. The concluding notice in v. 33 would seem to suggest that the crowds are once again the audience for these two parables. However, v. 34b may imply that Jesus supplied for the disciples the kind of allegorical explanation that unlocked for them the "mystery" of the Sowing parable.

37. Cf. Jeremias, *Parables,* 151.

38. The growth process is explained in v. 28: "The soil brings forth fruitfulness by itself (literally, 'automatically' [Greek *automatē*])."

39. A note of strong contrast is signaled by the Greek *hotan de* introducing this final stage; cf. Taylor, *St. Mark,* 268.

40. "Harvest" is a stock image for the final judgment in Jewish apocalyptic literature. Here it is spoken of in terms derived from Joel 3:13. The "sending out" *(apostellein)* of the sickle will have an echo in the later description (13:27) of the coming of the Son of Man to finally institute the Kingdom, when he will "send out" his angels to the four corners of the earth to gather the elect.

course. As in the parable of the Sowing and its interpretation, the present time is when the Kingdom is taking hold and finding growth in the "soil" of receptive human hearts. God allows that to happen, delaying the "harvest" until the "fruit" is ripe.

This parable has been the despair of interpreters from the beginning.[41] I make no claims to have offered here a definitive interpretation. But it seems to me that, understood along these lines, the parable continues the instruction about the true nature of the Kingdom that has been running through the whole sequence. Disciples, both then and now, should understand that the absence of visible and dramatic signs does not mean that the Kingdom is not already at work; it is present and active, producing the "fruit" that will be "harvested" in God's good time.

The Mustard Seed: 4:30-32

This small parable addresses the same issue: the present insignificance of the Kingdom. Where the previous parable dwelt on the hidden nature of the Kingdom's growth, the point now lies in the contrast between tiny beginnings and the vast scale of the final outcome. The mustard seed is not in fact the smallest of seeds[42]—though proverbially it was considered to be so. Nor is the mustard bush the greatest of trees: in Palestine it is a shrub that grows to a height of two to three meters. Jesus takes an example with which his hearers would be familiar: mustard bushes grew vigorously and could take over vegetable gardens.[43] His audience would also know that birds could shelter in the shade of their large branches.[44] This final detail contains more than a hint that the Kingdom as finally constituted will embrace the vagabonds of society and, most especially for Mark, members of the nations of the world.[45] So again this parable, by indicating the true nature of the Kingdom as proclaimed by Jesus, gives assurance and hope to

---

41. Mark's earliest literary interpreters, Matthew and Luke, omit the parable, though Matthew's parable of the Weeds (13:24-30) may represent an early attempt to make sense of it.

42. That distinction belongs to the orchid; cf. Marcus, *Mark 1–8,* 324.

43. Matthew and Luke, in their versions (Matt 13:31-32; Luke 13:18-19), render the image less real by speaking of the seed becoming a "tree" *(dendron)* rather than a bush.

44. Again Matthew and Luke exaggerate the picture by having the birds build nests in the branches, something a mustard bush would hardly support.

45. The description of the birds finding shelter echoes LXX Dan 4:12, 21; Ezek 31:6, texts where birds finding shelter symbolize the nations of the world sheltering under the sway of great empires.

those who may be presently dismayed by what appear to be its unimpressive beginnings.

Conclusion: Jesus' Use of Parables: 4:33-34

The entire sequence concludes with a summary indicating that the three parables featured here illustrate a wider practice on Jesus' part: always to speak to the crowds in parables. The added note that he did so "inasmuch as they were able to hear" (v. 33b) and the further information that he explained all to his disciples privately returns to the distinction between "outsiders" and "insiders" elaborated in vv. 11-13. The crowds would go beyond finding the parables mere "riddles" if they were able to "listen" with converted hearts. The implication, in line with that earlier reflection, is that this is what they were not able to do. Hence the sequence ends with a sense of the crowd left for the time being in darkness, while the disciples, Jesus' new family, retain their privileged access to the "mystery of the Kingdom of God" (v. 11). The following scenes, however, will show just how far even they have to travel on the journey to full understanding.[46]

---

46. Cf. Gnilka, *Markus* 1:191; Marcus, *Mark 1–8,* 331.

Jesus Displays
the Power of the Kingdom: 4:35–6:6a

Jesus' teaching in parables (4:1-34) has disclosed to those with understanding the effective presence of the Kingdom, however limited the external evidence might seem to be. Now the Teacher confirms his words with a series of acts in which the power of the Kingdom confronts destructive demonic rule in a variety of manifestations: in nature (4:35-41), in demonic possession (5:1-20), in life-destroying illness (5:25-34), and in death itself (5:21-24, 35-43). Each scene drives further the issue of Jesus' identity (Story 1) and, correspondingly on the human side, the importance of faith.

The Storm on the Lake: 4:35-41

In the first scene, as Mark tells it, there is a striking oscillation between the human and the divine. In the evening of the same day (v. 35) on which he had taught the crowds in parables, Jesus makes the suggestion that they should cross the lake "to the other side," that is, to the Gentile region on the eastern shore. Whether it was advisable to make the crossing as evening was falling we do not know. The disciples, at any rate, do not demur but take him "just as he was, in the boat."[1] While it was he who suggested the crossing, they are now very much in control. Most of them are, after all, fishermen; the sea is where they are competent. A detail peculiar to Mark is the information that "other boats were with him" (v. 36d). We learn nothing more about these extra crafts. But "to be with him [Jesus]" is a technical phrase for discipleship in Mark's gospel (cf. also 3:14; 5:18). As in 4:10, the text

1. The phrase "just as he was in the boat" suggests that Jesus has not left the boat from which he had been speaking to the crowds. The detail underlines the continuity between Jesus' teaching and the powerful acts to follow.

92

is signaling the presence of an extended group of disciples beyond the Twelve. Readers of the gospel can enter the narrative by placing themselves in these "other boats."

A "great storm of wind"[2] disturbs the progress of this little flotilla, stirring up waves that threaten to swamp it (v. 37). Water out of control is a standard image of chaos in biblical literature (e.g., Ps 42:7); the original act of creation represented divine victory over watery chaos (Gen 1:6-9; Ps 104:5-9)—a victory that the swelling waters of the great flood (Genesis 6–7) threatened to reverse. Meanwhile, in sublime indifference to the present danger, Jesus lies asleep in the stern of the boat, having commandeered the helmsman's cushion as a headrest.[3] At one level his sleeping adds a human touch to the story;[4] at another it displays confidence that the forces of chaos, soon to be revealed as demonic, will not overwhelm the Agent of the Kingdom and his new family.[5]

This confidence is not something the disciples share. Desperate, they wake him up (v. 38b), rudely asking if he cares at all that they are about to sink. In Mark's account they are not necessarily asking for a miracle, but simply that he help in some way. Though not a sailor, he could at least bail out water or the like![6]

Swiftly, the One who moments before had been so humanly asleep like a child rises and majestically "rebukes" the wind and "silences" the sea (v. 39), bringing about "a great calm" *(galēnē megalē)*. The language of rebuke and silencing recalls the exorcism in the synagogue at Capernaum (1:25; cf. 3:12; 9:25), suggesting that behind the destructive natural forces unleashed on the lake lies the malevolence of the demonic world. In what is in effect an exorcism, the Agent of God's Rule beats back a deadly attack on himself

---

2. The Lake of Galilee remains vulnerable to such sudden wind squalls to this day; cf. Moloney, *Gospel of Mark*, 98, n. 140.

3. The discovery in 1986 of a surprisingly well-preserved boat, dating from around the time of Jesus, in the mud on the shores of the Sea of Galilee suggests that the stern had a raised platform on which the helmsman stood. Meier, *Marginal Jew* 2:1005, pictures Jesus sleeping underneath this platform. The "cushion" may refer to a leather cushion or bag used to protect the helmsman's thigh against the wall of the boat.

4. This sleep of the main character while others on a voyage battle with a storm is just one detail in which the account in Mark 4:35-41 is reminiscent in both language and motifs of the voyage of the prophet Jonah (Jon 1:1-17; cf. v. 7). See further Marcus, *Mark 1–8*, 337–38, who sets out both the similarities and the differences.

5. Even the sleep of Jesus before he is aroused by the disciples could be seen as revelatory of his divinity in view of a biblical tradition in which God is called upon to awaken from sleep and bring rescue: Pss 35:23; 44:23; 59:4; cf. Marcus, *Mark 1–8*, 338.

6. This is shown in Mark's account by the address, "Teacher." Contrast Matt 8:25, "Lord, save us; we are perishing!"—almost a liturgical invocation.

and on the nucleus of the community he is forming as a beachhead of the Kingdom. In this fresh contest with the Strong One (Satan) Jesus has once again proved "Stronger" (cf. 1:7; 3:27).[7]

The storm subdued, Jesus turns to the disciples, questioning them about their fear and lack of faith (v. 40). The second question ("Have you still no faith?") underpins the first ("Why are you afraid?"). Had they at this stage sufficient faith to have some inkling of who he was, they would not have given in to such fear.[8] Did they not understand that with him present, even if asleep, there was no chance that the forces of chaos and destruction could overwhelm them?

The faith of the disciples, then, still has a long way to go before being adequate to the mystery of Jesus. But at the end (v. 41) they at least ask the right question: "Who is this, whom even the winds and the sea obey?" The biblical tradition teaches them that such command of the forces of chaos belongs to the Creator alone (cf. Pss 65:7; 89:9; 106:9; 107:23-30; Job 26:11-12; 38:8-11; Isa 51:10); they know that they have witnessed an exercise of divine power. Hence they are "filled with great awe"—the human response to the presence of the divine (cf. 16:8).[9] In the compass of this one short scene the Markan narrative has swiftly moved from a view of Jesus as very human to one in which he displays divine power in a most dramatic way.

In this way the scene intensifies on the lips of the disciples the key question at this stage of the gospel: "Who is this . . . ?" (Story 1). It has further symbolic resonance in that, as in all four gospels, the boat is a symbol of the church, while the sea—especially the sea out of control—represents the world dominated by forces that are hostile to the church and seek to destroy it. Yet to fulfill its mission and win people ("fish") for the Kingdom, the church must go out upon the sea that is the world. There are times in the history of the church when its Lord seems to be absent or asleep, times when faith in the divine presence and power is put to the test, times even when the forces of death do prevail and lead to martyrdom in the cause of faith and justice. The Lord who rescued the disciples from death at sea will not always preserve the faithful from death—just as the Father did not preserve the Son from death, but raised him from the dead when his "obedience unto

---

7. Cf. Marcus, *Mark 1–8,* 336.

8. The Greek word here, *deilos,* expresses a cowardly, timid fear.

9. Literally, "they feared a great fear" *(ephobēthēsan phobēn megan).* This reverential fear is of quite a distinct order from the cowardly fear of which Jesus accused them in v. 40. The adjective "great" runs like a connecting thread throughout the narrative: "great storm of wind" (v. 37); "great calm" (v. 39); "great awe" (v. 41).

death" had run its course (Phil 2:8-9). The story calls those who place themselves "in the boat" with Jesus to faith in the God who saves through and beyond death but not necessarily from it.[10]

Liberation of a Deeply Troubled Person in the Land of the Gerasenes: 5:1-20

The story of Jesus' rescue of a man possessed by a "legion" of demons in the land of the Gerasenes is the longest single episode in Mark's gospel. Despite some unevenness in the telling,[11] it is also the most compelling in terms of literary power. The most sustained and dramatic exorcism in the gospel, it offers a paradigm of Jesus' whole mission to reclaim human lives for the freedom of the Kingdom. Significantly, it takes place after Jesus and his disciples have crossed the sea to land, for the first time, in non-Jewish or Gentile territory.[12] He has confronted the demonic in a Jewish context (the synagogue: 1:21-28) and withstood its onslaught in the forces of nature (1:35-41). Now he is to confront its "possession" of the wider Gentile world that is the principal context of those for whom Mark's gospel was written.

The long account breaks down into four distinct sections:

1. Jesus' encounter with the possessed man: vv. 1-10
2. The episode with the herd of pigs: vv. 11-13
3. The reaction of the people from the nearby town: vv. 14-17
4. The mission of the formerly possessed man: vv. 18-20.

As Jesus disembarks from the boat from which he has calmed the storm he is immediately confronted with a man "from the tombs (possessed by) an unclean spirit" (v. 2). Mark's description of the man is graphic and prolonged:

> [3]He lived among the tombs; and no one could restrain him any more, even with a chain; [4]for he had often been restrained with shackles and chains, but the chains he wrenched apart, and the shackles he broke in pieces; and no one

---

10. Cf. Boring, *Mark,* 146.

11. The unevenness is evident in the repeated description of the man's approach to Jesus in vv. 2b and 6. Jesus' demand to know the demon's name (v. 9) seems to come rather "late" in the interaction, since he has already been commanding it to depart (v. 8). The keepers of the pigs make two reports about what had happened to the herd: vv. 14 and 16. Mark is presumably reliant on separate sources from which he has not put together a completely coherent account; see further, Boring, *Mark,* 149–50.

12. This is clear both from the geographical reference (the eastern shore of the lake was not a place of Jewish settlement) and from the raising of animals (pigs) unclean for Jews.

had the strength to subdue him. ⁵Night and day among the tombs and on the mountains he was always howling and bruising himself with stones.

The man presents the very image of self-destructiveness and social isolation: one who lives in the realm of death among the tombs (as we are told no less than three times [vv. 2, 3, 5]) and whom no one has the strength to "bind." The repeated emphasis on the human impossibility of "binding" the man immediately recalls Jesus' image of Satan as "a strong man" whose "house" can only be burgled if a "stronger one" succeeds in binding him first (3:27). In the personal encounter between Jesus and this possessed man we are to see the paradigm of Jesus, the Stronger One (cf. the Baptist's description: 1:7), binding with divine power the One against whom all human efforts are of no avail.

Like a watchdog guarding its patch, the demon makes the possessed man run out toward Jesus with a loud cry (vv. 2, 6a). The prostration, the protest ("What have we got to do with each other?"),[13] the address to Jesus as "Son of the Most High God" (vv. 6b-7):[14] all represent an acknowledgment of superior power. In the presence of this Stronger One the demon already feels subject to the punishment (lit. "torment") God was expected to inflict on the demonic world at the final judgment (v. 7a).[15]

The contest moves to a wider plane when Jesus compels the demon to yield knowledge of its name: ". . . Legion, for we are many" (v. 9). The admission explains the extremity of the man's condition: he is possessed by a large number of demons. Beyond this, it hints that the demonic world has occupied him and the surrounding milieu much as the military forces of Rome occupied and controlled the greater part of the known world.[16]

13. The protest, which echoes exactly that of the demon in the earlier confrontation at Capernaum (1:24), means: "We belong to totally separate realms. What are you doing invading ours?!"

14. This address to the divinity is found in both Jewish and pagan sources; cf. Gnilka, *Markus* 1:204; Marcus, *Mark 1–8,* 344. It is appropriately placed here on the lips of one living in a non-Jewish region.

15. The Matthean parallel (8:29a) makes this eschatological reference more explicit: "Have you come to torment us before the time?" (cf. also Rev 20:10).

16. Whether the appearance of the Latin military term "legion" in the name wrung from the demon implies an identification of the Roman military occupation with the demonic (so especially Myers, *Binding the Strong Man,* 191–94; also Marcus, *Mark 1–8,* 351–52) is much discussed. Some (e.g., Donahue and Harrington, *Mark,* 134; Moloney, *Gospel of Mark,* 104, n. 170) are skeptical of sociopolitical interpretations on the grounds that Jesus is not here expelling demons from Jewish lands since he is in a Gentile area, possibly quite sympathetic to Roman rule. The sociopolitical reference, however, can be understood more generally, not with reference solely to Palestine but to the Gentile world considered subject as a whole to the power of Rome.

The information that Jesus is confronting a plurality of demons gives way to what is perhaps the most bizarre aspect of the entire episode: the demons' request that, instead of being expelled from the region, they might enter into a large herd of pigs that happens to be grazing nearby, and the resultant headlong stampede and drowning of the pigs when Jesus allows them to do so (vv. 11-13). Readers of the gospel have long found this the most troubling feature of the entire incident. How could Jesus be so indifferent to the destruction of so many animals—not to mention the loss of stock and livelihood for those who owned and pastured them? The concerns are reasonable, but they import into the text considerations stemming from a literal understanding going well beyond the limits of its concentrated symbolic focus.[17] The desire to enter into animals regarded by Jews as unclean and the subsequent drowning in the sea reinforces the sense of the uncleanness of the demons and the destructiveness they communicate to those they possess, something already patent in the behavior of the demoniac himself (v. 5). The episode further displays Jesus' power, in that he outwits the demons. They had attempted by bargaining with him to gain the least worse deal: not expulsion from the land (cf. v. 10) but occupation of animals at least, if not human beings. But the stratagem ends with their return via the sea to the underworld, their habitual abode, and the cleansing of the land from their presence.

The report of the swineherds introduces the next stage of the drama: the reaction and response of the people of the region on learning what had happened (vv. 14-17). Skillfully, the author lingers on the impression made by what the people see when they come to Jesus: "the (previously) possessed man sitting there, clothed and in his right mind, the man who had had the legion," and, we are told, "they were afraid" (v. 17). What they see is a human being totally transformed: the one whom they had previously known as a raging and self-ravaging outcast now sits there in peace, the very image of humanity regained. The transformation repeats on a human level the "great calm" Jesus brought about in the previous scene when he "rebuked" the rage of the sea (4:39).

The reaction of the locals is also in the first instance similar to that of the disciples in the boat: "they were afraid" (v. 17d).[18] Their fear stems from realization that what they were seeing could only have been brought about by an exercise of more than human power. But their further response is curious. Instead of asking who this might be who has come among them with such liberating effects, they urge Jesus to leave their region. They were more

17. See further Boring, *Mark,* 152–53.
18. Greek *ephobēthēsan,* as in 4:17.

comfortable, it seems, with having a demon-possessed maniac on the out-skirts of their town than with the presence among them of one who could exercise divine power in such liberating ways.[19]

The episode closes, as it had begun,[20] with an interaction between the (formerly) possessed man and Jesus (vv. 18-20). The man wants "to be with Jesus," the technical expression in Mark's gospel for close discipleship (cf. 3:14). Jesus does not allow this, but sends him off in another direction: he is to return "to his house, to (his) own people" and tell them what the Lord has done for him and the mercy he has received (v. 19). In other words, the previously outcast person is to seek reintegration into his house and family by explaining how his transformation has come about. In fact, however, the man goes well beyond Jesus' instruction (v. 20): he goes and begins to pro-claim in the Decapolis (that is, throughout the largely Greek cities east and southeast of the Sea of Gennesareth) what *Jesus* had done for him.[21] This preaching on his part prefigures the mission to the Gentiles that subsequent believers will undertake when "the Gospel of God" (1:15) has become "the Gospel (about) Jesus Christ" (1:1).[22] The liberation from captivity to the demonic experienced by this man foreshadows what it means for members of the pagan world addressed by the Gospel to be claimed and transformed by the power of the Kingdom. The reaction to the man's proclamation was "that all wondered"—by no means an expression denoting conversion.[23] But a door has been opened for the mission to that wider world. The Gentile centurion who reacts to Jesus' death (15:39) will be its first convert.[24]

Like the former demoniac, the original readers of the gospel—and all subsequent believers down to ourselves—may wish that they could have

19. One could argue that it was the destruction of their pigs that made them want to be rid of Jesus. But in that case their reaction would more likely have been described as anger rather than fear; cf. Donahue and Harrington, *Mark,* 167.

20. The genitive absolute construction, "as he was getting into the boat" (v. 18a), picks up inclusively the same construction, "as he was getting out of the boat," in v. 2a.

21. It is possible to see in vv. 19-20 a further infraction of the "messianic secret" command (cf. 1:45): Jesus restricts the man to explaining his transformation to his own household; the man disobeys by spreading the news far more widely; so Gnilka, *Markus* 1:206–07. But the Markan text does not seem to place the command and the response at odds: "The man interprets Jesus' command expansively but not wrongly" (Marcus, *Mark 1–8,* 346).

22. The change from "what the Lord (= God) has done" in v. 19 to the parallel "what Jesus had done for him" in v. 20 is a further indication of Mark's high christology (cf. 1:2-3); cf. Marcus, *Mark 1–8,* 354.

23. Apart from this occurrence, the word *(thaumazein)* denotes Jesus' amazement at his townsfolk's lack of faith (6:6) and twice describes the reaction of Pilate during the Passion (15:5, 44).

24. Cf. Moloney, *Gospel of Mark,* 106.

been disciples of Jesus in the sense that the Twelve and other close disciples were during his historical life. The passage of time has denied them (and us) this privilege. But the man Jesus liberated in this Gentile region can be our point of insertion into the narrative. Like him, we can hear Jesus missioning us to spread the good news of liberation in our own time and place.[25] We may even find aspects of our own life and character reflected—albeit not perhaps in such extreme measure—in the description of the man's condition before Jesus set him free: ways in which we find ourselves living in isolation "among the tombs," bound in self-destructive patterns of behavior from which we cannot escape. We can be grateful, I think, that Mark has chosen to narrate this episode in such detail and with so much dramatic force. Perhaps more than any other in the gospel, it takes us into a disturbing mythic world. But precisely as such it goes to the heart of the liberation God is offering human beings through the power of Jesus.

Two Persons of Faith:
Jairus and the Woman Healed of a Hemorrhage: 5:21-43

The interwoven story of the healing of the woman with a hemorrhage and the raising of Jairus' daughter is perhaps Mark's masterpiece in terms of narrative art. Rich in detail and human touches, it also offers the most notable example of the evangelist's "sandwiching" technique: enclosing one episode within a wider framework in a way that enhances the dramatic effect and allows each element to shed light on the other. Both the main characters in this interwoven story emerge as persons of faith, but they illustrate different aspects of faith, enabling the story as a whole to provide a rounded instruction on this key disposition. In the first episode in the miracle cycle, when Jesus calmed the stormy sea (4:35-41), he chided the disciples for having "no faith" (v. 40). The cycle will conclude with a visit to his home town, Nazareth, where he is "astounded at their lack of faith" (6:6a). Against this negative background, Jairus and the woman who touches Jesus' clothing stand out as complementary examples of the kind of faith required if human lives are to be grasped by the transforming power of the Kingdom.

Jairus (1): vv. 21-24

As Jesus returns across the lake from Gentile territory, a large crowd is once again waiting for him on the lakeshore (v. 21). He is all set, presumably, to teach them there (cf. 4:1-2) when a leading synagogue official,

25. Cf. Trainor, *Quest for Home,* 118.

Jairus,[26] approaches him in great anxiety: his little daughter is at the point of death. Falling at Jesus' feet, he implores him to come and lay his hands on her "so that she may be made well and live" (v. 23). It is unusual for a representative of the religious establishment to approach Jesus in this way, but Jairus' desperation as a parent[27] leads him to cast aside his dignity and have recourse to this prophetic figure whose capacity to heal has become well known. Immediately acceding to the plea, Jesus sets out for Jairus' house, accompanied and hemmed in by a large crowd (v. 24; cf. v. 21b).

The Woman with a Hemorrhage: vv. 25-34

The press of the crowd provides the context for the interruption that now occurs. While Jairus waits in ever-growing fear that his daughter's life is ebbing away (a fear we readers share), Jesus pauses to deal with another desperate person. Mark lingers on the description of the unnamed woman and the condition that has led her to approach Jesus: her twelve-year suffering from a hemorrhage and her lack of relief from human medical resources, which have only made her worse and reduced her to penury besides. Her condition has rendered her a chronic menstruant and hence, under the prescriptions of the Law (Lev 12:1-7; 15:19-25), not only permanently unclean but liable to communicate uncleanness to anyone she touches. It is not easy for us to understand the concept of ritual uncleanness and the socioreligious exclusion from society it entailed. We should remember, however, that the gospel constantly applies the epithet "unclean" *(akathartos)* to the demonic spirits (1:23, 26, 27; 3:11, 30; 5:2, 8, 13; 6:7; 7:25; 9:25) who are the principal foes of Jesus' messianic mission. Her condition has placed this unfortunate woman within the grip of the demonic world, from which no human power (medical resources) has been able to free her. Metaphorically at least she, like the Gerasene demoniac, has had "to live in the tombs" (vv. 3, 5).

She has, however, heard about Jesus (v. 27), and the press of the crowd gives her the opportunity, as she supposes, to break through the purity barrier undetected and so to access his power. As Jesus subsequently points out (v. 34), this is a genuine exercise of faith that brings about a release of divine

26. The term *archisynagōgos* indicates some kind of leading office in the synagogue governance structure—a presiding official at worship or a functionary in the nature of a business manager. It is unusual for Mark to give the names of characters in miracle stories (elsewhere only Bartimaeus, the blind beggar, in 10:46-51). Meier, *Marginal Jew* 2:787, suggests this may be evidence that behind the narrative lies a genuine historical reminiscence.

27. The use of the Greek diminutive form *thygatrion* expresses affection. Jairus is the first of three parents in Mark's gospel who seek help for afflicted children: cf. 7:26-27; 9:17-24; cf. Marcus, *Mark 1–8,* 365.

power. The rude protest of the disciples (v. 31; cf. 4:38b) when Jesus, aware of the power that has gone out from him, asks who touched him, brings out the difference between the jostling he receives from the crowd and the touching in faith that channels healing.

We might think that it would have been more considerate of Jesus simply to have let the woman, now free of so embarrassing an affliction, slip away unnoticed. But such an anonymous and "mechanical" dispensing of healing, without personal interaction, is not his way. The woman's coming forward "in fear and trembling," her falling at his feet and acknowledging "the whole truth" (v. 33) amounts to a christological confession: an acknowledgment of the divine power present in him that has rescued her from the clutch of the demonic.[28] His response (v. 34) expresses both personal reassurance and social rehabilitation. By addressing her as "Daughter" he proclaims her reinclusion within the community and perhaps also within the "new family" of the Kingdom. His explanation, "Your faith has saved you; go in peace," makes her a model of faith's power to rescue ("save") people from the demonic and reclaim them for the fullness of life ("peace") associated with the messianic age. Saved from her twelve-year affliction, both personally and socially she has regained her life.

Jairus (2): vv. 35-43

As Jesus is speaking these words of assurance, messengers come from Jairus' house with what must be the most brutal of all announcements in the gospels: "Your daughter is dead. Why trouble the teacher any longer?" (v. 35). While Jesus has been attending to the woman, we have shared the anguish of Jairus as he waits for Jesus to resume his journey. Now his worst fears are confirmed. Harsh though they be, the words of the messengers, like those of the disciples earlier (v. 31), express plain common sense. The "teacher" might have been able to do something for his daughter while she still had some hold upon life. But now she is dead, what more is there to hope for?

Jesus, however, has "overheard"[29] the blunt message. In the face of it he invites Jairus to go further with him on the journey of faith: "Do not fear; just keep on believing" (v. 36). The use of the present imperative in the Greek

---

28. The phrase "fear and trembling" represents not so much human timidity but the characteristic biblical response of awe in the presence of the divine; cf. Phil 2:12; Gnilka, *Markus* 1:216; Marcus, *Mark 1–8,* 359-60.

29. The Greek participle *parakousas* could also have the sense "ignore," but the context— Jesus' consoling words—makes "overhear" more likely; cf. Hooker, *Saint Mark,* 149.

brings out the sense of a faith that has to persevere and indeed take on a whole new dimension: beyond grave illness it must now confront the fact of death itself.[30]

Jesus resumes his journey to the house of Jairus, taking with him only Peter, James, and John, the "inner circle" of his new family (v. 37) who will also be with him on two other significant occasions: his transfiguration (9:2-9) and the hour when he confronts the prospect of his own death in the garden of Gethsemane (14:32-42). Arrived at the house (v. 38), he finds there another crowd gathered and loudly engaged in the rituals of death, weeping and wailing. Death, it would appear, already has possession of the scene. But that is a conclusion Jesus defiantly challenges: "The child is not dead, but asleep!" (v. 39c).[31] The statement is ambiguous—doubtless deliberately so. In the context of the divine power about to be displayed, death is indeed a "sleep" from which people can be awakened.[32] But for those already engaged in the rituals of death this is pure nonsense. They simply laugh at him (v. 40a).

Jesus "expels" from the house this ring of unbelief (v. 40b)—much as he was wont to "expel" demons.[33] He then creates a domestic context of faith, taking with him into the inner part of the house the child's father and mother and the three select disciples (v. 40cd). There, taking the child by the hand, he addresses her in words Mark has preserved in the original Aramaic and then translated: "Little girl, I say to you, Arise!" (v. 41). The conquest of death is complete when the girl instantly gets up and begins to walk about (v. 42a).

In a seemingly casual afterthought to this stupendous event, Mark adds the information, "She was about twelve years of age" (v. 42b). The information is not casual. The number of years (twelve) inevitably associates the girl with the woman whose twelve-year-long flow of blood Jesus had cured en route to her family's house. That cure has enabled the woman, after her twelve-year captivity to "uncleanness," to resume full life in both the private and societal sphere. The girl had died just as she was on the cusp of marriageable age.[34] By freeing her from the realm of death, Jesus has given

---

30. This aspect of going beyond grave illness to confront the fact of death, caused by a delay on the part of Jesus, is one feature this episode has in common with the long narrative of the raising of Lazarus in John 11; cf. Byrne, *Lazarus,* 41, 49, 56, 84–89.

31. Cf., again, Jesus' initial words about Lazarus: John 11:11-14.

32. Cf. other references to death as "sleep" in early Christian parlance: 1 Thess 4:13; 1 Cor 15:20, 51; etc. "Death is called 'sleep,' not to pretend it is not real, but to deny that it is ultimate" (Boring, *Mark,* 162).

33. The Greek verb appearing here, *ekballein,* regularly occurs in cases of exorcism (1:34, 39; 3:15, 22, 23; 6:13; 7:26; 9:18, 28, 38; [16:9, 17]).

34. Cf. Moloney, *Gospel of Mark,* 110 and the further references given there in n. 198.

her—at the end of twelve years—the same possibility as that to which he had restored the woman. Both are now capable of giving birth to new life.[35] As in the case of the leper (1:41), Jesus has stretched out his hand and touched what was supremely unclean, namely, a dead body. *He* has not contracted uncleanness through that touch; on the contrary, life and wholeness have flowed from him into the realm of uncleanness and death, claiming this young person for life in terms ("arise" *[egeire]*; "get up" *[anestē]*) that foreshadow his own resurrection.[36]

It is this connection with the resurrection that explains Jesus' otherwise totally unrealistic command that those present tell no one about what had happened (v. 43a). How, after the great public display of mourning at the girl's death, could her restoration to life be kept secret? But realism of narrative yields here to theology. The meaning of the raising that has taken place can only be grasped by those who are being schooled in belief in Jesus' own resurrection, which is never to be separated from its prelude: his obedient death on the cross.[37] For the readers of the gospel who do share that faith, Jesus' conquest of death in a family dwelling that has become a house of faith is a guarantee and illustration that the same lifegiving power is at work in their own house churches and gatherings. For all his standing and authority in it, the synagogue has not helped Jairus in his hour of need. In leaving that world and coming to faith he has experienced in his own home a "saving" and giving of "life" vastly beyond what he had hoped for when he pleaded with Jesus to come and lay his hand on his daughter.[38]

Of course, for parents who have themselves suffered the loss of a child the gospel story will be very painful. Fine in the end for Jairus and his wife; where was Jesus when our son or daughter died? There is no easy answer, but one can at least point to the fact that God let Jairus' daughter die; delayed by the woman, Jesus arrived too late on the scene. But his overcoming of physical death in this one case points, in a sacramental sense, to a deeper truth. In and beyond the physical death he himself tasted to the full he is the

---

35. Cf. Boring, *Mark,* 158.

36. The strong expression of amazement on the part of those present (literally, "They were beside themselves in great amazement *[ekstasis]"*) recurs in the description of the women's state as they flee from the empty tomb of Jesus (16:8).

37. Cf. Jesus' similar injunction to the same three disciples after they have witnessed his transfiguration (9:9); cf. also Hooker, *Saint Mark,* 111; Moloney, *Gospel of Mark,* 111.

38. In this sense we have in this scene the same movement from the synagogue to the domestic scene that we saw at the beginning of Jesus' ministry in 1:21-31. See further Trainor, *Quest for Home,* 118–20.

One through whom God remains for all believers the author and giver of eternal life.[39]

In this way the scene pushes further the question of Story 1: Who is this person exercising what amounts to divine power over the allied forces of "uncleanness" (the demonic) and death?[40] At the same time the interwoven miracle stories equally contribute to our knowledge of the faith that is required to allow that power into human lives. The woman illustrates how faith must overcome barriers—those erected by status and society but also those resulting from deep-seated personal self-doubt. Suffering extreme social isolation, she could have thought to herself, "I am too 'unclean,' too dirty and worthless, for him to be interested in healing me." But her faith drove through that barrier to access Jesus' healing power. Jairus too had a social barrier to overcome: the synagogue ruler had to humble himself before this popular prophet. His part in the drama illustrates how faith must frequently go on a journey, confronting in the process greater challenges than were present at the start. Jairus asked Jesus to come and lay his hands on a daughter who was grievously ill. In the end he saw him grasp her by the hand and summon her from death to life. He saw what all believers experience sacramentally in baptism and will experience ultimately in the mystery of death: the powerful tug of the Lord of life.

Jesus Meets with Lack of Faith in his Home Town: 6:1-6a

Jesus has just performed two outstanding miracles in the context of faith. The sequence concludes with a scene in which Jesus, visiting his home town of Nazareth,[41] experiences by contrast a striking absence of faith. At one level the scene presents Jesus in all his humanness. It locates him within his natural family, whose members it lists at some length (v. 3),[42] and indi-

---

39. "The daughter is 'allowed' to die—as Jesus will die—so that the whole becomes a story of victory over death" (Mark McVann, "Destroying Death: Jesus in Mark and Joseph in 'The Sin Eater,'" in Robert Detweiler and William G. Doty, eds., *The Daemonic Imagination: Biblical Text and Secular Story*. AARSR 60 [Atlanta: Scholars Press, 1990] 123–35; see p. 128).

40. Cf. Gnilka, *Markus* 1.217.

41. Jesus' home town *(patris)* is not named, but 1:9 makes clear that it must be Nazareth.

42. The designation of Jesus as "son of Mary" is unusual; the normal practice was to identify a person through the father, even if he were dead. Gnilka *(Markus* 1:231–32) sees here a Markan hint of the motif of the virginal conception of Jesus later found in the infancy stories of Matthew and Luke. The subsequent listing of Jesus' "brothers" and "sisters" does not impugn that motif. If those named are taken to be Jesus' siblings, this does run counter

cates his powerlessness to perform any "mighty work" because of their want of faith (v. 5). At another level the questions of those who hear him teaching in the synagogue on the Sabbath acknowledge that he is displaying a wisdom and power mysteriously "given" to him from a source they cannot fathom (v. 2). We, the readers of the gospel, know the source of that wisdom and power. We know it derives from his being empowered, as Son of God, by the Spirit (1:9-11). We see the Nazarenes wrestling with the issue and ultimately being "scandalized" (v. 3d) because, as their questions show, in their view he is no different from themselves.[43]

The episode shows that the greatest enemy to faith can simply be "familiarity": a refusal to believe that God's presence—and prophetic agents of that presence—could come to us in so familiar a form as the person next door. The Nazarenes had their own fixed ideas as to when and where and how the Messiah should come to Israel—and the one they knew as the carpenter, Mary's son (v. 3), simply did not fill the bill. So the only place that really missed out on Jesus' works of power was his own home town.[44]

Progress in the spiritual life—growth in the Spirit—almost always shows itself in the ability to recognize God more and more in the ordinary, the everyday. The great saints never ceased being filled with wonder at the mysterious presence of God they constantly sensed all around them. The full meaning of the Incarnation is not only that the Son of God became a human being, but that he took human form in a town as ordinary and insignificant and out of the way as Nazareth (cf. John 1:46). The gospel invites us to identify and name the "Nazareth" in our own selves.

---

to the secondary motif, treasured in the Catholic and Orthodox tradition, of Mary's perpetual virginity. On this issue see Byrne, *Lifting the Burden,* 26–27; Moloney, *Gospel of Mark,* 112, n. 212; Donahue and Harrington, *Mark,* 187–88.

43. Cf. Donahue and Harrington, *Mark,* 183.

44. The proverb Jesus quotes in response—about prophets being recognized everywhere save in their own home town (v. 4)—draws to himself the biblical motif of the "rejected prophet" (Jer 35:15; Ezek 2:15; Hos 9:5; etc.). Luke builds on this scene at Nazareth (cf. Luke 4:14-30) to make "rejected prophet" a key christological category in the Third Gospel.

III
JESUS EXTENDS HIS MINISTRY
6:6b–8:21

Jesus Shares His Ministry: 6:6b-56

A fourth major section of the gospel begins at this point. Like the two preceding sections of the Galilean ministry (1:14–3:6 and 3:7–6:6a), it begins with a summary (6:6b) and a new mission of the disciples (6:7-13) and ends on a note of unbelief (8:14-21; cf. 3:6 and 6:1-6a). In this section the issue of Jesus' identity (Story 1) intensifies, particularly in regard to the disciples. While they share Jesus' mission, their continual failure to understand him and act appropriately becomes a major theme, replacing the more overt conflict with the demonic featured in the earlier sections. At the same time Jesus extends his ministry, first by sharing it with the Twelve (6:6b-13, 30-31) and then by moving more and more in the direction of non-Jewish (Gentile) territory (7:24-37). Thus, while certain patterns can be discerned, there is an interplay of several themes in the section as a whole.

From a structural point of view this part of the gospel falls roughly into two subsections: (1) 6:6b-31: Jesus extends his ministry by sending out the Twelve, the period before their return being taken up by a description of the death of John the Baptist; (2) 6:32–8:21: a longer subsection dominated by two "Feeding Sequences" (6:32–7:23 and 8:1-21), each of which begins with a miraculous feeding (6:32-43 and 8:1-10) and then features (in differing order) a boat scene (6:45-52 and 8:14-21) and a dispute with Pharisees (7:1-23 and 8:11-12). Between the two feeding sequences are two miracles Jesus works in Gentile regions (cure of the Syrophoenician woman's daughter [7:24-30] and cure of the deaf-mute in the Decapolis [7:31-37]).

We can set it out schematically as follows:

Part 1: 6:6b-31

Summary Statement: 6:6b:

Sending out of the Twelve: 6:7-13

Herod's Reflection about the Identity of Jesus: 6:14-16

Herod's Execution of John the Baptist: 6:17-29

Return of the Twelve and Withdrawal: 6:30-31

Part 2: 6:32–8:21

Feeding Sequence 1: 6:32–7:23

Feeding of **5000**: 6:32-43
Boat Sequence (Jesus appears/Disciples fail to understand): 6:45-52
    Summary Statement: 6:53-56
Dispute with Pharisees (Breaking of 'clean' and 'unclean'): 7:1-23

Cure of Syrophoenician (Gentile) Woman's Daughter: 7:24-30

Feeding Sequence 2: 8:1-21

Feeding of **4000**: 8:1-10
Dispute with Pharisees: 8:11-12
Boat Sequence (Disciples fail to understand): 8:14-21

Jesus Sends Out the Twelve on Mission: 6:6b-13

Following his unsuccessful visit to his home town (6:1-6a), Jesus makes a tour around the surrounding villages teaching (v. 6b). This short summary presents Jesus in his characteristic role of teacher, with perhaps the implication that these villages, in contrast to his own, were receptive to his message. At any rate, his own renewed activity forms the background for his beginning to share his mission with the Twelve. "Beginning" suggests the start of a process that will continue beyond the mission of his immediate disciples into the life of the later church. As risen Lord he will continue in the church the personal mission he begins to share here with the disciples.[1]

Jesus had, of course, already chosen and appointed the Twelve "to be with him, and to be sent out to proclaim the message, and to have authority to cast out demons" (3:14-15). Now (v. 7) he activates that appointment, sending them out "two by two." In pairs they can give reliable witness to the inbreaking of the Kingdom.[2] Empowered with Jesus' authority to cast out demons, they will enlarge the space already won for the Kingdom by reclaiming more people from the rule of Satan.

Jesus adds instructions on how they are to travel (vv. 8-9) and what they are to do about lodging (vv. 10-11). They are to travel very "light," submitting themselves to the risk of hospitality: no bread—because food should be provided for them; no traveler's bag[3]—because lodging should also be provided; and, for the same reason, no money. Sandals, yes, and a staff because they will be constantly "on the way."[4] If they do meet with inhospitality and rejection in any place (as Jesus has just experienced in Nazareth), they are to shake the dust from under their feet (a prophetic gesture indicating judgment)[5] and then move on. The "lightness" with which they

1. Cf. Gnilka, *Markus* 1:238–39.

2. The biblical legislation required two witnesses for valid testimony: Deut 17:6; 19:15; cf. Hooker, *Saint Mark,* 155.

3. The Greek word *pēra* refers to a leather pouch used by travelers; the modern equivalent would be a sleeping bag.

4. The allowance of sandals and a staff (a walking stick, but also to ward off dangerous animals or robbers) is a feature that distinguishes the Markan account from the stricter Synoptic parallels influenced by the "Q" source (Matt 10:1-14; Luke 9:1-6; cf. also 10:1-16). The exception reflects Mark's sense of Jesus and the disciples being continually on a journey impelled by the divine urgency of the Kingdom; cf. Moloney, *Gospel of Mark,* 122.

5. This is the gesture Paul and Barnabas perform on leaving Pisidian Antioch, according to Acts 13:5. Later Jewish texts suggest that the action was performed by Jews returning to the Holy Land on leaving pagan territory—so as not to bring any particle of "uncleanness" with them; cf. Moloney, *Gospel of Mark,* 123. The gesture would, then, be tantamount to consigning towns that had rejected the preaching to the "unclean" demonic world.

are to travel will show trust in the divine authority that has been given them; it will also ward off any suspicion of self-seeking. They must have confidence that the treasure they are bringing in the shape of the Gospel so vastly outweighs any burden their stay might impose that they will receive ready hospitality from all destined to be won for the Kingdom.

Thus instructed, the Twelve go out (vv. 12-13), taking up Jesus' summons to repentance in view of the Kingdom (1:14-15) and testifying to its presence by "expelling many demons." Like Jesus, they also heal many (6:5b)—employing for this purpose anointing with oil.[6]

The mission of the Twelve foreshadows that of the church, establishing something essential for its life: that it is always a community on mission, entrusted with the supreme treasure of the Gospel and the healing ministry carried out in the sacraments. How the contemporary church is to imitate these first missionaries in the "lightness" of their travel is far more of a problem, granted the massive institutionalization and wealth that have accrued in the course of the centuries. There are no facile solutions to this, save perhaps the otherwise traumatic experience of persecution. But the Gospel reminds the church that the effectiveness of its prophetic role—its critique of prevailing cultural assumptions and practice—will largely be in proportion to the lightness with which it travels, the trust in the goodness (hospitality) of ordinary people, and the lack of self-seeking its ministers present to the world.

The Prophetic Witness and Death of John the Baptist: 6:14-29

While the Twelve are out on mission Mark provides a narrative interlude with the account of Herod's execution of John the Baptist.[7] Leading up to this is a short passage (vv. 14-16) telling of Herod's awareness of Jesus and reporting the popular belief that the "powers at work in him" mean he must be John the Baptist risen from the dead—or Elijah or one of the other prophets (v. 15). Herod, however, satisfies himself that he is John risen from the dead—an ominous conclusion since Herod has been responsible for John's death, as Mark now proceeds to tell (vv. 17-29). Herod's questions and conclusion intensify the issue of Jesus' identity (Story 1) that runs through this first half of the gospel.

---

6. The anointing with oil reflects the practice of the later church; cf. Jas 5:14-15.

7. The Herod in question is Herod Antipas, Tetrarch of Galilee and Perea (4 B.C.E.–39 C.E.). The account of John's death in Mark is notably at odds with the other account provided by the Jewish historian Josephus (*Ant.* 18.116-19). For a full discussion of the historical issue see Marcus, *Mark 1–8,* 394–96, 399–400.

The account of John's death (vv. 17-29) is unique in that it is the only sustained episode in the gospel from which Jesus himself is absent. It is also distinctive in the sense that none of the players in it—save John himself, the totally passive victim—emerges with any credit. On the contrary, we have a superbly told story about a banquet of sensual voyeurism that comes to a horrific climax with the "serving up" of a severed human head presented by a young woman to her mother "on a dish" (v. 28). Through a combination of vengeful cruelty (Herodias) and rash folly (Herod) a righteous prophet (John) suffers a violent death when a weak ruler is compelled by circumstances he himself has created to act against his own better judgment and inclination.[8]

We might well ask what this totally unedifying tale is doing in the gospel—save perhaps to serve as a negative warning against the vices and folly it so vividly illustrates. We recall that the last we heard of John the Baptist was the brief notice preliminary to the first appearance of Jesus: "After John had been given up" *(paradothēnai),* Jesus came into Galilee" (1:14a). We now appreciate the deeper implications of the enigmatic expression "given up": John has preached (1:4-8; 6:18) and John has been given up, beginning a pattern ("you preach and you are given up") that will also apply in the case of Jesus (3:19; 9:31; 10:33; 14:10, 11, 18, 21, 41, 42, 44; 15:1, 10, 15) and that of his disciples (13:9, 11, 12). The Twelve have just been sent out to preach, and that preaching has been successful (v. 13). The intervening account of John's death serves as a reminder that winning people for the freedom proclaimed in the Gospel will not proceed without cost. It will regularly challenge and provoke the combination of human viciousness, self-interest, and folly patent in the events that brought John to his lonely death.

Moreover, while Jesus may be physically absent from the story, from a narrative point of view he is not really absent at all, since in several respects the fate of John prefigures that of Jesus. The arrest and binding of John (6:7) looks forward to the arrest and binding of Jesus (14:46; 15:1).[9] Likewise, in a repetition of Herod's weakness in the face of his guests, the Roman governor, Pilate, through fear of a mob getting out of hand, will hand over Jesus, whom he recognizes to be innocent (15:10, 14a, 15a).[10] In one respect, however, there is a difference. At the end of the story John's disciples, learning of his fate, come and reverently bury his body in a tomb (6:29). No such

8. The circumstances of John's death further link him with the prophet Elijah, with Herodias playing the part of Jezebel and Herod that of King Ahab (cf. I Kings 18–19). For more detailed comparison see Boring, *Mark,* 178.

9. Cf. Marcus, *Mark 1–8,* 400.

10. Cf. Moloney, *Gospel of Mark,* 127.

relieving touch attends the death of Jesus. He will be buried by a stranger (Joseph of Arimathea), all his disciples having deserted him and fled (15:42-47). Jesus' death in this respect will be even more lonely than that of John. But the clear parallels that do exist between the deaths suggest that the otherwise meaningless suffering of John—and that of all who suffer in similar circumstances—is bound up with that of Jesus, the "rejected stone," whom God vindicated by raising him from the dead and making him the keystone of a new "temple" (12:11-21).[11] From this wider perspective the account of John's death, so unedifying at first sight, is not without significance for all who bear costly and often lonely witness to the Gospel and its social implications.

The Return of the Twelve: 6:30-31

The apostles return and inform Jesus of "all that they had done and taught" (v. 30).[12] One detects in the report a breathless sense of novice enthusiasm—matching the increased enthusiasm of the crowds that prevents them having any time even to eat (v. 31). For Jesus this popular response is ambiguous. It is not without threat to the true direction of his messianic mission. The disciples have a long journey to make with him before they will be spiritually ready to "handle" it: hence his summoning them to withdraw for a time into a deserted place (cf. 1:35-37; 6:45).

The Shepherd King Provides God's Hospitality in the Wilderness (The Feeding of the 5000): 6:32-44

The enthusiasm of the crowds thwarts Jesus' attempt to withdraw for some rest and recreation. They observe his departure by boat and, proceeding on foot, are ready there to greet him in the deserted place when he disembarks (vv. 32-33).[13] When he does so, the sight of them "overwhelms him

---

11. Cf. Marcus, *Mark 1–8,* 404.

12. They are here called "apostles" not in the later technical Christian sense of "the Twelve Apostles" but in the literal meaning of the Greek word *apostolos* = "one sent out." The addition of "teaching" to the activity originally indicated (cf. vv. 7, 12-13) implies that they—and the ministers of the church they foreshadow—are now equipped for all the ministries hitherto reserved to Jesus.

13. That the large, disorganized crowd, taking the roundabout land route, could arrive before Jesus is, in historical terms, unrealistic. The Markan narrative is making a theological point, stressing the enthusiasm of the crowds; cf. Marcus, *Mark 1–8,* 417.

with compassion."[14] They appear to him as "sheep without a shepherd," a stock biblical expression to describe the people of Israel suffering from lack of leadership through corrupt or negligent rulers (Num 27:17; 1 Kgs 22:17 [// 2 Chron 18:16]; Jdt 11:19; cf. Ezek 34:8; Zech 10:2), of which Herod has just provided such a notable example. In contrast, Jesus will reveal himself to be a true shepherd ruler after the model of Moses and David—both shepherds who were called to leadership of the people—by first teaching (v. 34d), and then ordering (v. 39) and feeding (vv. 41-42) the people. Mark's characteristic portrayal of Jesus as teacher and now as the one who provides food for the people lends the total episode that now unfolds a "word and sacrament" duality prefiguring the later ministry of the church.[15]

Jesus' miraculous feeding of thousands of people in the wilderness is told no fewer than six times across all four gospels (Mark 6:32-44 // Matt 14:13-21 // Luke 9:10-17; Mark 8:1-10 // Matt 15:32-39; John 6:1-13).[16] It was clearly a tradition of immense significance for the early believing community for what it reveals both about Jesus himself and about God's designs for human beings in the context of the full arrival of the Kingdom. Various Old Testament motifs hover about the account, notably the prophet Elisha's feeding of a hundred people from twenty loaves, in the face of his servant's protestation, and with some residue after all had eaten (2 Kgs 4:42-44). Getting the people to recline on the green grass (v. 39) and feeding them evokes Psalm 23 ("the Lord is my shepherd") and the sense of Jesus as the Davidic King who will truly shepherd his people (in contrast to the [non-Davidic!] Herod).[17] The provision of food in the wilderness also recalls God's feeding of Israel with manna following the Exodus from Egypt.[18] Looking in another direction, to the future, the description of Jesus' gestures

14. The narrative uses the strong Greek expression *splagchnizomai* = "moved to the depths of one's being"; in Luke's gospel the same word expresses the response of the Good Samaritan (10:33) and the father of the Lost (Prodigal) Son (15:20).

15. Cf. Donahue and Harrington, *Mark,* 211.

16. For a thorough discussion of the likely origins and interrelationships of the traditions behind the accounts see Meier, *Marginal Jew* 2:950–67, who concludes in regard to historicity: "Whether something actually miraculous took place is not open to verification by the means available to the historian. . . . a decision pro or con will ultimately depend upon one's worldview . . ." (966).

17. Passages such as Jer 23:1-6; Ezek 34:22-24 speak of the future Davidic ruler as a shepherd of the people; cf. the later development of this in a messianic direction in *Ps. Sol.* 17:40-41; cf. Hooker, *Saint Mark,* 165.

18. The parallel in John 6, and especially the discourse Jesus subsequently delivers in the synagogue at Capernaum (6:22-66), develops this aspect very explicitly, portraying Jesus over against Moses. The presence of Mosaic overtones in the Markan accounts of the multiplication (so Marcus, *Mark 1–8,* 406) is, to my mind, less clear.

as he "takes" the five loaves and two fish, "blesses," "breaks," and "gives" them to the disciples to set before the people (v. 41), anticipates the gestures of Jesus at the Last Supper, where he will indicate the cup of wine as the last he will share with them until he drinks it "new" in the Kingdom of God (14:22-23).[19]

The feeding tradition, then, looks in two directions. It looks back to the Exodus traditions, where God fed his wandering people in the desert, and also to the promise of a Davidic Shepherd King who would gather and feed the people, a promise now being fulfilled in the person of Jesus. It looks forward to the Eucharist instituted by Jesus at the Last Supper and celebrated by the church. Beyond that still, it anticipates the banquet of the final Kingdom. Along this wide continuum the feeding fills out the picture of the divine hospitality of which the Eucharist is both pledge and sign. The concluding note, "all ate and were satisfied" (v. 42), suggests the complete satisfaction of all human longing, physical and spiritual, associated with the Kingdom. The amount left over (v. 43), together with the note about the number fed (v. 44), underlines the unstinting—carefree even—abundance of the divine hospitality, while the gathering up of the leftover fragments in twelve baskets hints that Jesus' provision of food, both physical and sacramental (the Eucharist), will continue in the ministry of the church.[20]

For the disciples the episode has, once again, been a learning experience. At the start they had made the humanly sensible and indeed responsible suggestion that the people be dismissed in order to buy food for themselves before nightfall (vv. 35-36). When Jesus responded by telling them "You give them something to eat yourselves" (v. 37a), they had—once again with some sharpness (cf. 5:31)—pointed out the human impossibility of making such provision (v. 37b).[21] Jesus further responds by involving them totally in the action that follows: he first makes them find out just how little food they have at hand (five loaves and two fish[22] [v. 38]), and then tells them to get the people to recline in ordered groups as if for a banquet, clearly creating the impression that food is to be provided.[23] There is no description of

19. On the eucharistic overtones see Meier, *Marginal Jew* 2:961–64; Donahue and Harrington, *Mark,* 210.

20. Cf. Marcus, *Mark 1–8,* 421.

21. Both Matthew (14:16-17) and Luke (9:13) spare Jesus from the rough protest of the disciples.

22. Bread and dried fish were the staple items of a meal.

23. The curious Markan phrase *symposia symposia* places in Semitic idiom the Greek word for a drinking or eating party, made famous by Plato's *Symposium.* The idiom is repeated in the next verse: "clusters" (*prasiai prasiai:* literally, "garden plots") of hundreds and fifties. The ordered arrangement may reflect Moses' division of the Exodus community of Israel:

how the abundance of food is created. The disciples simply receive from Jesus the capacity to provide for the people the hospitality that, on purely human reasoning, had seemed impossible. They had already received from him the capacity to expel demons from people and to teach them (6:7-13). Now they have received the capacity to feed them—their own meager resources taken up into the divine generosity to be multiplied beyond all imagining.[24] The miraculous feeding, as key foretaste and sign of the Kingdom, powerfully communicates the sense that God's whole intent in regard to human beings is to have us as honored guests at the banquet of life.

Jesus Walks on the Sea: 6:45-52

Following his feeding of the people, Jesus compels his disciples to get into their boat and go ahead of him "to the other side"—that is, to Bethsaida—while he himself sees to the dismissal of the crowd (v. 45). The strong expression "compel" *(ēnagnasen)* suggests a desire on his part to remove them as quickly as possible from the dangerous enthusiasm of the crowd— dangerous, that is, for the proper understanding of his mission (cf. vv. 31-33). Presumably, it is to renew the true direction of that mission that he himself goes up to a mountain to pray (v. 46).

The temporary physical separation of Jesus from the disciples, now out at sea and hard pressed by a contrary wind, allows him to come back to them in a way that creates the most intense moment of self-revelation in the gospel. To appreciate this fully, we have to be more than ordinarily conscious of the biblical (OT) allusions behind the scene.[25] Jesus' ascent of the mountain to commune with God (v. 46) recalls the description of a similar ascent by Moses (Exod 24:15-18). His coming to them in the fourth watch of the night,[26] walking on the sea with the intent of "passing them by" (v. 48), implies, however, a status far beyond that of Moses. To walk on the sea—to trample down and subdue the forces of primeval chaos and destruction—is

---

Exod 18:21, 25; cf. Deut 1:15; similar ordered arrangements for the eschatological people of God feature in later Jewish literature such as the Dead Sea Scrolls to enhance the sense of identity as the final Israel; cf. Moloney, *Gospel of Mark,* 131; Donahue and Harrington, *Mark,* 206.

24. The link between the multiplication and the Eucharist was probably more palpable in the early church, where the sacrament was celebrated in the immediate context of a communal meal; cf. Paul's complaint and instruction in 1 Cor 11:17-34.

25. For a thorough survey of these and their implications for Markan christology see Meier, *Marginal Jew* 2:914–19.

26. That is, just before dawn; according to the Roman military reckoning of the night as divided into four three-hour periods, the fourth watch runs from 3 a.m. to 6 a.m.

the prerogative of God.[27] The otherwise puzzling detail about his intent "to pass them by" discloses its meaning in light of the virtually technical usage of the phrase "pass by" in biblical accounts of theophanies (encounters with the divine), notably those experienced by Moses and Elijah.[28] Moses cannot look upon God's face and live, but God promises to place him in the cleft of the rock while the divine glory "passes by" (Exod 33:19, 22; 34:6). Elijah experiences a similar theophany on a mountain when told: "Go out and stand on the mountain before the LORD, for the LORD is about to pass by" (1 Kgs 19:11; cf. [LXX] Dan 12:1 [Michael]; Gen 32:31-33).[29]

In light of this biblical background, what the disciples in the boat see and what in their terror they think is a ghost (vv. 49-50a) is nothing less than Jesus as personal revelation of God, the God who created the world out of primeval watery chaos (Gen 1:2-3) and saved Israel by parting the waters of the sea (Ps 77:16-20). The final element of revelation comes with his words of reassurance: "Be of good heart; it is I *(egō eimi); fear not*" (v. 50d). On a surface level the Greek phrase *egō eimi* is a simple self-identification such as anyone might make when surprising a person in the dark. In the context of a further biblical motif going back to Moses' experience at the burning bush (Exod 3:14) it is a solemn expression of the divine presence and power to save (Deut 32:39; Isa 43:10; 41:4).[30]

The appearance of Jesus in this form renders the disciples "utterly beside themselves" (v. 51b)—an expression of being completely at a loss in the presence of divine power (cf. elsewhere in Mark: 2:12; 5:42). The final verse (v. 52) very cryptically—at least as far as we are concerned—seeks to account for their state: they had not understood about the loaves, for their hearts were hardened. The implication is that if they had rightly grasped the revelation involved in Jesus' multiplication of the loaves, in which they were so actively involved, they would not have been so surprised by this present manifestation of his divine status. The episode, then, sheds light retrospectively on the multiplication of the loaves and is its essential continuation. What the disciples should have grasped when they were distributing the loaves is that the exercise of divine hospitality in which they were then involved was a sign both of the inbreaking of the Kingdom and of the presence

27. Cf. Job 9:8 [LXX]: "who alone stretched out the heavens and trampled, as if on dry ground, the waves of the Sea" (cf. 38:16); Ps 77:20: "Your way was through the sea, your path, through the mighty waters"; also Hab 3:15; Isa 51:9-10.

28. This understanding takes the final statement in v. 48, beginning with the Greek conjunction *kai,* in an explanatory sense; cf. Meier, *Marginal Jew* 2:917.

29. Cf. Marcus, *Mark 1–8,* 426.

30. Cf. Moloney, *Gospel of Mark,* 134.

of the One who is the instrument of its arrival in the world. What they have experienced in the boat is simply the extension of that divine presence in another sphere. Had they made that connection, they would not now be at such a loss.

More difficult, though, is the final comment: "Their hearts were hardened" (v. 52b). The biblical motif of "hardening" has till now appeared only with reference to the adversaries of Jesus (3:5). Its reference here to the reaction of the disciples suggests that in some way, from the aspect of their incomprehension at least, *they* are now ranged on that opposing side.[31] The disciples' "hardness of heart" will become the principal opposition Jesus has to contend with until the Passion. They will remain his collaborators, but the front line of battle will shift more and more from overt clashes with demons and hostile human authorities to this difficult terrain of the disciples' hearts.

The physical separation at the start of the episode between Jesus communing with the Father on a mountain and the disciples battling a headwind on the boat points symbolically to the situation of the later church that keenly senses the absence (and delay in coming; cf. Mark 13) of its Lord while it struggles against all the forces that oppose it in the world. Jesus may be physically absent (in heaven until the *parousia*), but he "sees" (cf. v. 48) the church in its struggle and supports it with his prayer (cf. Rom 8:34). His subsequent coming to the disciples in the revelatory way described guarantees his ever-present readiness to intervene and save. It is "hardness of heart"—refusal to believe at sufficient depth—that blocks disciples in every age from discerning the presence of the Lord, especially at those times when there is more than ever a sense of "rowing against the wind" (v. 48).

Jesus' Power to Heal Attracts the Crowds Once More: 6:53-56

As Jesus lands with his disciples on the shore at Gennesaret,[32] he is once again "mobbed" by crowds who recognize him and begin to bring their sick to him on stretchers (vv. 53-54). This is only the beginning of a wider movement to flock to him wherever he goes—towns, villages, or fields (vv.

---

31. The passive expression—"were hardened"—suggests the action of God. The disciples have not shown adequate faith in the divine presence in Jesus. As in the case of "those outside" in 4:11-13, God has responded by "locking" them in to this disposition of heart (cf. 8:17).

32. Mark is again (cf. 4:35) either careless or ignorant about geography. According to 6:45 the disciples were heading in the boat for Bethsaida, which is a town on the northeastern side of the Sea of Galilee. Gennesaret, not so much a town as a small fertile plain, is on the western side between Tiberias and Capernaum.

55-56b). The description, ever growing in intensity as it proceeds,[33] climaxes with the sick ("set down in the market places") seeking to touch even the fringe of his garment (v. 56c). This final extended summary is the culmination of a series of statements stressing the enthusiasm of the crowds to access the healing power that radiates, almost automatically, from him.[34] We hear no word from Jesus himself, no mention of exorcisms or faith. There is just a laconic note at the end that all who touched him were healed (v. 56d). One has the sense that the healings are something of a byproduct of his mission; they are not central to its direction nor do they reveal his true identity.[35] That will require a much longer journey of faith.

33. Cf. Marcus, *Mark 1–8,* 437–38.

34. There is a sense of climax in this, too: in 3:7-12 people touch Jesus; in 5:21-34 the woman touches his garment; here, 6:56, people only have to touch the fringe of his garment; cf. Marcus, *Mark 1–8,* 438.

35. Cf. Gnilka, *Markus* 1:273.

Into the Gentile Regions: 7:1–8:21

The enthusiasm of the crowds who rushed Jesus as he stepped ashore at Gennesaret (6:52-56) contrasts with the hostility of the religious authorities who now reappear on the scene (cf. 2:1–3:6; 3:22-30). The controversy over "clean" and "unclean" they initiate (7:1-23) bears upon a Jewish issue and takes place presumably in a Jewish region (unspecified). But Jesus' breaking through the "clean/unclean" barrier in a legal and theological sense opens the way for his physical "breaking out" into the formally "unclean" Gentile regions in the scenes that follow (7:24–8:21). It is appropriate, then, to take the sequence 7:1–8:21 as a unit. It is also held together, as well as linked to what has gone before, by a recurring "feeding" or "bread" motif.

The Controversy over "Clean" and "Unclean": 7:1-23

The presenting issue in this long sequence is the fact that Jesus' disciples—or at least some of them—were eating with unwashed hands (v. 2). For the benefit of non-Jewish readers Mark turns aside (vv. 3-4) in a brief parenthesis to explain Jewish practice in regard to multiple washing of objects considered unclean (vv. 3-4). The summary is rather unfriendly and distancing in tone; it is also not entirely accurate since not "all the Jews" followed the Pharisaic practice outlined here. The legal prescriptions concerning clean and unclean appear in Leviticus 11–15. They stem from the sense of Israel as a holy people living before God in a holy land with a holiness that must be preserved and that requires restoration when injured through contact with what is alien and unholy. The Pharisaic aim was that the Jewish people should live out their vocation to be the holy people of God in the mixed society that was the Palestine of Jesus' day. They extended the stricter purity the Jewish Law required of priests to the people as a whole, and to this end developed a whole body of traditions they traced back to an oral law communicated to Moses alongside the written Torah.

Here (v. 5) the Pharisees and scribes seem to presuppose that Jesus shares their view of a binding oral law when they complain that his disciples go against the "tradition of the elders" (that is, the tradition purportedly handed down from antiquity) by eating bread with unwashed hands.[1] Jesus, however, will have none of it. He immediately goes on the offensive, broadening the issue from the washing of hands before eating to a wholesale assault on the "tradition" to which they have appealed (vv. 6-8). He cites a divine complaint against Israel voiced in Isa 29:13:

> "This people honors me with their lips,
> but their hearts are far from me;
> in vain do they worship me,
> teaching human precepts as doctrines."

The first part of the quotation, while not immediately relevant to the present issue, introduces the all-important truth that what is central in human relationship to God is the "heart," the moral core of a person from which all else proceeds—a focus that will return later in the sequence (vv. 19, 21). The second part of the text does speak disparagingly of "human precepts," with which Jesus can link the "tradition of the elders."[2] On prophetic authority, then, he can accuse his critics of setting aside the commandment of God in order to hold fast to (mere) "human tradition" (v. 8).

Jesus substantiates the accusation by citing at length (vv. 9-12) a case in which use of the tradition appears to subvert the Torah. The example chosen is the practice (somewhat cryptically described in the text) whereby people exempt themselves from the Law's solemn injunction to honor one's father and mother (Exod 20:12; Deut 5:16)—specifically to see to their welfare in old age—by declaring their property *"korban,"* that is, vowed to the Temple treasury and hence unusable for the purpose of parental support. The Pharasaic "tradition" either condones this practice or else fails to remedy it by forbidding those who have rashly made such a vow to rescind it, on the grounds that the commandment to observe a vow remains binding (Num 30; Deut 23:22-23). In the latter case the ruling mandated by the tradition woodenly pits one commandment of the Law against another, without any

---

1. The connective "but" (Greek *alla*) between the clauses suggests that it is all one complaint: eating with unwashed hands is but a single, typical instance of a wholesale rejection of the tradition.

2. The negative judgment on human tradition is better grounded in the LXX translation (which Mark cites) than in the original Hebrew of Isa 29:13.

sense that the overriding principle ought be what most benefits human beings.[3] Whichever way the abuse Jesus deplores is to be understood, the practice serves as a typical example (v. 13b) of setting aside the word or will of God in favor of "your" tradition.

The narrative affords the Pharisees and scribes no right of reply. Instead, Jesus summons "the crowd" (v. 14) and, reverting to the original issue, makes a fundamental pronouncement on the question of "clean" and "unclean": "there is nothing outside a person that by going in can render that person unclean, but the things that come out of a person are what render unclean" (v. 15).[4] The crowd are left to make of this statement what they will. The disciples, however, when they are alone with Jesus in a house (cf. 4:10), press him for an explanation.[5] In a way that is now becoming characteristic in dealing with the disciples, he begins by expressing irritation at their lack of understanding (v. 18b; cf. v. 14b). He then radically subverts the entire purity legislation of Leviticus 11–15 by expanding on his previous statement (v. 15) in its double aspect: first from the aspect of what enters a person from outside (vv. 18b-19c), then, in the opposite "direction," from what comes out of a person from inside (vv. 20-23).[6] In both cases it is the heart that is the core consideration. Food entering a person from outside goes through a familiar physiological process that does not affect the heart but rather bypasses it (v. 19a-c). With this statement, the narrator notes in an aside (v.

---

3. This is the explanation of Jesus' criticism of the "Qorban" practice that is usually adopted: cf. Nineham, *Saint Mark,* 195–96; Hooker, *Saint Mark,* 141; Moloney, *Gospel of Mark,* 140–41. A problem is that it makes the issue a conflict between two prescriptions of the Law rather than one between the Law and the "tradition," which is what Jesus is indicating. "Tradition" has then to be brought in as a false interpretation favoring the "vow" law against the fourth commandment (cf. Moloney, *Gospel of Mark,* 141). In my reading v. 11 describes a person acting not so much rashly as coldly: cynically seeking a way to freeze assets so that they could be preserved for later use—much as declaring bankruptcy can function today; cf. Gnilka, *Markus* 1:283–84.

4. The argument seems to presuppose that the Pharisees think that unwashed hands transmit uncleanness to what is eaten and thence to the one who eats; on the problems this poses in regard to our knowledge of the historical Pharisees see Marcus, *Mark 1–8,* 446.

5. Literally, they "asked him about the parable"—"parable" being understood here in a broad sense as something requiring explanation.

6. It is not certain how much the attitude recorded here in the gospel reflects that of the historical Jesus. It is difficult to account for the lengthy controversy over the matter in the early church (cf. 1 Cor 8–10; Gal 2:11-14; Rom 14:1–15:13; Acts 10:9-16; 15:1-21) if key players in that controversy, such as Peter, could report a clear directive from Jesus on the matter. For an excellent discussion of the issue see Donahue and Harrington, *Mark,* 227–30.

19d), Jesus declared all foods clean.[7] While that may clear up the matter as regards food, the truly profound ruling occurs when Jesus states what does in fact render a person unclean, namely what comes out from the heart: evil intentions, issuing forth in a variety of actions and vices, of which the text lists twelve (vv. 21-22).[8]

While, as noted above, Jesus is here undermining the purity legislation by insisting on the primacy of moral over ritual holiness, he is at the same time standing within Israel's prophetic tradition (cf. the appeal to Isaiah in vv. 6-7).[9] "Cleanness" or holiness is primarily a matter of the heart. If you want to know whether a person is holy or not, that is, whether they are in touch with the true source of holiness (God), see what comes out of their heart. The list of vices is a kind of checklist, to which we could add examples relevant for our time. By the same token, on the more positive side, we might think of qualities that demonstrate true holiness of heart.[10]

Jesus Liberates the Daughter of a Syrophoenician Woman: 7:24-30

In his ruling on what does and does not render a person "unclean," as earlier in his contact with the leper (1:40-45) and the woman with the hemorrhage (5:21-36), Jesus has redefined holiness. Holiness is a quality emanating from God as the Kingdom, proclaimed and enacted by Jesus, pushes back the realm of the truly "unclean"—the demonic—and reconstitutes God's holy people. A crucial issue for the early believing community concerned where the limits of that people were to be drawn. Could it include non-Jewish, formerly "unclean" Gentiles? The scene that follows—Jesus'

---

7. Matthew's gospel, more sensitive to the radical nature of this declaration in a Jewish context, omits this clause (cf. Matt 15:17). It does closely correspond to Paul's pleas for tolerance in the matter of food in Rom 14:14, 20.

8. The first six items, listed in the plural, have to do with actions; the second six, listed in the singular, are more indicative of vices and tendencies. Such lists are conventional and occur in several places in the New Testament (Rom 1:29-31; Gal 5:19-21; 1 Pet 4:3; cf. 1 Cor 6:9-10; cf. also Wis 14:25-26).

9. Donahue and Harrington, *Mark,* 228–29, insist that, apart from v. 19d, Jesus is not presented by Mark as contrasting moral integrity with ritual observance, and maintain that Leviticus also holds both together (cf. especially Lev 19:11-18). But the paradox remains that the Markan Jesus accuses the adversaries of frustrating the Law through their own tradition, and then proceeds himself to abrogate the Law at least in its ritual prescriptions. Mark may understand him to have the authority, as Son of God, to give preference to some parts of the Law over others—as, e.g., in the Sabbath incidents: 2:23-28; 3:1-6a; cf. Hooker, *Saint Mark,* 179–80.

10. Cf. Paul's list of the "fruits of the Spirit" in Gal 5:22-23.

encounter with a Syrophoenician woman in the regions of Tyre—is the first of several scenes that address this issue.

The opening phrase, which reads literally "rising up, Jesus went away to the region of Tyre" (v. 24a), signals a fresh move on his part.[11] Tyre, the most important seaport in Phoenicia, was the leading city in an area of mixed population where Jews lived as a threatened and oppressed minority.[12] Jesus may be branching out in a new direction, but he is not "on mission"; on the contrary, he is hiding in a house, not wanting to be noticed (v. 24b).

As so often, his attempt to lie low is not successful. A woman of the region, a Gentile[13] but seemingly aware of his reputation for healing and expelling demons, approaches, falls down at his feet (cf. 5:22, 33), and begs him to drive out a demon that is possessing her daughter.[14] Jesus' response, "Let the children be fed (lit. "be filled" *[chōrtasthēnai]*) first; it is not fitting to take the children's food and throw it to the house dogs" (v. 27), is of a harshness unparalleled in the gospels. The first phrase is not too harsh. Within the domestic image he is framing, "children" picks up the Jewish sense, based on several biblical texts, of Israel as God's "child" and Israelites as God's "sons and daughters," a privileged designation never extended to non-Jews.[15] Jesus is addressing the woman as a Gentile and making the point that his mission of bringing about the "fullness" of the Kingdom (anticipated in his feeding the five thousand [Jews] in the wilderness, so that "all were filled" [6:42]) is first and foremost for Jews.[16] The word "first" leaves open the possibility that a time may come when others beyond "the children" might also be fed. But the second statement,

---

11. Jesus "rises up" at turning points in his mission: 1:35-37; 10:1; and, of course, the same Greek expression refers to his resurrection (8:31; 9:10; 9:31; 10:34); cf. Donahue and Harrington, *Mark,* 232.

12. Cf. Boring, *Mark,* 207.

13. "Syrophoenician" identifies her as a Phoenician from Syria rather than from other regions, e.g., Libya, settled by Phoenicians. Mark also calls her "a Greek," not in an ethnic sense but to identify her as a Gentile (cf. Rom 1:16; 1 Cor 1:22-24).

14. Mark describes the child's condition as "having an unclean spirit" (v. 25b), referred to simply as a "demon" (vv. 26, 29, 30). "Unclean" links the passage with the preceding controversy (vv. 1-23). In light of the later episode (9:14-29) in which a similarly distressed parent begs Jesus to drive a demon from his son and the condition is described at length, and in view of the ending of this episode, when the child lies peacefully on a bed, we are justified in thinking of some psychophysical condition involving convulsions, perhaps a chronic epileptic condition, which the ancient worldview attributed to possession. On this difficult interpretive matter see the wise observations of Meier, *Marginal Jew* 2:661 and 677, nn. 77 and 78.

15. See Byrne, *"Sons of God"–"Seed of Abraham,"* 9–78.

16. The same sense of Israel's priority rings through Paul's letter to the Romans (1:16)—mysteriously inverted though it be in a temporal sense (11:26-32); see further Byrne, *Romans,* 349–53.

extending the image to include not only the children but also house dogs,[17] seems harshly to close this off. Dogs were considered unclean in the Palestine of Jesus' day. To call someone a "dog" was a great insult, and yet Jews did refer to Gentiles, conventionally considered "unclean," in such terms.[18] Jesus' words reflect a sense of the huge socioreligious barrier separating God's holy people from the "unclean" Gentile world around them.

Seizing Jesus' image, the woman exploits it in a way that breaks right through that barrier. Her polite "Yes, sir" (v. 28),[19] accepts the Jewish priority Jesus had stated. But then, perhaps from her greater knowledge of domestic affairs, she points out that the house dogs under the table do manage to get some of the scraps that fall while the children eat.[20] Her wit—and, though it is not made explicit in the Markan account, her faith—bring about a complete change. Jesus tells her to go on her way: the demon has already left her daughter (v. 29). Trusting in his word, she departs for her house, where she finds the situation exactly as he had said: the demon departed and the daughter lying (peacefully, we may suppose) on a bed.

Jesus has not come to her house. But her faith, breaking through the barrier,[21] has opened the way for his power to reach there. The house to which she returns, a Gentile house, has become a site for his authority to liberate people from the "unclean" demonic world and claim them for the Kingdom. This unnamed woman becomes the pioneer and paradigm of all Gentile believers who, while they recognize that Jesus' earthly mission was confined to Israel, have come to experience in their own homes his presence and power as risen Lord. They too can feed and "be satisfied"—as when Jesus repeats the feeding miracle for the benefit of the (Gentile) four thousand (8:1-10).[22] This story, challenging though it be to conventional piety, is a

17. The diminutive Greek form *kynarion* probably refers to domestic animals as distinct from dogs that roamed the streets.

18. Cf. Marcus, *Mark 1–8,* 463–64.

19. "Sir" (Greek *kyrios*) is ambiguous: as well as the polite form of address to a stranger, there may also be a hint here of the "Lord" of Christian confession (cf. Rom 10:9; 1 Cor 12:3; Phil 2:11).

20. In Matthew's parallel (15:27) the crumbs "fall from the table"—perhaps because children eat untidily. Mark's less detailed account is open to the suggestion that the children deliberately feed (literally "throw" crumbs to) the house dogs under the table. Boring, *Mark,* 212, points out that only in Gentile houses would dogs have been allowed inside.

21. Beyond the ethnic ("Jew/Gentile") divide, the woman has also broken through the social gender barrier preventing women from approaching unknown males (cf. John 4:9, 27); cf. Moloney, *Gospel of Mark,* 148.

22. In both cases—that of the woman who seeks help for her daughter and that of the four thousand—the "bread" and "the crumbs," the "feeding" and "being filled," may have a eucharistic resonance; cf. Trainor, *Quest for Home,* 135.

key place in the gospel where the situation of the later church—our church—washes back over the portrayal of Jesus in his own lifetime, inviting us to identify with the woman in her desperation and her faith. It also suggests that the tight boundaries of "righteousness" the church is prone to draw around itself will often "suffer violence" (Matt 11:12) from outsiders who, under the prompting of God's inclusive grace, seek access to its treasures.[23]

Healing of a Person with a Hearing and Speech Impediment: 7:31-37

Leaving the regions of Tyre, Jesus makes a long, roundabout journey, first north to Sidon, then east across the north of Galilee to the Decapolis region (v. 31). The route makes little sense geographically, but it communicates the sense of Jesus moving through Gentile areas bordering on Palestine.[24] It establishes that the man healed, along with those who bring him and react to the healing, are Gentiles, forerunners of those who will respond to Jesus from the nations of the world.

The man is described as "deaf" and "having an impediment in his speech" (v. 32).[25] Jesus accedes to the request of those who bring him in a most physical way. He takes the man aside, away from the crowd, and then performs a lengthy series of gestures: putting his fingers into the man's ears, touching his tongue with spittle, looking up to heaven, concluding with a command, expressed in Aramaic *(Ephphatha)* and then translated: "Be opened!" (vv. 33-34). The gestures recall descriptions of magical cures in the Hellenistic world,[26] but there is no working of magic here. The healing comes about through the summoning of divine power (looking up to heaven and groaning) and then by an authoritative word of command. That command, and especially the remark that "the bond *(desmos)* of his tongue was

---

23. It is regrettable that the compilers of the Roman Catholic Lectionary did not see fit to include this episode (Mark 7:24-30), along with that of the Gerasene demoniac (5:1-20), among the Sunday Gospel readings for Year B—a misguided attempt, surely, to "protect" the faithful from more challenging aspects of the Gospel.

24. On the meaning of the journey see especially Meier, *Marginal Jew* 2:712.

25. The second phrase renders the rare Greek word *mogilalos,* which can have the sense either of being simply unable to speak (= dumb) or of being unable to speak distinctly. That the latter is the sense here is shown by the statement that, after he was healed, the man could speak "correctly" (v. 35b). It is, of course, a fact that inability to hear creates problems with speech. The only other occurrence of *mogilalos* in the Greek Bible appears in (LXX) Isa 35:6, alluded to in the final acclamation (v. 37c).

26. Cf. Meier, *Marginal Jew* 2:713; Donahue and Harrington, *Mark,* 242.

loosened," lend the healing a strongly exorcistic note:[27] here too Jesus is reclaiming a person from the grip of the demonic.

The healing of the man in private and Jesus' instruction not to say anything about it (v. 36) is, once again, completely ineffectual. The response to the healing is widespread enthusiasm on an unprecedented scale and general acclaim: "He has done all things well; he has made the deaf hear and the dumb speak" (v. 37). The acclamation alludes to Isa 35:5-6, a text serving as a key vehicle of the hopes for the messianic age. These people from the Decapolis, like the Syrophoenician woman whose daughter Jesus has just freed, foreshadow all those Gentiles who will gain access to the riches of the Jewish Messiah.

The very physical nature of this healing has made it particularly open to symbolic interpretation in the Christian tradition. The man is deaf and has an impediment in his speech. His condition places him at a great disadvantage as regards communication: he cannot receive it verbally or freely communicate his own thoughts and feelings; his condition is lonely and isolated. Through word and touch Jesus brings him into the hearing and speaking world of interpersonal communication. In this experience the man represents all believers. Apart from the grace of God we are "deaf" to the Word of life spoken to us by the Creator. By opening our ears Jesus gives us the capacity to hear his life-giving Word, which he then speaks to us in the Scriptures proclaimed by the church.[28] Having heard that Word in the context of our own life-experience, we then can turn to testimony and praise. We can join in the chorus of the community of faith: "He has done all things well" (v. 37).

Once Again:
Hospitality in the Wilderness (Jesus Feeds Four Thousand): 8:1-9

Presumably still on his "tour" of the Decapolis region (7:31), Jesus repeats the miracle of feeding a multitude of people in the wilderness (6:35-44). The account differs only in detail from that of the previous feeding and we might wonder why this short gospel includes two such episodes.[29] The

---

27. Inability to speak is explicitly attributed to demonic possession in Mark 9:17, 25; cf. Marcus, *Mark 1–8,* 475, 478.

28. Jesus' gestures have, of course, found their way into the rite of Christian baptism, at the beginning of which the minister touches the ears of the person and proclaims *"Ephphatha."*

29. The two feeding stories (as well as that in John 6:1-15) most likely stem from two independent pre-Markan traditions; cf. Meier, *Marginal Jew* 2:950–67.

best explanation is that Jesus performs the second miracle for the benefit of the inhabitants of the Gentile region in which he is now moving.[30] In the earlier account he acted as the Shepherd King of Israel, having compassion on the multitude, who seemed to him "sheep without a shepherd" (6:34). Here Jesus simply expresses compassion for the people's want of food after three days with him, especially as "some have come from a long way away" (v. 3). The seven baskets of fragments collected after this second feeding may hint at the later mission to the nations of the world, conventionally reckoned to number seventy; they also, of course, will have "come from a long way away."[31]

As in the preceding account, Jesus' gestures over the loaves[32] (giving thanks, breaking, giving to the disciples to set before the crowd) foreshadow the institution of the Eucharist (Mark 14:22-25). Likewise, the concluding remark, "and they ate and were satisfied" (v. 8a), suggests again the fullness and satisfaction of the final banquet of the Kingdom, to which both the feeding and the Eucharist point. In the first feeding (6:31-44) Jesus fed "the children" (Israel); in this one he displays acceptance of the Syrophoenician woman's insistence that "even the dogs under the table" (Gentiles) should share the crumbs of the children. Taken together, the two feeding miracles point to the divine intent, begun in Jesus' ministry to Israel and carried to nations by the church, to draw the whole human family into the hospitality of God.

A puzzling aspect of this second feeding concerns the disciples. In light of the earlier feeding in which they had played a key role, their exclamation concerning the problem of feeding so many people in the wilderness (v. 4) shows them up as at least very forgetful, if not downright stupid.[33] But, at the expense of some narrative consistency, the evangelist probably retained the exclamation from an early tradition because it highlights something he is constantly at pains to point out: a state of affairs impossible to account for or remedy in human terms to which the exercise of divine power will respond (cf. 5:26; 5:39-40; 9:3).[34] The question "*Whence* would anyone be

---

30. This view is widely, though not universally, accepted. Against those skeptical that Gentiles are in view (e.g., Hooker, *Saint Mark,* 187–88), see Moloney, *Gospel of Mark,* 154–56.

31. Cf. Moloney, *Gospel of Mark,* 155.

32. The reference to the "few fish" is something of an afterthought in Mark's account (v. 7).

33. Cf. Hooker, *Saint Mark,* 189; Moloney, *Gospel of Mark,* 153–54.

34. Cf. Eduard Schweizer, *The Good News according to Mark* (London: SPCK, 1970) 156.

able to satisfy with bread these people in the wilderness?" begs for the response: "From the power and generosity of God operative in Jesus." It once again brings to the forefront the central issue of this half of the narrative: "Who is this among us?" (Story 1).

The Pharisees Seek a Sign: 8:10-13

After the feeding and dismissal of the crowd (v. 9b), Jesus leaves the Gentile area of the Decapolis and returns by boat with the disciples to Jewish territory on the opposite side.[35] Here he has a brief encounter with Pharisees, who begin to argue with him demanding from him a "sign from heaven" (v. 11). We might wonder why, in view of his extensive miracles, they make such a demand. But "a sign from heaven" is more than a miracle. The phrase suggests a cosmic wonder such as would indicate the end of the present age—the kind of phenomenon he will himself later point to as heralding the arrival of the Son of Man (13:24-25).[36] Their intent is hostile; they are "testing" him *(peirazontes),* as Satan tested him in the wilderness (1:13).

Jesus' response (v. 12)—his groaning in the spirit followed by a solemn oath of refusal—suggests that behind the demand for a sign he sees yet another ploy of the demonic.[37] His proclamation of the Kingdom carries its own authority (1:22, 27). To seek to bolster it with a "sign" would fatally compromise that authority and lead him into the trap being laid in the request.[38] The "generation" that seeks such a sign shows itself to be heir to the rebellious generation of the Exodus, who immediately after being fed with the manna from heaven (Exodus 16) tested God by demanding a further sign (Exod 17:1-7; cf. Ps 95:7b-11).[39] For human beings to demand of God a sign is to treat God as a partner whose trustworthiness has yet to be proven. It is the exact opposite of faith. In fact, the demand for a sign shows the same fixedness in unbelief that "those outside" displayed on hearing Jesus' teaching in parables (4:11-12); it will recur in the mockery directed at Jesus as he hangs on the cross (15:32).[40] Jesus can do nothing with these Pharisees but simply get back on board the boat and leave them to it (v. 13). A curtain

---

35. The location specifically mentioned, "Dalmanutha," has long defied identification; cf. Donahue and Harrington, *Mark,* 245–46.

36. Cf. Donahue and Harrington, *Mark,* 248.

37. See especially Marcus, *Mark 1–8,* 501.

38. Cf. Vincent Taylor: "If He tries to give a sign, he will fail; if He refuses he will lose popular support" (*St. Mark,* 362).

39. Cf. Marcus, *Mark 1–8,* 503.

40. Cf. Donahue and Harrington, *Mark,* 250.

now descends on his dealings with these sign-seeking representatives of Israel's religious leadership.[41] From now on the principal contest will be with misunderstanding on the part of his own disciples.

The Forgetful Disciples: 8:14-21

We arrive now at the last of three boat scenes that play a key role in revealing both Jesus' identity and the disciples' difficulty in coming to terms with it.[42] In the first (4:35-41) Jesus had displayed a Godlike capacity to command the winds and the sea, leading his awestruck disciples to ask "Who is this . . . ?" (v. 41). In the second (6:45-52), following the first multiplication of the loaves, he had again shown a Godlike capacity, treading underfoot the waves of the sea as "he made as if to pass by" (v. 48). At the close of that episode, we are told, the disciples were utterly astounded: "they had not understood about the loaves, for their hearts were hardened" (v. 51b-52). The final boat scene does not involve a further revelation of Jesus' status. Rather, he reminds his disciples about the two miracles with the loaves and upbraids them severely for not drawing from those events the right conclusions about his identity, his presence, and his power. The scene, then, for all the difficulty of interpretation it presents, draws together a number of motifs and themes that have been running through the first half of the gospel. In particular it brings to a climax the motif of the disciples' spiritual incomprehension. Under the image of "blindness" this will be the major preoccupation of the central section of the gospel (8:22–10:52).

The episode begins with the information that the little company of Jesus and the disciples had set off on their trip across the lake without provisions: they have forgotten to bring loaves of bread—though they do have one loaf with them in the boat (v. 14). Suddenly—and rather intrusively as far as the narrative flow is concerned—Jesus warns them against "the leaven of the Pharisees and the leaven of Herod" (v. 15). The mention of "leaven" seems to trigger in the disciples an awareness of their lack of bread. Disregarding the warning, they begin to argue with one another about this lack, which in turn leads Jesus to issue a sustained reprimand in the shape of no less than eight searching questions (vv. 17-21). Like a frustrated schoolmaster, Jesus catechizes them about their lack of understanding in language ("hardness of heart," "having eyes and not seeing," "having ears and not hearing") till

---

41. Cf. Paul: "For Jews demand signs and Greeks desire wisdom, but we proclaim Christ crucified, a stumbling block to Jews and foolishness to Gentiles" (1 Cor 1:22-23).

42. Cf. Watts, *Isaiah's New Exodus,* 220–39.

now reserved for adversaries and "those outside" (3:5; 4:11-12).[43] The final questions concern their failure to "remember" (v. 18c), their failure to advert to the implications of the two feedings, each of which Jesus recalls in exact detail (vv. 19-20).[44] The interrogation comes to a climactic halt (v. 21) with the bald "Do you not yet *(oupō)* understand?"—the "not yet" at least seeming to leave open the possibility that a time might come when they will.

But what precisely is the leaven of the Pharisees and that of Herod against which Jesus warns the disciples? And what was it that they should have deduced from the repeated feedings, such that, had they remembered it, they would not have been concerned about an insufficiency of bread? These two questions are not easily answered and the relationship of the first to the second is obscure.[45] To take the second first, we have to ask what it was that the feedings ought to have revealed about Jesus. The answer can only be that they reveal him to be the One in whom the Creator is providing— for Israel and potentially for the nations of the world—the hospitality of the Kingdom, and doing so with a generosity (seen in the abundance of leftovers) that is truly divine. If, in this context, five loaves supplied more bread than was necessary for five thousand, and seven loaves for four thousand, how could it be that in the company of Jesus the one loaf would not suffice for them? Had they grasped that, they would not have been so preoccupied with food as to miss or, at worst, ignore his warning about "leaven."[46]

In biblical and related literature leaven or yeast, an essential ingredient for baking, occurs as an image for a hidden element secretly and insidiously working moral corruption (cf. 1 Cor 5:6-8; Gal 5:9).[47] Jesus speaks separately of the "leaven of the Pharisees" and "the leaven of Herod" (v. 15), suggesting two distinct evil influences. The Pharisees have consistently appeared as critics of Jesus, proceeding from a refusal to acknowledge that, with the

43. The language of v. 18 recalls not only Jer 5:21; Ezek 12:2; Ps 115:5-6 (LXX 113:13-14) but also the phrases from Isa 6:9-10 cited in the strongly negative statement about "those outside" in 4:12.

44. The detail extends to recalling the different terms for the containers of the leftover fragments: *kophinoi* for the 5000; *spyrides* for the 4000.

45. The passage would flow much more smoothly in the absence of the warning in v. 15, which in Luke's gospel occurs in a different context (12:1). With v. 15 in place, the Greek conjunction *hoti* in v. 16 is best understood in the sense: "They discussed with one another that he said this because they had no bread"; cf. Marcus, *Mark 1–8*, 507.

46. This is to take primarily a christological approach to the passage: cf. Hooker, *Saint Mark*, 192; Nineham, *Saint Mark*, 213–14; Gnilka, *Markus* 1:311. To find also a eucharistic reference in the "one loaf" (so Marcus, *Mark 1–8*, 510; Moloney, *Gospel of Mark*, 162; Trainor, *Quest for Home*, 140; Donahue and Harrington, *Mark*, 254; Boring, *Mark*, 226–27) seems to me to go beyond the evidence.

47. Cf. Marcus, *Mark 1–8*, 510; Donahue and Harrington, *Mark*, 252.

onset of the Kingdom, restrictive barriers of the old era (sinners/just [2:15-17]; fasting/celebration [2:18-22]; Sabbath/human need [2:23-28; 3:1-6a]; clean/unclean [7:1-5]) have been cast down. They have just demanded a sign from heaven to show that the new age has really dawned (8:11-13).[48] In all of this they display a "hardness of heart" (cf. 3:5) that renders them enemies of the saving project now under way, a danger against which Jesus warns his disciples (8:17d; cf. 6:52). Herod, on the other hand, represents worldly power, exercised in a foolish, brutal, and ultimately murderous fashion (cf. 6:17-29), absolutely contrary to the path Jesus is taking as messianic King. Each tendency, in its own way, constitutes a "leaven" of temptation that the disciples must guard against if they are truly to be his followers. This scene, then, prepares the way for much of the gospel that is to follow in showing that the disciples suffer from a spiritual "blindness" that Jesus will have to enlighten.

---

48. They will further test Jesus (on divorce [10:1-12]) and, again in consort with the Herodians, seek to trap him in regard to payment to Caesar (12:13-17).

IV
THE "WAY" TO JERUSALEM
8:22–10:52

The Messiah Who Must Suffer and Die:
8:22–9:29

We now approach the chief turning point in Mark's gospel. The issue that has existed from the start, "Who is this person, armed with such striking power to teach, to heal, and to set free?" is about to be resolved—at least for the disciples. In the person of Peter, at least, they will recognize him as "the Christ" (8:29) and so get some purchase on what I have called "Story 1": the truth, known to the reader—and to the demonic world—that Jesus is the Messiah, the Son of God. But the moment the disciples arrive at this knowledge they have to begin to cope with a further revelation: that precisely as Messiah and God's "Beloved Son" he is destined to suffer and die (Story 2 [8:31-33]). Jesus' sustained and largely unsuccessful attempt to communicate to his disciples this deeper truth about his person and mission forms the main "agenda" of the journey to Jerusalem that now lies ahead.

The disciples have already shown themselves to be spiritually blind and forgetful of much of what they have heard and seen Jesus do: "having eyes, (they) have not seen" (8:18). Blindness now becomes a sustained metaphor for the fresh difficulty they will have as they struggle with what appears to them a radical inconsistency between Story 1 and Story 2. Mark brings this image to the fore with the healing of the blind man at Bethsaida (8:22-26). The journey to Jerusalem will approach its end with a similar cure of a blind man (Bartimaeus) at Jericho (10:42-50). The two cures of men physically blind thus "frame" Jesus' sustained attempt to cure the disciples' "blindness" as they travel together along the way. At this center point of the gospel the first cure gathers up the emerging "blindness" theme from what has gone before and prefigures the difficult process of enlightenment that lies ahead.[1]

---

1. Meier, *Marginal Jew* 2:691, aptly speaks of the scene as in this respect having a "Janus-like" character, looking both ways; cf. also Moloney, *Gospel of Mark,* 163.

Jesus Cures a Blind Man at Bethsaida: 8:22-26

Like the cure of the man with a hearing and speaking impediment in 7:31-37, with which it has much in common, this miracle story occurs only in Mark. Again like that earlier cure, it also involves highly physical gestures: the use of spittle and the laying on of hands. It is unique in that it is the only miracle recorded in the gospels in which the cure takes place in two stages.[2] After an initial, partially successful opening of the man's eyes (he can see people, but only "like trees walking about" [vv. 23-24]),[3] Jesus lays his hands on the man's eyes again, whereupon he at last sees everything clearly.[4] The cure ends, in characteristic Markan fashion, with Jesus sending the man home, forbidding him to enter the village—presumably because then the cure, very deliberately conducted in private (v. 23a), would become known.[5]

As stated above, the main function of the scene in Mark's story is symbolic. The two-stage "enlightenment" of the man foreshadows and il-lustrates in advance the two-stage enlightenment of the disciples. They will soon arrive at partial vision of Jesus' identity (8:29: Story 1) but will remain fixed on that level till the end of the story. Their enlightenment will not be complete until, beyond the narrative of the gospel itself, they will glimpse in risen glory (cf. 16:7) the Lord whose arrest, suffering, and death (Story 2) had shattered them so completely.

Along with this symbolic function, the scene is attractive in its richness of human detail and in the sacramental aspect of the physical attentiveness Jesus displays toward the man—even if some details, for example the spit-ting, may challenge modern taste.[6] In particular, the man's two-stage arrival at full vision speaks to most people's journey of faith, which is usually a gradual process with many stages of blurred vision along the way. The scene invites us to feel Jesus taking us by the hand and leading us to a place where

---

2. The two-stage working of the cure may have led both Matthew and Luke to omit the story as suggesting some limitation on Jesus' power.

3. The fact that he can name what appear to him to be trees suggests that the man, unlike the man cured by Jesus (again rather "physically") in John 9:1-5, was not blind from birth.

4. The description is quite detailed: literally, "he stared with wide open eyes (*dieblepsen;* cf. BDAG 125) and (his sight) was restored *(apekatestē)* and he saw everything clearly *(eneblepsen tēlaugōs hapanta)*. The last phrase, featuring the rare adverb *tēlaugōs,* literally means "to see things at a distance clearly." On the verbs see Donahue and Harrington, *Mark,* 257.

5. The manuscript tradition at v. 26 is notoriously variant; for details see Meier, *Marginal Jew* 2:739, n. 59.

6. As in the case of the earlier healing (7:31-37), the gestures parallel those found in healing accounts from the Hellenistic world; cf. Meier, *Marginal Jew* 2:693.

he can enlighten us stage by stage until we see both his own face and the world around us with the clarity of vision that mature faith provides.

The Messiah Who Is to Suffer and Die: 8:27-33

From Bethsaida (8:22) Jesus has led his disciples to the region of Caesarea Philippi, the northernmost point of his travels as recorded in the gospels. From here he will turn around and begin a long journey south that will bring him to the gates of Jerusalem (11:1). Alongside the physical journey will run a deeper journey into the mystery of his identity and his mission. The gospel has from the start portrayed Jesus as a teacher; his authoritative teaching no less than his actual exorcisms have rescued human lives from the grip of the demonic and reclaimed them for the Kingdom. From this point forward that teaching will be directed to the disciples and focused more precisely on the resistance in their hearts to the direction in which he is leading them. As his rebuke to Peter will show, that resistance is no less a manifestation of the demonic than the more overt instances he has countered in his exorcizing activity.

While "on the way" to Caesarea Philippi Jesus puts his question on the issue concerning his identity that has been running through the narrative: "Who do people say that I am?" (v. 27b). As readers of the gospel, we have known from the start that he is "the Messiah, the Son of God" (1:1 [Story 1]), but this has been concealed from other human participants in the drama. As his ministry in the cities and towns of Galilee unfolded, the disciples wrestled with the question they voice immediately after he has calmed the sea: "Who is this, then, that even the winds and the sea obey him?" (4:41). The people too have been struck by the authority of his teaching and his powerful works of healing and exorcism, but, as the disciples now report (8:28; cf. already 6:14-15), they see him as John the Baptist *redivivus* or one of the figures—Elijah or some other prophet—whose return was anticipated as a harbinger of the Kingdom.[7] Only the demons, feeling the force of his messianic power, have acknowledged his identity as Son of God (1:24; 3:11; 5:7). But Jesus has silenced them; his identity is not to be revealed from malign sources such as these. Likewise, he has tried—usually without success (cf. 1:45; 7:36-37)—to suppress reports about his healings, presumably to dampen the kind of popular enthusiasm that could arouse misguided messianic expectation.

---

7. On these figures see further Donahue and Harrington, *Mark,* 260.

Now the moment has come for Jesus to draw from the disciples an explicit acknowledgment of his identity. The prior question and the report about the inadequate views of people at large place the disciples in a special category both in regard to the question ("Who do *you* say that I am?") and the response it receives. The question corresponds to the one Jesus put to the blind man after the first stage of his healing: "Can you see anything?" (v. 23d).[8] Peter, speaking for them all, gets it right: "You are the Christ (the Messiah)." In contrast to the people, and like the man who could now see men walking about like trees (v. 24), the disciples have an accurate, if incomplete, grasp on Story 1: Jesus is the Messiah of conventional expectation.

Jesus neither confirms nor applauds Peter's response. Instead, he strictly enjoins the disciples not to pass on this knowledge to anyone else (v. 30) and then goes on immediately to speak of his coming Passion and death. That is, no sooner have the disciples gained some purchase on Story 1 than Jesus lays alongside it—plainly and openly (v. 32a)—what I have called "Story 2": the destiny of this Messiah to suffer and die before rising again on the third day.[9] The knowledge of Jesus' messianic status is not to be separated for a moment from the kind of Messiah he is destined to be: not one who will be served and honored, as is customary in the case of rulers of this world, but one who is "to serve and give his life as a ransom for many" (10:45). For the remainder of the gospel the disciples will struggle to hold these two truths together: that Jesus is indeed the long-awaited Messiah (Story 1) and that he will fulfill his messianic role by entering into the pain and suffering of this world, even to the point of death (Story 2)—something totally unforeseen in conventional Jewish messianic expectation.[10]

Peter's remonstration (v. 32b) voices just this sense of incompatibility between the two. How can it be that the Messiah should suffer in such a way? How could God allow this to happen to the chosen instrument of Israel's rescue? The sharpness of the rebuke it earns, "Get behind me, Satan" (v. 33a), shows that Jesus senses in it a ploy of the demonic.[11] To attempt to hold Jesus back from his divinely ordained path is to play Satan's game to frustrate God's gift of life to the world through the costly "service" (10:45)

---

8. Cf. Moloney, *Gospel of Mark,* 166.

9. Jesus does not refer to himself as Messiah but as Son of Man, employing this self-designation for the first time since 2:10 and 2:28. "His messiahship is to be found in his future as the Son of Man" (Moloney, *Gospel of Mark,* 173).

10. For "conventional messianic expectation" I again refer the reader to the discussion of the term "Messiah" in the introductory chapter, "The Worldview Behind Mark's Gospel" above; see also Moloney, *Gospel of Mark,* 166, n. 261.

11. Cf. Boring, *Mark,* 242.

he must render. Peter and all the disciples (included in Jesus' sweeping glance: "turning and seeing his disciples") are to "get behind" him in the sense of following him along his "way" rather than standing *in* his way through the protest voiced by Peter.[12] To do otherwise is to be on the side of human beings rather than of God (v. 33c). This last comment voices the "divine-human" dichotomy that is a constant theme in Mark's gospel. It is not "antihuman," but expresses the truth that the radical rescue of the world that is under way must challenge and overthrow many human views and values that are part of its captivity to the demonic. The messianic expectation lurking behind Peter's protest is exactly the view Messiah Jesus has to challenge if his mission is achieve its end.

Let us not, however, be too hard on Peter. It is natural to wish to preserve those we love from suffering—even if we acknowledge some measure of suffering to be an unavoidable byproduct of what for them and for ourselves leads to fuller life. The fact that a disciple (Peter) who has just got something so splendidly right (the confession of Jesus as Messiah) straightaway stumbles so badly at the thought of suffering can be an encouragement: a recognition in the gospels that we all do badly at suffering. Each fresh trial that comes our way may be an invitation into this scene, to hear Jesus' command "Get behind me . . ." as a call to a closer, more "enlightened" following of him along "the way."

The Challenge and Hope of Discipleship: 8:34–9:1

Jesus has plainly outlined what the future holds for himself (v. 31). He now goes on to make equally plain what it will involve for those who follow him. These are in the first instance his immediate disciples, but the reference to his "summoning the crowd" (v. 34) incorporates readers of the gospel and all subsequent believers into the audience. The instruction states a basic principle (v. 34b) and then justifies this with a series of further statements (vv. 35-38), culminating in the assurance of future vindication in 9:1. The basic principle sets two conditions for being a disciple: being prepared first to "deny oneself," and then to take up one's cross and follow after Jesus (v. 34b). "Denying oneself" means placing the demands of discipleship above all other desires and plans a person might cherish or hold to be significant.[13] It does not necessarily exclude such aspirations, but subordinates them to

---

12. Cf. Moloney, *Gospel of Mark,* 174.
13. Cf. Gnilka, *Markus* 2:23.

the overriding demands of discipleship.[14] The second condition, under the stark image of "carrying one's cross," requires readiness to follow Jesus to the point of death.[15] In the world of Mark's gospel, where crucifixion was an all-too-familiar form of execution, such language would have a chilling resonance. In a more extended sense (seen already in Luke's formulation: take up one's cross *daily* [9:23]), the image suggests that each disciple, even if not required to follow Jesus to the point of physical death, is nonetheless called to a lifelong dedication to his cause and readiness to make a costly entrance into the world of suffering in union with him.

In justification of this self-surrender, the following sentences (vv. 35-37) play upon a double meaning in the word "life" expressed by the Greek term *psychē,* which occurs or is referred to no less than six times. *Psychē* can refer simply to the span of a person's everyday life that will end in physical death. Within the wider eschatological framework presupposed by the gospel it can also refer to the deeper core of a human being that, under God's power, can transcend the limitations of physical mortality and participate in the resurrection. Thus Jesus can formulate the paradox that whoever wants at all costs to preserve his or her "life" in the former (limited) sense runs the risk of losing it in the latter (extended) sense (v. 35a), while whoever is prepared to lose her or his life in the former sense, for Jesus' sake and that of the Gospel, will save it in the latter sense (v. 35b). The next two sentences (vv. 36-37) explore this rationale more deeply. Even in a purely this-worldly perspective it is pointless to gain all the riches in the world, along with the pleasures and security such wealth may seem to promise, if a further span of life in which to enjoy them will be lacking. How much more "useless" is it, then, to gain all that at the expense of losing one's "life" in the deeper, eternal sense! If (v. 37) no amount of worldly wealth can be given in exchange for a further span of physical life,[16] how much less can it "buy" the eternal life that will be entirely the gift of God.

Continuing in eschatological vein, the final sentences (vv. 38-39) spell out the ultimate justification for embracing the costly life of discipleship. Those who reject this way—those, that is, who, captured by the values of the present "adulterous and sinful generation," find Jesus, his words, and his

---

14. We are close here to the principle laid out in the First Principle and Foundation standing at the head of the Ignatian *Spiritual Exercises* (§23).

15. Simon of Cyrene, constrained to carry the cross of Jesus after him to the place of crucifixion, will later (15:21) "model" this image.

16. The Greek word *antallagma* has the sense of something given in exchange for the acquisition of some goods in a commercial transaction; cf. BDAG 86. The thought is similar to that in Ps 49:7-9, 15.

fate "shameful"—will themselves be a source of shame to the Son of Man when he comes in the glory of his Father with the holy angels (v. 38); before that full heavenly court he will in turn reject them. Jesus, who has referred to himself as "Son of Man" in relation to his Passion and death (v. 31), now does so in relation to his coming as eschatological judge (the event I have referred to as "Story 3," appearing here in the narrative for the first time). The expression "in the glory of my Father" implies on his part the sense of divine sonship already declared after his baptism (1:11) and soon to be confirmed at the transfiguration (9:7). That divine status may now be hidden as he pursues his costly way. It will be revealed in all its glory when the heavenly court appears on earth for the final reckoning (14:62).

What Jesus states here is the negative case—what those who have been "ashamed" of him will face. The threat, however, implies a positive counterpart: those who have "lost their (physical) lives" for the sake of Jesus and the Gospel (v. 35) will "save" their lives in the deeper sense. The Son of Man, of whom they have not been ashamed, will vouch for them at the heavenly court as worthy to share the eternal life to which he has been raised (cf. 13:24-27).

The inclusion of "and the Gospel" (v. 35) in the cause for which they have lost their lives is a significant Markan detail. It makes the point that discipleship involves not only union with Christ but commitment to his cause, a cause destined to continue after his own physical departure from the scene. Taking up his proclamation of the Rule of God that is ousting the grip of Satan (1:14-15) will inevitably involve suffering.[17] The present order of things is an "adulterous and sinful generation" (v. 37) since it reflects the values and structures of that hostile allegiance. It will not surrender its hold without exacting a cost—a cost supremely shown in the Passion of Jesus and one that continues in the sufferings, at times to the point of death, of all those who proclaim the Gospel and seek to realize its values in the human sphere.

The final statement of this sequence (9:1) has long caused difficulty in that Jesus' assertion about the arrival of the Kingdom before "some of those present" were to die has clearly not been borne out in fact (cf. also his stated "ignorance" about the timing of "that day" in 13:32). It is best understood not as prediction of particular events but as an assurance, couched in terms of prophetic exaggeration, that, whatever cost discipleship may demand at the present time, the vindication just outlined will, through God's faithfulness,

---

17. See especially Nineham, *Saint Mark*, 227–28.

most certainly take place.[18] That will be the moment when the Kingdom, at present hidden and seemingly unfruitful in many ways (cf. chapter 4) will be displayed "in power." In terms of the formulation I have been using in this interpretation of Mark's gospel the tension created by the placing of Story 2 alongside Story 1 finds resolution in the prospect of the vindication announced in Story 3.

God's Beloved Son Revealed: The Transfiguration: 9:2-8

With the mysterious episode traditionally known as "the transfiguration" we arrive at the midpoint of Mark's gospel. It is the second of three scenes in which Jesus is declared to be God's Son, the first occurring after his baptism (1:11), the third on the lips of the centurion immediately after his death (15:39). As I explained in the short chapter devoted to the design of Mark, these three moments of revelation are the "pillars" on which the entire narrative rests. What is more, each follows a description of or allusion to Jesus' obedient entrance at depth into the human situation alienated from God.[19] The first follows his submission, along with the mass of repentant Israelites, to baptism at the hands of John (1:9). The transfiguration follows his first announcement that he is to suffer and die (8:31). The third and final declaration is a reaction to his death, which has just occurred. In each of these "pillars," then, the mysterious interplay of Story 1 and Story 2 emerges plainly. It is as the One who has obediently made a costly entrance into the depths of the human condition that Jesus is revealed as Messiah and Son of God.

The transfiguration is, then, a revelation of Jesus' full identity made to Peter, James, and John, the inner group of three disciples who have seen his power over death displayed in the raising of Jairus' daughter (5:37) and who will later witness his anguished wrestling with the "cup" that lies before him in Gethsemane (14:33). They will experience the revelation on the mountain, but they will not understand it. As readers we will watch them in this new phase of their halting journey from "blindness" to some measure of vision.

---

18. So Hooker, *Saint Mark,* 212, who also provides a helpful survey and critique of suggested interpretations (pp. 211–12). A widespread view holds that for Mark at least the assurance made in 9:1 receives at least partial fulfillment in the experience of Peter, James, and John in the scene of the transfiguration that follows. But, as Hooker points out, the fact that this experience occurs only a week later renders absurd the solemnity of Jesus' assurance about "some" not "tasting death" before undergoing it (p. 212).

19. Cf. Dorothy Lee, *Transfiguration,* New Century Theology (London and New York: Continuum, 2004) 24–30.

The episode itself is richly laden with symbolism, though there is little agreement on the meaning of many of the features that appear. In biblical thought mountains are natural locations for divine-human encounter; on mountains the air is "thin" in more senses than one.[20] The indication of time, "after six days" (v. 2), ties the episode to the preceding instruction on the fate of Jesus and the cost of discipleship (8:27-38). It probably also alludes to Moses' ascent of Mount Sinai, where the glory of the Lord in the shape of a cloud settled upon the mountain for six days, after which, on the seventh day, the Lord addressed Moses from the cloud (Exod 24:13–25:1). Here on this mountain[21] before the eyes of the disciples Jesus undergoes a "metamorphosis" (Greek *metamorphē*), displayed particularly in the whiteness of his garments, something beyond human capacity to produce (v. 3). In Jewish literature "whiteness," particularly white apparel, denotes belonging to the heavenly/divine realm, while the Greek term *morphē* refers to the way in which the inner being of a person displays itself outwardly. Hence what is being described here is a transformation in which Jesus' divine status is outwardly disclosed.[22]

The appearance (v. 4) of "Elijah with Moses," both conversing with Jesus, lends a particular nuance to this revelation.[23] In the biblical tradition both figures enjoyed the unique privilege of converse with God on a mountain (Moses: Exod 33:11; 34:35; cf. Deut 34:10; Sir 45:5-6; Elijah: 1 Kgs 19:8-18). Both, following severe trials and persecution, experienced mysterious conclusions to their lives, which in Elijah's case explicitly (2 Kgs 2:9-11) and in Moses' case implicitly (Deut 34:5-6),[24] involved transport to the heavenly realm. Both were expected to play a role in the events associated with the final establishment of the Kingdom—either as precursor (Elijah: Mal 3:1; 4:5-6) or as model for an end-time prophetic figure (Moses: Deut

---

20. Ibid., 15.

21. The mountain is not specified, though it has traditionally been identified with Mount Tabor in central Galilee. Mount Hermon would be a more significant location, both in view of its height (cf. "high mountain" [v. 2c]) and its location, closer to the region (Caesarea Philippi) where the previous episode took place. Mark may leave the mountain unspecified in order to facilitate allusion to Mount Sinai, which of course makes no sense in terms of strict geography.

22. The transformation is, then, the reverse of what is said of Jesus in the Christ-hymn embedded in Phil 2:6-11: "Though he was in the *morphē* of God . . . he emptied himself, taking on the *morphē* of a slave" (vv. 6-7); Donahue and Harrington, *Mark,* 269.

23. Contrary to strict biblical chronology, Elijah is mentioned before Moses (contrast Matt 17:3; Luke 9:30) because of his importance in Mark's gospel.

24. Post-biblical Jewish tradition interpreted the information in Deut 34:5-6, that no trace of Moses' tomb was to be found, as indicating his "assumption" to heaven.

18:15-18). It is not clear which of these allusions is dominant here. My sense is that for Mark it is the first that is to be preferred. Moses and Elijah now converse with Jesus as once they conversed with Israel's God on Mount Sinai (Horeb).[25] Their presence and their converse in this sense reinforces what the transformation of Jesus' clothing already displays: that in his person the presence and power of God is interacting with human beings.[26]

Once again, as in 8:29, Peter speaks up (v. 5). His initial exclamation, "Rabbi, it is wonderful (*kalon*) for us to be here," hardly catches the true dignity of Jesus here being revealed. But "wonderful . . ." gives utterance to human longing for vision of God and communion with the divine; it is an experience of "consolation" in the highest degree. Where he does begin to falter, as Mark's comment about his ignorance suggests (v. 6a), is in his proposal to build "three tents" *(skēnai)* to accommodate each of the heavenly figures. This detail has, again, been variously interpreted,[27] but "tent" suggests a desire to retain the wonderful experience indefinitely by providing places where the three heavenly figures might dwell.[28] Peter has forgotten or else not truly "heard" Jesus' instruction about a costly "way" and a fate that lies ahead (8:31).

The overshadowing cloud (v. 7) signals the presence of God and prepares the way for a solemn, corrective declaration. Jesus is not just "Rabbi": No, "This is my Son, the beloved. Listen to him!" The full status of Jesus (Story 1), declared simply to him (and the reader) following his baptism (1:11), is now made known to the three disciples. But they are also to "listen" to what he has been saying and to what he will continue to say despite their failure to understand: that his immediate destiny is to suffer and die and rise again on the third day (8:31; 9:31-32; 10:32-34). This makes clear that Jesus is to undergo this fate (Story 2) not just as Messiah but as "Beloved Son." What God did not in the end require of Abraham—the sacrifice of his beloved only son (Isaac: Gen 22)—God will require of Godself for the salvation of the world (cf. Rom 8:32). This is the supreme issue with which the disciples will have to wrestle for the remainder of the gospel: how can Jesus be

25. The Greek expression *syllalountes* ("conversing") echoes Moses' *syllalein* with God in LXX Exod 34:35 (cf. Sir 45:5).

26. Contrary to what has often been maintained, the scene is not a resurrection appearance transferred back into the life of Jesus, nor, strictly speaking, is it an anticipation of the *parousia* of Jesus as Son of Man, since there is no suggestion of judgment or vindication of the elect (cf. 13:24-27). It is a momentary tearing aside of the "veil" between the divine and the human to reveal the true identity of Jesus.

27. For a critical review of the main proposals see Lee, *Transfiguration,* 19–21.

28. Cf. Gnilka, *Markus* 2:35; Moloney, *Gospel of Mark,* 179; Donahue and Harrington, *Mark,* 270; Lee, *Transfiguration,* 20.

Messiah—and indeed God's beloved Son—and yet be destined to die on a cross? The transfiguration, then, is not simply a revelation of Jesus' divine status; it is a revelation of the profound mystery lying at the heart of the Gospel: God's costly personal involvement in the evil of the world.

Contrary to Peter's bid to hold the experience, when the voice from the cloud has spoken, the vision disappears. The disciples look about but find themselves in the presence of "Jesus alone" (v. 8), the human Jesus familiar to them. Once again we experience Mark's penchant for ringing the changes on the divine and human with striking speed (cf. 4:35-41). But all has changed: even if the disciples still struggle to understand, we know that the narrative is taking us on a journey in which, without laying aside his divine status as God's Son but rather in obedience to that relationship, Jesus will enter most deeply into the pain and suffering of the world to set it free (10:45).[29]

The transfiguration remains, as I have said, a mysterious episode. But it is really about the closeness rather than the remoteness of God. The "thinness" of the divide between human and divine on the mountain reveals an equal thinness on the plain: a translucence of the divine that mystics see in everyday human life and that the sacraments of the church disclose. We will sometimes be with Jesus on the mountain, mostly on the plain; whatever we feel at any particular moment, we will never be truly far from the One who is the source of our life and our hope.

Down from the Mountain: "What about Elijah?": 9:9-13

As Jesus and the three disciples make their descent back to the plain we overhear a conversation between them. Characteristically, Jesus warns them to say nothing about the vision "until the Son of Man has risen from the dead" (v. 9). The glory they have witnessed is not to be divorced from the Passion and death that lie more immediately before him. The warning leaves the disciples puzzled about what "rising from the dead" might mean (v. 10). The idea of resurrection was abroad and debated in the Jewish world of the time, as the controversy with the Sadducees will show (12:18-27). Where it was accepted it came in the shape of expectation of a *general* resurrection of the dead (cf. Dan 12:1-2), not the raising of an individual preceding that event. The disciples, invoking the scribal tradition that Elijah must come "to restore all things" before the resurrection can take place (Mal 4:5 [LXX

---

29. Again, we are very close to the vision expressed in the Christ-hymn: Phil 2:6-11.

3:23]), ask where, then, the coming of that eschatological figure fits into the picture Jesus is outlining (v. 11).

In response Jesus reinterprets the scriptural traditions both in respect to Elijah and to himself. Elijah *has* already come in the shape of John the Baptist (v. 12a)—as the opening description of John (1:2-6) has hinted—and this Elijah/John the Baptist has already "put everything in order," not only through his preaching but also by prefiguring in his faithfulness and death (6:17-29) the fate of the One whose "way" he had prepared (1:2). Likewise there is scriptural warrant for the suffering and rejection of the Son of Man (v. 12b) if "one like a son of Man" in Dan 7:13-14 is taken in the sense of an individual who receives glory and dominion following faithfulness in great suffering. What the Scriptures foretold has already taken place in the experience of Elijah/John the Baptist, and will soon take place in the experience of Jesus as Son of Man.[30] Like Elijah and like John, Jesus will follow the pattern of vindication following faithfulness in suffering that Daniel foretold for the Son of Man. The eschatological "script" indicated in Scripture is on track and already under way.

Jesus Liberates a Possessed Boy
His Disciples Could Not Help: 9:14-29

As Jesus, with his three companions, rejoins the remaining disciples, a sharp reminder of Satan's continuing hold on the world immediately confronts him. In contrast with the earlier exorcism stories the focus in this one, in line with the overall theme of the second part of the gospel, is on the disciples' inability to remedy the situation: to assist in any way a father whose son is possessed by a very violent demon. They are impotent in the face of this evil because they belong to a "faithless generation" (v. 19), whereas, Jesus insists (v. 23), "all things are possible" to the one who has faith.[31] In touching dialogue with the father of the boy (v. 24) Jesus builds up the required context of faith. This enables the expulsion of the demon and the rescue of the boy from what, to the onlookers, appeared to be nothing short of death itself (v. 26).

---

30. Cf. Moloney, *Gospel of Mark*, 182, to whose discussion of this pericope in the light of Dan 7:13-14 I am much indebted.

31. Many interpreters find in this statement at least an initial reference to Jesus' own faith; so, e.g., Gnilka, *Markus* 2:48, 50; Hooker, *Saint Mark*, 224; Moloney, *Gospel of Mark*, 184. But ". . . the power that Jesus possesses is in virtue of his status as God's son and Messiah, not in virtue of any faith relationship to God" (Nineham, *Saint Mark*, 247). Jesus is exhorting the father to have faith.

While these are the major themes, the story in itself is rambling and complex.[32] Nonetheless, as with similar long narratives in Mark (notably the Gerasene demoniac [5:1-20]), there is a wealth of detail and other features that render it attractive and compelling. As readers we are immediately engaged by the anguish of the father as he describes at length the symptoms of his son's condition (v. 18)[33] and begs Jesus to exercise his compassion (v. 22b).[34] In the face of the violent reaction of the demon-possessed boy on seeing him, Jesus' response seems coolly clinical at first: "How long has he been like this?" (v. 21a). This draws from the father a second description of the boy's behavior that makes clear the utterly destructive nature of the demon in its attempts to burn or drown the boy (v. 22a; cf. 5:5, 13). Our sympathy comes to a peak as the father, grappling with Jesus' somewhat testy demand for faith (v. 23), cries out in anguish: "Lord, I believe; help my lack of faith" (v. 24). This cry, long a comfort to those struggling with faith, recognizes that Jesus is the solution to all aspects of the problem: not only does he have the power to cast out demons, he can also create the depth of faith required for channeling that power into the situation of need presently at hand. The father's faith may be small, but he is at least looking for help in the right direction.

The exorcism itself follows a pattern familiar from those described earlier in the gospel (1:21-28; 5:1-20). Jesus "rebukes" the "unclean spirit," commanding it to depart and never enter the child again (v. 25).[35] The demon does not go quietly: with a howl, it makes a final attempt to destroy the boy, rending him so severely as it departs (cf. 1:26) as to leave many with the

---

32. The crowd seems to arrive twice (v. 15 and v. 25); the "pathology" associated with the possession of the boy is twice described in detail (v. 18 and vv. 21b-22a); the scribes mentioned at the start (v. 14) play no further role. The unevenness is probably due to Mark's reliance on more than one tradition, or else on his introduction of the disciples and their incapacity into the basic miracle story tradition; see further Moloney, *Gospel of Mark*, 182–83, n. 50.

33. As has long been recognized (first in fact by Matthew: 17:15), what the boy is suffering from is a severe epileptic condition, regularly attributed in the ancient world to demonic possession. This attribution, now of course completely outmoded by medical science, requires sensitive handling so as not to add to the burdens and distress of sufferers and carers today; on the pastoral issue see further Donahue and Harrington, *Mark*, 281–82.

34. Literally "to have compassion *(splagchnistheis) on us*"; the plural first person pronoun indicates that the condition affects the whole family.

35. The narrative curiously suggests that Jesus begins to deal with the demon in response to the sight of a crowd that is gathering—as if the former crowd (vv. 14-15) had in the meantime disappeared. As in the case of the raising of Jairus' daughter, Jesus may want to cure the boy—in effect bring him back to life—in a domestic rather than a public situation (cf. 5:37).

impression that he is dead. Jesus takes him by the hand and raises him so that he "stands up" (v. 27). Once again, as in the case of Jairus' daughter (5:35-43), Jesus has reached into the realm of "uncleanness" and death. In a family context of faith he has grasped and drawn a young person from the grip of death, making him "stand up" to share his own risen life.[36]

Following a standard pattern in the gospel, there is a kind of denouement when the disciples "in the house" (v. 28) ask Jesus why they were unable to expel the demon. We might have expected, in view of its significance in the story so far, that his response would underline the necessity of faith. Instead, he speaks of prayer. The response is not all that surprising when we consider that prayer is a primary exercise of faith and an attempt to align one's life and activity completely with the design and power of God. We have seen Jesus retire to pray (1:35; 6:46) before renewing his ministry and the contest with Satan. If the disciples, when Jesus is in fact no longer (cf. v. 19c) with them, are to carry on his work of reclaiming people for the life of the Kingdom, the kind of access to the power of God that prayer creates will be indispensable (cf. Eph 6:10-20).

36. "The Christian language of resurrection rings out as the miracle story comes to a close" (Moloney, *Gospel of Mark,* 185).

The Disciples Instructed on the "Way": 9:30–10:52

Jesus now (v. 30a) begins the long journey south that will eventually bring him to Jerusalem. He passes through Galilee, the scene of his public ministry so far, but does so quietly. He avoids public notice to concentrate on what is now his chief task: the instruction of his disciples (vv. 30b-31a).

A Second Passion Prediction and a Lesson for the Disciples on Humble Service: 9:30-37

Once again the instruction bears upon the fate that awaits him as Son of Man (Story 2): that he will be given up[1] into the hands of men, be killed, and rise after three days (v. 31b). The disciples are still impervious to this truth and are "afraid to ask him about it" (v. 32). Half knowing what he is saying, in an understandable human way they shrink from full knowledge of the unpalatable truth. They prefer to cling to the exciting prospect for their future that being close associates of the Messiah (conventionally understood) would seem to entail.

An aspect of this has, in fact, been the subject of an argument they have been having "on the way" (vv. 33-34). They have been arguing about which of them is the greatest—and so first in line to enjoy a leading role in the coming messianic kingdom. Nothing could run more counter to what Jesus

---

1. As I remarked in connection with the "giving up" of John in 1:14, the Greek verb *paradidōmi* has a range of meanings including both "give up" and "betray," and so in the passive, as here, can include both the betrayal of Judas and the divine purpose ("divine passive") operative behind all the human agency in Jesus' Passion and death.

has been attempting to teach them. Hence their guilty, half-knowing silence when Jesus questions them in the house at Capernaum.

In response Jesus sits down (the posture of teaching), summons the Twelve—the leading group—and lays down the principle that must govern the exercise of leadership in his messianic community: the one who would be first must be last of all and servant *(diakonos)*[2] of all (v. 35). He dramatizes the lesson (v. 36) by taking a child from the house and setting it in front of them. He wraps his arms around the child and then makes an extraordinary statement of self-identification: "Whoever welcomes one such child in my name welcomes me, and whoever welcomes me, welcomes not me but the One who sent me" (v. 37).[3]

To grasp the full force of this action on Jesus' part we have to put aside the idealization of childhood that arose in the nineteenth century. In the ancient world children were precious, no doubt, to their parents, but they had no social status or value whatsoever; until adulthood they were nobodies.[4] For someone outside the family to "welcome" a child would be to turn prevailing values and social mores upside down; it would require putting aside all one's ideas of self-importance and adult status to simply meet the child as an equal, as "child" to child. That, says Jesus, is what the disciples must "practice." In so doing they will be welcoming him, and not only him but the Father who stands behind his entire life and mission, which is not one of dominance and being served but one of service, destined to culminate in the supreme "service" *(diakonia)* of giving his life as a ransom for many (10:45).

It is hard to exaggerate the significance of this gesture of divine identification with a child. Not only does it challenge the disciples' notion of messiahship, it goes to the heart of their—and our—understanding of God. Is God to be thought of as a kind of extraterrestial Ruler to whom nothing but fear and service is due? Or is the God revealed by Jesus a God whose primary gesture toward human beings is that of One who serves, One who comes among us in the guise of a child? Jesus' gesture of hugging the child

2. A *diakonos* in Greek is basically one who conveys something to someone on behalf of a third party. In a parallel passage in Mark 10:41-45 Jesus will describe his mission as not one of being served *(diakonēthēnai)* but of serving *(diakonein)*.

3. This statement could perhaps be more appropriately located in Jesus' second instruction involving children in 10:13-16, that is, after 10:14, while the statement about receiving the Kingdom as a little child (10:15) would be appropriate in the present instruction, replacing 9:37 (as in the Matthean parallel: 18:1-5). Hooker, *Saint Mark,* 228, suggests that the sayings may have been accidentally reversed during the oral stage of the tradition. Nonetheless, both pericopes make good sense as they stand.

4. Cf. Gnilka, *Markus* 2:57; Donahue and Harrington, *Mark,* 285.

in front of all shows more powerfully than any words could express the preciousness of each and every human life in the sight of God, no matter how small, how insignificant. We are all—in our "littleness" rather than our achievement—hugged by God in this moment.

The lesson, the challenge to worldly values and estimation, that the disciples found so difficult confronts the church in every age. After the early centuries of persecution, at the time of Constantine (early fourth century C.E.) the church emerged from the catacombs to take on many of the trappings and roles of Roman officials. We are now witnessing the end of that "Constantinian church" in which leaders were accorded honors and symbols of rank more reflective of worldly power than the values of Jesus, and where the institution itself was built into the fabric of society. The pain that goes along with the loss of status and honor is perhaps akin to that experienced by the disciples of Jesus as they struggled both to hear and to resist what he was saying. Like them, we are all on the way to Jerusalem with Jesus.

Good Outside the Community; Scandals Within: 9:38-50

At this point the gospel presents Jesus instructing or correcting his disciples on a number of topics that at first sight seem rather disconnected. Closer inspection reveals that the particular instructions link with each other through a number of terms or phrases they have in common: "name" (vv. 37, 38, 41); "children/little ones" (vv. 37, 42); "stumble" (vv. 42, 43-47); "fire" (vv. 48, 49); "salt" (vv. 49, 50).[5] The connections presumably served as an aide-memoire for catechists in the oral stage of the tradition. Though the connections and hence the flow of thought are in this respect artificial, the overall sequence falls into two main sections: the instructions in vv. 38-41 deal with good *outside* the community, while vv. 42-50 warn against severe consequences of evil (scandal) *within*.

John, the son of Zebedee, singled out as an individual on this sole occasion and, like Peter in 8:29, speaking in the name of all, draws attention to the fact that when the disciples saw someone using Jesus' name to cast out devils they sought to stop him. They took this action because "he was not one of us" (v. 38). Instead of the approval they probably expected for this action, what the disciples receive from Jesus is a mild rebuke (v. 39). He does not mind his name being used by another for a good purpose; such a person is unlikely to speak badly about him (v. 40a). The main thing is that human beings are being set free from the power of Satan and reclaimed

---

5. See Taylor, *St. Mark,* 409, for a comprehensive setting out of this pattern.

for the fullness of life associated with the coming of the Kingdom.[6] The disciples' action, on the contrary, shows them to be less focused on the objective good being done and more concerned about an outsider's use of what they see as their own prerogative and possession: the "brand name" of Jesus.

After a more general maxim (v. 40), Jesus reinforces the lesson by pointing to outsiders who give members of the community (possibly traveling missionaries are particularly in view) a cup of water to drink "because they belong to Christ"[7] (v. 41). Such outsiders show the kind of service to others that is supposed to be a hallmark of the followers of Jesus. What determines the "reward" one will receive (at the judgment) is not whether one is inside or outside the community but whether one has performed the service expected of the community.

Taken together, both elements of Jesus' instruction show a remarkable openness to the possibility of goodness and effective ministry outside the community of disciples strictly so defined. They invite the disciples to look away from their own sense of distinctiveness and privilege and be prepared to find and rejoice in goodness wherever it exists. This is not to play down the importance of being associates of Jesus. It is simply to insist that what is supremely important about such belonging is being prepared for costly service rather than resting on privilege and power.

So much for *good* found *outside* the community. The remaining instructions (vv. 42-50), in a balancing way, take up the issue of *evil* that may exist *inside* the community. Any community consists of strong and weak, people whose faith is mature and people whose faith is still growing. "These little ones" (v. 42) are either children or else simply the more vulnerable in the latter sense: those whose faith—and hence salvation—can be "scandalized," that is, placed in jeopardy by bad example or exploitative behavior on the part of the stronger members.[8] Presupposed is a sense to which Paul gives memorable expression: "The life and death of each of us has its influence on others" (Rom 14:7 [Jerusalem Bible translation]). The sense that wrong-

6. Numbers 11:25-29 offers an instructive biblical precedent for this episode. It tells of a similarly misguided response on the part of Joshua when two individuals (Eldad and Medad), who were not numbered among the designated seventy elders appointed to assist Moses, manifest the same spirit of prophecy the seventy had shown. The large-heartedness of Moses stands out in contrast.

7. The unique reference to "Christ" in the sense of a surname for Jesus reflects the usage of the later Christian community.

8. "To scandalize" (Greek *skandalizein*) in the biblical sense is literally to place an obstacle *(skandalon)* in a person's way to cause that individual to fall. Here the sense is to fall away from the community of salvation.

doing ought be a community concern rather than simply a private affair accounts for the severity of the alternative that Jesus, with prophetic exaggeration, suggests would be better: being tied to a large stone and thrown into the sea.[9]

The following statements (vv. 43-48),[10] commending sacrifice of various parts of the body (hand [v. 43], foot [v. 45], eye [v. 47]),[11] continue the "cause to stumble" theme but focus on the effect on the agent (the person giving scandal) rather than on those affected by it. What seems to be in mind is a surgical operation in which a diseased limb is sacrificed in order to save the whole body.[12] Jesus applies the principle involved—the sacrifice of a part in order to save the whole—to the gain or loss of eternal life (entry "into the kingdom of God" [v. 47]). The drastic measures suggested are clearly not meant to be carried out in a literal sense, but the prophetic sharpness of tone and in particular the reiterated mention of the negative fate—entrance into "Gehenna" with its unquenchable fire (reinforced at the end by a quotation from Isa 66:24)—are challenging for modern readers.[13] Jesus must be allowed to speak out of the apocalyptic worldview that was the background of his preaching and with a prophetic sharpness derived from the seriousness of the issues at stake. Rather than concentrating solely on the negative, however, it is important to see what is being so strongly *affirmed:* the supreme value of life in the Kingdom of God.[14] One's own salvation and that of other members of the community is of such overriding importance that

9. The Greek phrase *mylos onikos* (literally: "millstone of a donkey") refers to the large upper stone on a mill that would have been turned by a donkey. Drowning by attaching a large stone to a person was a Roman form of execution.

10. Verses 44 and 46, which duplicate after vv. 43 and 45 the quotation from Isa 66:24 in v. 48, are missing in several early manuscripts and are generally regarded as unoriginal; cf. Donahue and Harrington, *Mark,* 288.

11. The choice of limbs may be influenced by Job 5:1 (hand), 5 (foot), 7 (eyes).

12. Also possibly in view is Roman penal practice whereby a person under sentence of death could save his or her life by opting instead to suffer various forms of mutilation.

13. "Gehenna" referred originally to the Valley of Hinnom, situated southwest of Jerusalem. A place of forbidden pagan worship during the early monarchical period, under the reforming King Josiah it became the city's garbage dump. The fact that fires burned there continuously led to its becoming a byword for the place where the wicked would be consigned for destruction. It is important to note that in Jesus' image it is the fire that is continuous ("unquenchable"), not the punishment; the wicked, once consigned to Gehenna, simply cease to exist; cf. Moloney, *Gospel of Mark,* 191, n. 94. "Gehenna" and especially the references in the present passage to "fires" should not, then, be simply identified with the traditional Christian understanding of Hell, which in any case has been the subject of considerable theological reinterpretation in recent years; see further Anthony Kelly, *Eschatology and Hope* (New York: Maryknoll, 2006).

14. Cf. Gnilka, *Markus* 2.66; Moloney, *Gospel of Mark,* 191.

one must be prepared to act vigorously against immediate self-interest or temptation in order not to lose it.

The added statements about fire and salt (vv. 49-50) are among the most puzzling in the New Testament; their meaning may have been lost beyond retrieval.[15] The reference to salt may stem from its use as a purifying and preserving agent, and "fire" may be a metaphor for the trials of persecution or the increased distress expected as a prelude to the final triumph of God's rule. If, as in Matthew 5:13, "salt" refers to the quality of the community as distinct from the way of life of the surrounding world, the sense of "everything will be salted in fire" may be that the fire of persecution will severely test the quality of the community and require the kind of sacrifice outlined in the preceding warning (vv. 43-48). The final injunction (v. 50c-d) may then have the sense of: if you maintain that quality of life, with all the sacrifice it entails, you will, despite all, live in peace with one another; there will be no "scandalizing" of the little ones (v. 42).

On Marriage and Divorce: 10:1-12

Having now left Galilee, Jesus continues his journey south into Judea, taking a route east of the Jordan river (v. 1a).[16] His presence attracts crowds and he begins again to teach them "as was his custom" (v. 1b). The report of this more general teaching (presumably announcing the Kingdom [1:14-15]) comes as something of a surprise since his main concern now, we have been told (9:30-31a), is to instruct his immediate disciples. For the same reason the question about divorce that some Pharisees[17] now introduce to test him (v. 2) might well have found a place during the Galilean ministry before the "watershed" scene at Caesarea Philippi (8:27-30). After the discussion with the Pharisees there is, as so often in Mark (cf. 4:10; 9:28), a more private scene of instruction for the disciples (vv. 10-12), so that in this sense the whole episode follows that model. A similar pattern will recur in the teaching about wealth and other attachments prompted by the inquiry of the rich man

---

15. For a good discussion see Hooker, *Saint Mark,* 233.

16. Mark's geographical reference is, as so often, vague and textually uncertain. I have adopted the suggestion that Jesus is depicted as taking a route south that avoids passing through Samaria; for other possibilities see Donahue and Harrington, *Mark,* 292 and, in exhaustive detail, Taylor, *St. Mark,* 416–17.

17. Explicit reference to "Pharisees" is wanting in some early manuscripts, leading some scholars to see it as an import from Matt 10:3. However, the Pharisees have not faded from the scene and will return to "test" Jesus again, along with the Herodians, in the controversy about payment of tax to Caesar (12:13).

(10:17-31). Both sections of the gospel bear upon areas of human life—fidelity within marriage and detachment from wealth—that set the standards required in the community of the Kingdom far beyond those of surrounding society, whether it be the Palestine of Jesus' day, the wider Greco-Roman milieu of the time when the gospel was written, or that of its readers today. Both touch on aspects of life in which the cost of discipleship that Jesus has been making clear to his disciples (8:31-32, 34-35; 9:31) moves from theory, so to speak, to practice.[18] In this sense both find an appropriate place in this section of the gospel, where instruction of the disciples is the main concern.

The Law of Moses made provision for divorce, albeit solely on the initiative of a husband, who was allowed to send away his wife with a bill of divorce if he found her displeasing in some respect (Deut 24:1). What was at issue in the Judaism of Jesus' day was not the legality of divorce per se but the grounds on which a husband might claim to find his wife displeasing and so justify her dismissal.[19] When the Pharisees, then, approach Jesus and question him about the legality of divorce as such (v. 2), they would appear to be operating out of prior knowledge that he excludes it[20] and so, as the remark about "testing him" suggests, are setting a trap for him: they want to expose him as setting himself in opposition to the Mosaic Law.

Jesus is more than a match for their ploy. He asks them to state what Moses "commanded" *(eneteilato)* them (v. 3). In reply they cite what Moses "allowed" *(epetrepsen),* citing Deuteronomy 24:1 ("to write a bill of dismissal and divorce [her]"). The distinction between the two verbs is crucial. Jesus has trapped them into an explicit admission that the whole matter of divorce was not something Moses "commanded" but something merely "allowed."[21] That is, the Mosaic Law took divorce as a fact of life and instituted what, in modern terms, we would call a "harm minimization procedure" in the sense of seeking to protect the rights of the woman, who might otherwise be suspected of infidelity.[22] In Jesus' eyes the Mosaic "concession"

18. Cf. Nineham, *Saint Mark,* 260n; Moloney, *Gospel of Mark,* 192–93.

19. The issue was a classic case of conflict between the school of Shammai, taking a stricter line in regard to the grounds, and that of Hillel, taking a more liberal position. The whole situation is set out with admirable clarity in Donahue and Harrington, *Mark,* 296–97. In the Matthean parallel (19:1-12) the Pharisees attempt to draw Jesus into this controversy rather than to engage him on the issue of the legality of divorce as such.

20. Cf. Gnilka, *Markus* 2:71; Moloney, *Gospel of Mark,* 194; Donahue and Harrington, *Mark,* 293, 295.

21. Cf. Donahue and Harrington, *Mark,* 293.

22. The main intent of the Deuteronomic legislation, as shown in Deut 24:2-4, was actually to prevent abuse, when a man sought to take back a wife he had dismissed and who had become the wife of another man who had also dismissed her.

in this regard reflects a fallen dispensation in which "hardness of heart" prevails (v. 5)—a "hardness" seen in the measure (bill of dismissal) instituted to protect women from the heartless operation of a custom slanted entirely toward the will and pleasure of the man. That "hardness of heart" is characteristic of the human state of affairs that the Rule of God is seeking to displace in the interests of establishing the original design of the Creator. Hence Jesus' appeal (vv. 6-8) to the account of creation (Genesis 1–2) where that original design is set forth. God made them "male and female" (Gen 1:27) and "for that reason[23] a man will leave his father and mother (and will be joined to his wife)[24] and the two will become one flesh" (vv. 7-8). Jesus, then, excludes divorce on the grounds that "what God (in creation) has put together, man must not divide" (v. 9). Over against the Mosaic legislation designed to lessen harm within a sinful dispensation biased toward the male partner, Jesus, in the name of the Kingdom, has reinstated the original vision in which marriage means an indivisible union of mutual companionship. He has not, as his adversaries hoped, been trapped into setting aside the Mosaic Law.[25] Rather, he has authoritatively reinterpreted it in the light of the original will of the Creator set forth in Genesis (of which Moses, in the prevailing understanding, was also the author).

The private instruction later given to the disciples (vv. 10-12) takes the issue somewhat further. In response to their query Jesus indicates that divorce followed by remarriage leads to infringement of the commandment against adultery.[26] In the Jewish understanding a woman could commit adultery against her husband and he could commit adultery against another man (by taking his wife), but since a wife was considered the property of her husband he could not, strictly speaking, be guilty of adultery against her. Against this bias in favor of the man Jesus raises the dignity of the woman by stating that in divorcing and remarrying he does commit adultery against her (v. 11). His second ruling, as recorded in verse 12, also raises her social status, albeit in the negative case, by envisaging a situation in which a woman might initiate

---

23. Jesus relates the explanation in Gen 2:24 to the first creation story in 1:27 rather than to the story of the creation of the woman from the rib of the man, as in Gen 2:21-24 as a whole; cf. Nineham, *Saint Mark,* 265.

24. This part of the quotation from Gen 2:24 is normally considered to have accidentally dropped out of the manuscript tradition; cf. Hooker, *Saint Mark,* 236.

25. Cf. Hooker, *Saint Mark,* 235.

26. Cf. Moloney: ". . . Jesus' words to his disciples show how disobedience to his interpretation of Torah leads to the breaking of Torah" (*Gospel of Mark,* 195).

a divorce—something not foreseen in the Jewish Law but allowed in the Roman milieu of the gospel.[27]

The overall instruction Jesus is recorded as giving here is so counter-cultural, not only in respect to its original setting but also to society today, that it is understandably heard more in terms of what it prohibits (divorce) than what it commends. But it is unfortunate if the negative note on which it ends (vv. 11-12) leads to a neglect of the positive and, in terms of his own society, innovative character of Jesus' teaching on marriage, in which the union of two in "one flesh" is simply the most intimate expression of a com-mitment, companionship, and intimacy embracing the totality of life. At the same time it is an undeniable fact that most congregations who hear the Gospel today will include a considerable proportion of people in second marriages or people affected by family members in that situation. In many if not most cases that situation will have come about through circumstances beyond their control or from which they cannot now responsibly free them-selves. To simply read out the rulings of Jesus in the Gospel without com-ment or nuance would be to turn Gospel into law and only add to a burden of guilt that may already be oppressive.

It does seem clear from the New Testament record that Jesus did rule out divorce and remarriage for the community he was forming as a beach-head of the Kingdom in the world.[28] At the same time, interpretation of his ruling must take several factors into account. First, life expectancy in the ancient world was less than half that prevailing in developed Western socie-ties today; marriages were rarely required to last much beyond twenty years before death did them part. Second, Jesus and the early community lived in the expectation that the world as then constituted was soon—perhaps in the very same generation—going to pass away (cf. Mark 9:1; 13:32). In such a situation contemplation of a second marriage is a very different proposition from what it is in societies in which people live much longer and where the sense prevails that the present shape of the world is going to be around in-definitely. Already in Matthew's gospel we see in the recording of Jesus' rulings on divorce (5:32; 19:9) some movement toward accommodation to new situations in which believers found themselves (cf. also 1 Cor 7:10-16). Moreover, the reality is that people make mistakes and relationships fail—something that longer lifespan and the high premium currently placed on personal freedom and development make more prevalent. While remaining faithful to the ideal taught by Jesus in the name of the Kingdom, the church

27. Cf. Donahue and Harrington, *Mark,* 295.
28. Cf. ibid., 297.

has to find a way to help people grow through failure, to find in it an experience of grace and deepened knowledge of God.[29]

Receiving the Kingdom as a Little Child: 10:13-16

Jesus' blessing of children follows naturally from the preceding discussion about marriage and, by implication, family life. But it also continues his instruction of the disciples who, once again, get something wrong. When people bring their children to Jesus for him to touch them—that is, for a blessing (v. 13a)—the disciples, acting as his "minders," try to shoo them away (v. 13b). They seem not to remember his embracing a child not long before and insisting that in welcoming a child they were welcoming him (9:36-37). Hence, presumably, the indignation with which he rebukes the disciples on this occasion (v. 14a). The children are not to be "prevented" from approaching him (v. 14b-c), for "of such is the kingdom of God" (v. 14d).

This explanation renders the incident an occasion for teaching about the nature of the Kingdom. Children cannot earn, or perform any useful work. Any benefit they receive can only come to them as pure gift. If, then, children are the paradigm recipients of the Kingdom, this means that it comes to everyone as pure, unmerited gift from God.[30] When Jesus summons people to "repent and believe in the good news" of the Kingdom (1:15), he is laying down the only condition for receiving it: a conversion of heart to believe that God is so good, so generous as to give the Kingdom—and all the blessings it entails—freely and without measure. That is how children receive gifts and that is how they "model" receiving the Kingdom. The added warning (v. 15) looks to the future, when the Kingdom is also something to "enter": that is, the "banquet of life" that is God's ultimate intention for human beings. It is only by receiving the Kingdom now as a child receives—that is, as pure gift—that one will be in line to enter into that final state when what one has of the Kingdom here and now (the renewed relationship with God) is extended to all other aspects of life.[31]

---

29. See further the sensitive reflections on this problem offered by Pheme Perkins, "Gospel of Mark," *New Interpreter's Bible* 8:646.

30. Cf. Donahue and Harrington, *Mark,* 301. The authors rightly warn against "careless theological discourse" (one might include phraseology of some popular folk hymns) referring to "our building up or bringing in the kingdom of God."

31. In this way Jesus' statements about the Kingdom here (vv. 14-15) bring out both the present and the future aspects of it in his preaching; cf. Hooker, *Saint Mark,* 239; Gnilka, *Markus* 2:81.

Jesus rounds off the "lesson" (v. 16) by more than amply fulfilling the original request: beyond merely touching the children (v. 13) he blesses them by enveloping them in his arms (cf. 9:36). The gesture illustrates perfectly the point he has been making. In their—doubtless delighted—reception of this free, loving embrace from the One who personally embodies the Kingdom, the children show how it is to be received by all.[32] Once again (cf. 9:36-37), to believe the "good news" is to be "hugged" by God.

Treasure on Earth or in Heaven: Riches and the Kingdom: 10:17-31

As Jesus continues his way (v. 17) the instruction he gives his disciples focuses once again (cf. 10:1-12) on a practical issue. A long sequence bears upon the question of possessions in relation to following Jesus and, indeed, entry into the Kingdom. The issue is sharply raised by the episode in which attachment to wealth prevents a rich man from achieving what he most deeply desires (vv. 17-22). This is followed once again by private instruction on the issue for the benefit of the disciples (vv. 23-27). Finally and more positively, the disciples, who have left everything to follow Jesus, are assured that they will not lack a deeper and more lasting "wealth" (vv. 28-31).

a. A Rich Man Goes Away Sad: 10:17-22

The account of the rich man[33] who approaches Jesus to ask what he must do to inherit eternal life (vv. 17-22) is yet another example of a Markan narrative rich in detail and human interest. We sense the eagerness of the man as he runs up to the journeying Jesus, falls on his knees and breathlessly, we may suppose, puts his question. Gaining eternal life is more or less a synonym for entry into the Kingdom of God. The man presumes that there is something he must "do" to gain it and he looks to this "good teacher" to tell him what it is.

Jesus, like the "good teacher" that in fact he is, does not give the man a simple answer but begins to explore the issue with him at a deeper level. He appears to bristle at the epithet "good," insisting that it applies to God alone (v. 18). He is not so much deflecting goodness from himself[34] as at-

---

32. Cf. Nineham, *Saint Mark,* 268; Gnilka, *Markus* 2:81.

33. In Mark's account (contrast Matt 19:20) the man is not said to be young; his protestation in v. 20 might suggest a certain advance in years. Note also that it is only at the very end (v. 22c), and with considerable dramatic effect, that we learn that he is wealthy.

34. The implications for christology have long troubled interpreters: see the lengthy review of proposed solutions set out in Taylor, *St. Mark,* 426–27; more recently Moloney, *Gospel of Mark,* 199, n. 144.

tempting to focus the man's attention away from what *he* must *do*[35] and onto the goodness and generosity of God, which will be the main consideration in the answer eventually given. Jesus then (v. 19) begins to list the commandments that the man, as a devout Jew, should "know." The items listed are the "social" commandments—those dealing with the neighbor.[36] All of them except the last (the fourth commandment dealing with duties to one's parents) list what one must *not* do. This, if it does not entirely convey a rather negative impression of the Torah way of life, at least suggests a gap waiting to be filled more positively. Hence we are not all that surprised when the man protests that he has kept all these things since his youth (v. 20), clearly implying that he is looking for something more.

The sense of emptiness in the man's life prepares the way for the invitation Jesus now sets before him (v. 21). In a detail peculiar to Mark we are told that before issuing the invitation Jesus "looking at him, loved him."[37] It is unnecessary to think that Jesus loves him because he has kept the commandments.[38] Rather, what is expressed here is the divine love that precedes and stands behind all vocations.[39] Jesus is calling the man to a way of life proceeding from and resting on intimate personal relationship with himself. The man, according to Jesus, is "wanting in one thing," but that one thing is, in a sense, everything. Instead of seeking to know what more he must *"do"* while basically retaining the present direction of his life (v. 17), the man is invited to a total transformation of life.

The first step in this transformation is to radically fulfill his obligation to the neighbor (cf. the "social commandments" listed in v. 19) by selling all he possesses and giving the proceeds to the poor (v. 21b). Wealth purports to be the best source of security in this life.[40] Abandoning it will mean loss of that security. But abandoning wealth in the way Jesus recommends (giv-

---

35. Cf. Moloney, *Gospel of Mark,* 198: "The question, 'What must I do?' is the wrong question."

36. To the list of prohibitions derived from the "Ten Commandments" in Exod 20:12-16 Jesus adds a further one, "Do not defraud," which has an exact verbal parallel in Sir 4:1 (cf. also Deut 24:14), where the context is that of a warning against taking advantage of the vulnerable situation of the poor—a temptation to which the wealthy would be particularly open (cf. Jas 5:4). Along with its relevance in the present context, the prohibition adds a socioeconomic dimension to the interchange; cf. Boring, *Mark,* 295.

37. The verb may imply that Jesus made his affection palpable through a gesture of some kind.

38. A standard explanation: cf., e.g., Donahue and Harrington, *Mark,* 303.

39. Cf. Gnilka, *Markus* 2:87.

40. Cf. Nineham: "For a man [*sic*] to give away his wealth, if it is great, is terribly difficult because it means depriving himself of the resources on which he has come to rely for status, security, interest, and enjoyment in life" (*Saint Mark,* 271).

ing it to the poor) simply transfers it into a far more secure "bank," a heavenly one, so that he will have "treasure in heaven." That is, security will now rest on the faithfulness and generosity of the "good" God (v. 18), the only security that reaches beyond this present life to transcend the barrier of death.

Divested of the dubious source of security provided by wealth, the man will be free to join Jesus ("and then come, follow me" [v. 21d]) in the way of life that is his, with the radical trust in the Father's goodness that is its base and inspiration.[41] Trusting God in this absolute sense, he will be open to receiving the Kingdom like a child (10:15): that is, as pure gift. He will be on the way to "entering" the kingdom of God, obtaining eternal life in accord with his original wish.

While the contrast with the man's path up to this point, following the way of the Torah, should not be overstated, the invitation he receives clearly involves crossing a threshold: from a way of life centered on the Torah and its commandments to one centered totally on the person of Jesus. Once again, as so often in Mark, we are very close to the theology of Paul.

> . . . whatever gains I had, these I have come to regard as loss because of Christ. More than that, I regard everything as loss because of the surpassing value of knowing Christ Jesus my Lord. For his sake I have suffered the loss of all things, and I regard them as rubbish, in order that I may gain Christ and be found in him, not having a righteousness of my own that comes from the law, but one that comes through faith in Christ, the righteousness from God based on faith. (Phil 3:7-9)

Sadly, the man balks at the invitation and goes away (v. 22), his disappointment patent in his downcast looks. What he sought with such eagerness (v. 17) he cannot win because the pull of his "many possessions" holds him captive. Unlike the man in an earlier incident (9:14-29) who, knowing his lack of the required faith, turned more insistently to Jesus ("Lord, I believe; help my unbelief" [v. 24]), he makes the fatal mistake of taking his eyes off Jesus and the relationship being offered, and thinks only of his wealth and his own incapacity to let go of it. He retains his wealth—and whatever security it may for a time offer—but in place of the joy and freedom he might have known in loving companionship with Jesus he has the sadness of knowing he is trapped, controlled, prevented from gaining his deepest desire. In this subtle way the demonic has its grip on him.

---

41. Jesus is, in effect, stating the conditions for following him in the itinerant missionary lifestyle commended in the instructions given to those sent on mission in 6:7-13; cf. Donahue and Harrington, *Mark*, 307.

b. How Riches Get in the Way: 10:23-31

The episode with the rich man is the only occasion in the gospel when Jesus' call proves ineffective (contrast 1:18, 20; 2:14). Jesus lets the man go; love does not control. But the unhappy outcome prompts him to gather his disciples[42] and make a more general reflection (vv. 23-27) on the difficulty wealth creates for entrance into the kingdom of God (v. 23b). When the disciples express "amazement" at this (v. 24a)—wealth was generally considered a sign of God's favor and blessing (cf. Deut 28:1-14; Job 42:12)—Jesus drives home the point with an exclamation: "How difficult it is (for anyone) to enter the Kingdom of God!" (v. 24b) and then intensifies it still further in regard to the rich with the highly arresting (and probably proverbial) saying about a camel passing through the eye of a needle (v. 25).[43] The disciples, even more staggered at this (v. 26), understandably conclude that what Jesus is saying is tantamount to making salvation (that is, entrance into the Kingdom) impossible: "Who then can be saved?" (v. 26).[44] This climactic sense of "impossibility" from the human point of view enables Jesus to drive home the fundamental truth: if human resources alone are looked to, the impossibility stands, but that is not the end of the matter, for "all things are possible with God" (v. 27).[45] The "good" God (v. 18) who gives the Kingdom as pure, unmerited gift (10:14-15) will also supply to human beings the capacity to adopt the costly lifestyle it presently requires. The rich man failed because he looked only to the sacrifice *he* would have to make. He did not grasp that in the context of the love and companionship (with Jesus) to which he was being invited he might have found himself given the capacity not so much to "do" as to *live* "the impossible."[46]

---

42. This is the effect of the participle "looking about" *(periblepsamenos)* with which the section begins (v. 23).

43. On attempts to rationalize this saying, see the wise observation of Morna Hooker: "It is only the extraordinary inability of commentators to appreciate the hyperbole and humour in the illustration that has led them to suggest that the camel *(kamēlos)* should be reduced in size to a rope *(kamilos . . .)* or that the eye of a needle should be enlarged to an imaginary gate in the wall of Jerusalem" *(Saint Mark,* 242–43).

44. Cf. Donahue and Harrington: "If the rich who have leisure to observe God's commandments and the resources to give alms find it difficult to be saved, how much more difficult must it be for everyone else!" *(Mark,* 304–05).

45. The phrase echoes the angelic visitor's response to Abraham in Gen 18:14 (also Rom 4:18-21); cf. also the similar assurance of Gabriel to Mary at the Annunciation: Luke 1:37.

46. Here, again, Mark's gospel aligns with Paul: salvation begins and ends with the grace of God (Rom 1:16-17; 5:17; 10:12-13; etc.).

This extremely challenging sequence concludes (vv. 28-31) on a hopeful note.[47] Peter, once more speaking for the group of disciples, points out that, unlike the rich man, *they* have left all things and followed Jesus. In response, Jesus makes a solemn and lengthy assurance (vv. 29-30). He lists in detail all that members of the community have left behind for his sake and that of the Gospel,[48] and then offers a parallel list of what they will receive back a hundredfold in this present age before, in the age to come, receiving what the rich man sought: "eternal life." The lists of what has been left behind and what will be received a hundredfold in the present age are identical save for one significant item: among the family members in the second list, "father" does not appear. The members of Jesus' new family share with him one "Father": God.

The whole amounts to an extraordinary assertion that life in the community of the Kingdom will more than compensate for all the family life that has been sacrificed for the sake of the Gospel.[49] This is not because all will be sweetness and light; the otherwise intrusive inclusion of "persecutions" is a bracing reminder of the external reality with which the community has to cope. The "hundredfold" comes from the sense of being God's beloved sons and daughters, already living the relationships belonging to the Kingdom, in the sure hope of its final "possession" in the age to come. What will shine forth at that time will be a great reversal of the situation currently in place: those who are now "last" in the world's estimation (the community of the disciples) will find themselves "first," while those now "first" in prestige, power, and wealth will be last (v. 31).[50]

Despite its conclusion on a positive note, this section of Mark's gospel presents perhaps the most radical challenge for contemporary readers. Is entrance to the Kingdom of God barred to all save those prepared to sell all and leave all, including their families, in order to adopt the radical insecurity and itinerant lifestyle of Jesus and his first companions? Had all followers

47. Moloney, *Gospel of Mark,* 202.

48. In the list the more material goods, houses and fields, appearing at the beginning and end, enclose the familial: brothers, sisters, mother, father, and children.

49. If, in contrast to the prevailing pessimism of Jewish apocalypticism, the Christian community can find something positive in "this age" ("the hundredfold"), this is because the community itself constitutes already in this age a beachhead of the Kingdom; cf. Donahue and Harrington, *Mark,* 306.

50. While this reversal primarily relates to those outside the community, the restriction in the opening phrase—"many . . ." (= "not all") may contain a hint of warning to leaders in the community: the final disposition of things in the Kingdom rests with God's sovereign free will; no "reservations" can be anticipated in view of status or presumed merits; cf. Gnilka, *Markus* 2:93.

of Jesus taken this way, abandoning all natural family ties to live simply as the "family of God," the messianic community gathered around faith in Jesus would hardly have survived beyond the first generation. Already in the New Testament itself we have attempts to incorporate a more settled existence within a faithful commitment to live out the Gospel. Luke, in particular, will explore the issue of poverty and riches at greater depth and sophistication. Mark's is not, then, the only voice to be heard. But the Markan Jesus summons all to consider their lifestyle in the context of the supreme goodness of God and the radical trust and hope that should spring from that perception.

A Third Passion Prediction: The Messiah's Ultimate Service: 10:32-34, 35-45

The instructions and incidents just described have all taken place in the course of Jesus' long journey southward in this second half of the gospel. Now (v. 32) the goal of that journey is explicitly stated to be Jerusalem. Jesus "goes ahead" of his disciples as if determined to confront what lies before him, but they trudge on behind him in an atmosphere of dismay, fear, and extreme reluctance to follow.[51] The impression conveyed is that of sensing that he is leading them into a situation of great danger, which they do not understand and really do not want to be clear about (cf. 9:32). Like the blind man at Bethsaida after the first stage of his healing (8:24), they can "see" just enough to be afraid; Jesus is leading them where they would rather not go.

In the context of this more general dismay Jesus takes the Twelve aside and informs them in the most detailed and explicit way of what is to happen to him ("the Son of Man") in Jerusalem. The prediction is a perfect summary of the main events of the Passion leading up to the resurrection. We are not told of any response on the part of the Twelve, but the request that two of them, James and John, make immediately afterward (v. 35) suggests that, once again, the prediction has not been "heard."

Nothing, in fact, could illustrate more powerfully the "blindness" under which the disciples are laboring than this request cutting right across all that Jesus has just been saying. The sons of Zebedee, James and John, form, along with Peter, the "inner three" who have been the privileged witnesses

---

51. The text of v. 32 suggests that a wider group of disciples beyond the Twelve is accompanying Jesus but does not make clear to which group or groups the emotions described (literally "amazement" and "fear") specifically pertain.

of Jesus' transfiguration on the mountain and auditors of the divine summons to "listen to him" (9:2-8). Their bold request[52] to sit, one on his right and the other on his left, when he shall have arrived "in his glory" (v. 37), shows they have not listened. The desire to sit on his right and left signals ambition to be his leading associates at the full realization of the messianic kingdom, imaged as a triumphant banquet when victory is won.[53] That is, they understand that he is the Messiah (Story 1) and in this sense "half see" (8:24). They completely fail to appreciate—or choose to ignore—that his path to messianic glory will run through suffering, death, and resurrection in Jerusalem (Story 2), about which he has just been so explicitly speaking.

Jesus does not brush aside their request, but attempts once more to educate them on its implications. He uses biblical imagery to hint at what lies in store—both for himself and for them—if what they desire is to be granted. Can they drink the "cup" that he must drink and undergo the "baptism" with which he must be baptized (vv. 38-39)? In the Psalms and prophetic literature "cup" frequently refers to the fate that lies ahead of a person: what he or she will receive from the hand of God[54] (cf. Mark 14:36). "Baptism" does not refer to the Christian sacrament, but evokes the standard biblical metaphor in which undergoing trials and dangers is depicted as a passage through stormy, turbulent waters.[55] Without fully realizing, it would seem, what they are letting themselves in for, James and John express readiness to share Jesus' fate (v. 39a). He accepts their declaration and affirms its realization (v. 39b)—something that James at least would experience in dying, according to Acts 12:2, a martyr's death.[56] But he goes on to explain (v. 40) that the allotment of places in his Kingdom belongs not to himself but to the Father.[57] The explanation shows that he himself is not going to his death in a calculating kind of way along the lines that, yes, the suffering will

---

52. The boldness comes out in their initial request for what is in effect a blank check: "Teacher, we want you to do for us whatever we ask" (v. 35b). The address "Teacher" often prefaces an inappropriate or distancing approach to Jesus (cf., e.g., 4:38; 5:35; 9:38; 12:14, 19; 13:1).

53. In an interesting background to this expectation "The Messianic Rule" from Qumran (1QSa) lays down detailed provisions for the final messianic banquet, with great attention to rank and honor and precedence; cf. Donahue and Harrington, *Mark,* 314. James and John may imagine that Jesus is going to Jerusalem to claim the Davidic throne; cf. Hooker, *Saint Mark,* 246.

54. This can be either good (Pss 23:5; 116:13) or ill (Ps 75:8; Isa 51:17-22; Jer 25:15; 49:12; Ezek 23:31-34; Lam 4:21; etc.).

55. 2 Sam 22:5; Pss 42:7; 69:2, 15; Isa 43:2; cf. Luke 12:50.

56. On John the tradition is less certain; cf. Moloney, *Gospel of Mark,* 206, n. 182.

57. A reference to the Father (explicit in Matt 20:23) is implicit in the ("divine") passive construction.

be terrible but it will all have a happy ending (resurrection). No, Jesus obediently follows the path laid out for him, surrendering the future entirely into
the hands of the God in whose power, faithfulness, and generosity he places
complete trust. Those who wish to be his associates must accompany him
in this trust as well.

The episode moves to a second stage (vv. 41-45) with the remaining
ten disciples expressing (understandable) irritation at what they see as an
attempt on the part of the sons of Zebedee to bag for themselves the highest
places in the messianic kingdom. Their indignation provides Jesus with an
opportunity to summon the whole group and explain the radical disjunction
between the exercise of leadership in his Kingdom and the understanding
of authority lying behind both the request of James and John and the irritation of the rest. The so-called rulers of the nations[58] lord it over their subjects
and exploit their power to their own advantage (v. 42b).[59] But this is not the
way authority is to run in the community of Messiah Jesus. On the contrary,
those who exercise leadership must think of themselves as servants and
slaves of all: that is, as people whose powers and capacities are not exercised
for their own benefit, but solely for the benefit and building up of others
(cf. 9:35).

In one of the most memorable statements in the Gospel tradition, Jesus
drives the point home by resting it on his own example: "the Son of Man has
come not to *be* served *(diakonēthēnai),* but to *serve (diakonein),* and to give
his life as a ransom for many" (v. 45). His ministry has from the start been
marked by great authority *(exousia:* 1:22, 27; 2:10). But that authority, displayed in his teaching and works of power (exorcisms), has been exercised
solely in setting people free from the grip of Satan and reclaiming them for
the Kingdom. Now his "service" is about to come to a climax in the costly
liberation he is to effect through his Passion and death. Again and again he
has tried to get across to his disciples the truth that he must die. Here, for the
first time, he communicates a sense of the significance and purpose of his
death. The giving up of his life *(psychē)* is to function as a "ransom for many."
"Ransom" *(lytron)* signifies a price paid to liberate people from some kind
of bondage (slaves, the kidnapped, prisoners of war). "For many" *(anti pollōn)*
may echo the closing lines of the Fourth Servant Song (Isa 52:13–53:12), in
which the Servant makes "many" righteous through bearing their sins (vv.

58. "So-called" (Greek *hoi dokountes*) communicates the sense that such rulers are really
only in power through the permissive will of God and stand under threat of the coming
judgment.

59. The description reflects the Markan community's knowledge of the way subject and
occupied peoples experienced the rule of Rome.

10, 12).[60] Jesus is going up to Jerusalem to discharge his messianic role, not in accord with conventional expectation (to which the disciples still cling), but according to a role traced out in the Scriptures (cf. 14:21, 27, 49). His "service" *(diakonia)* will consist in bearing the sins of others ("many" in Semitic idiom)[61] in order to achieve for them freedom and life ("ransom").

As will be clear, at the end of verse 45 what began as an attempt on Jesus' part to counter the false ambition of the disciples has concluded with a profound statement of the meaning of the death that lies before him in Jerusalem. The statement grounds the community's exercise of authority as "service" on nothing less than the redemptive action of Christ. If James and John, and the other ten disciples—and indeed all who would be disciples—wish to enter into and share Jesus' glory, the only "way" is to follow him in the self-sacrificing service of humanity that will have its high point of concentration on the cross.

The End of the Journey: a Blind Man Becomes a Disciple: 10:46-52

The healing of the blind beggar Bartimaeus on the outskirts of Jericho is the last episode before Jesus' entry into Jerusalem, the goal of his long journey from Galilee. Jesus' main task during the journey has been the instruction of his disciples on the true nature of his messianic mission and how it will be accomplished in Jerusalem—an instruction they have again and again resisted. Coming at the close of the long journey, the cure of blind

---

60. Many interpreters are skeptical of an allusion to Isaiah 53 here; cf. Hooker, *Saint Mark,* 248–51; Moloney, *Gospel of Mark,* 214; Dowd and Malbon, "Significance of Jesus' Death," 283–85. The verbal echoes are not close to either the Hebrew or, what is more significant in view of Mark's usage, the Greek (LXX) of Isa 53:10-12. However, it is difficult to understand the appearance of the Semitic idiom "for many" here (as also in the words over the eucharistic cup in 14:24) without reference to the thought of this passage from Isaiah where the suffering of an individual functions in a representative sense for the benefit of others; cf. Gnilka, *Markus* 2:104; Donahue and Harrington, *Mark,* 313, 315; Watts, *Isaiah's New Exodus,* 269–87. The notion of representative suffering appears later in the books of the Maccabees: 2 Macc 7:37-38; 4 Macc 6:28-29; 17:20-22, where the death of the martyrs functions as an atoning sacrifice for the sins of the nation. Mark may have expressed an allusion to Isaiah 53 in language more meaningful to his audience in a Greco-Roman milieu, where the motif of a "noble death" on behalf of or in place of others was familiar (cf. also Paul in Rom 5:6-7); cf. Adela Yarbro Collins, "The Signification of Mark 10:45 among Gentile Christians," *Harvard Theological Review* 90 (1997) 371–82.

61. The Semitic idiom "many" should not be understood in an exclusive sense ("many but not all"), but inclusively: "the contrast is not between the many who are saved and others who are not, but between the many and the one who acts on their behalf" (Hooker, *Saint Mark,* 249).

Bartimaeus corresponds to the earlier healing of a blind man at Bethsaida just before the journey began (8:22-26). Positioned at the beginning and end of the journey, the two cures play a symbolic role, bracketing Jesus' attempt to overcome the (spiritual) "blindness" of the disciples with respect to his true identity and mission. The difficult two-stage cure of the blind man of Bethsaida foreshadows the partial healing of Peter's blindness when he correctly identifies Jesus as the Messiah (Story 1) but strongly resists any further enlightenment about the way in which he is to carry out his messianic mission (Story 2), a resistance that persists all through the journey. The instant healing of Bartimaeus' blindness in the context of his vigorous faith, along with his subsequent following of Jesus on the way, shows up the present blindness of the disciples but also points forward in hope to the eventual overcoming of that blindness (the "second stage") when, after his death and resurrection, they will go to Galilee where they will "see him" (16:7).[62] The cure of Bartimaeus, then, plays a significant bridging role. It rounds off the only partially successful enlightenment of the disciples that began (symbolically) at Bethsaida and introduces the new stage of enlightenment that begins with Jesus' arrival in Jerusalem.

Bartimaeus is sitting, presumably at the gate of the city, begging for alms from the pilgrims passing through on their way to Jerusalem. Learning that among the large crowd going by is the miracle-worker from Nazareth, he begins to make a great commotion, crying out "Son of David, Jesus, have pity on me" (v. 47). Previously in the gospel Jesus has silenced messianic acclamations of this kind. That he does not do so here may be because the moment of his Passion, which will define his messiahship, is now close at hand.[63] On the contrary, it is the crowd who attempt to suppress—unsuccessfully, as it turns out—the blind man's cries (vv. 48-49). An acute sense of his own need drives him to break through the barrier created by the crowd to get access to Jesus. We are presumably to understand the vigor he displays—flinging off his cloak,[64] jumping up and going to Jesus—as the outward manifestation of the faith behind his cries (v. 50).

---

62. Cf. Meier, *Marginal Jew* 2:687.

63. Cf. Gnilka, *Markus* 2:112. The address paves the way for the Davidic, and hence messianic, overtones of Jesus' entry into Jerusalem in the very next scene: Mark 11:1-11. The response to the healing of the deaf and dumb person recorded in 7:31-35 shows that miracle-working was integral to messianic expectation; cf. also the Qumran "Messiah of Heaven and Earth" text (4Q521).

64. Casting off the cloak may convey readiness to abandon his only possession: like the first four disciples (1:18, 20) he leaves all he has in order to follow Jesus. It may also signify a more general transformation of life associated with conversion; cf. Boring, *Mark,* 306.

Jesus' question, "What do you want me to do for you?" (v. 51a), and Bartimaeus' response, "Master, that I may see again" (v. 51b), may seem redundant; the man's need is obvious. But we cannot forget that the question is exactly the same one Jesus put to the sons of Zebedee in the preceding scene (v. 36). They wanted for themselves places at his right and left in his glory, showing thereby their continuing spiritual "blindness." Bartimaeus' request to "see again" highlights what they so badly needed but failed in their ignorance to ask for: the capacity to "see" and really understand.

In contrast to the laborious two-stage process in the healing of the blind man at Bethsaida, here there is no gesture or word of healing in itself. Jesus just tells the man to go on his way because his faith has "saved" *(sesōken)* him (v. 52). He has received his physical sight, but at a deeper level he has experienced salvation. In fact, he does not "go away," but with sight restored "he follows (Jesus) on the way." That is, in contrast to the disciples who are having so much difficulty in following Jesus on his "way" (cf. especially 10:32), Bartimaeus follows Jesus on his journey to Jerusalem, his faith ready to witness all that will take place there. The blind beggar becomes, then, a model of discipleship and faith.[65] With open eyes of faith like his we are all invited to accompany Jesus to Jerusalem.

---

65. Cf. Gnilka, *Markus* 2:111; Hooker, *Saint Mark,* 253.

V
THE MESSIAH IN JERUSALEM
11:1–13:37

Jesus Enters Jerusalem and
Purges the Temple: 11:1-25

With Jesus' entry into the Messiah's city, Jerusalem, the final events of his life begin to take shape. Mark, with certain indications of time,[1] compresses all those events into a week. This has given rise to the Christian liturgical tradition of "Holy Week." Taken in historical terms, the week would be a crowded one indeed. Mark's timescale more likely reflects a desire to communicate the sense of everything coming rapidly to a climax in accordance with the will of God.

The "week" begins with Jesus' messianic entry into the city, followed by his purging of the Temple, an action that also symbolically presages its end as place of worship and reconciliation with God (11:1-25). Sparked by the question about the authority with which Jesus pursues this action (11: 28), there follows a series of encounters with leading groups in the city in which Jesus, verbally and morally at least, gains the upper hand (11:27–12:44). Sitting on the Mount of Olives, he delivers a long discourse looking to the future: he foresees and foretells the destruction of the Temple and of Jerusalem, the sufferings of the disciples, and their ultimate vindication at the advent of the Son of Man (13:1-37). The Passion proper begins with the plot to arrest Jesus and continues down to his death and burial (14:1–15:47). A new week begins with the women's discovery of the empty tomb, the explanation of its emptiness they receive from the angel, and the instruction that they are to tell the disciples to go to Galilee, where they will see the risen Jesus (16:1-8).

Jesus Enters the City of Jerusalem: 11:1-11

As described in Mark's gospel (and indeed all the gospels), Jesus' approach and entry into the city of Jerusalem is a carefully stage-managed

---

1. See 11:11, 20, 27; 14:1, 12; 15:1, 42; 16:1.

affair. Before entering the city proper he pauses on the Mount of Olives near two villages, Bethphage and Bethany.[2] From here he sends two disciples into one of the villages to procure a colt for him to ride into the city. The detailed instructions he gives them and the fact that all turns out exactly as he had foretold communicates the sense of deliberately and calmly following a divine plan of which he has special knowledge. The choice to enter the city riding on a colt on which no one had yet ridden evokes Zech 9:9 (LXX):

> Rejoice greatly, O daughter Zion!
> Shout aloud, O daughter Jerusalem!
> Lo, your king comes to you . . .
> humble and riding on a donkey,
> and on a new colt.[3]

While riding on a donkey may communicate a sense of humility, it was also a royal means of transport in biblical tradition.[4] The provision that no one had yet ridden upon it indicates its fitness for sacral usage.[5] Finally, the explanation the disciples are to give when questioned about untying the colt, "Its *kyrios* has need of it" (v. 3), is sufficiently ambiguous to signal a divine as well as human requisitioning: the *kyrios* at one level may refer to its human master, but for readers of Mark the *kyrios* is also the "Lord" for whom the "way" has been "prepared" (1:3) and who is now to complete his "way" by entering the Messiah's city.

All this preparation allows Jesus to make an entry into the city that is royal and messianic, though carefully defined by the fact that he is following a biblical (Zechariah) script rather than acting like a worldly ruler.[6] His disciples add to the sense of a royal occasion by laying their garments upon

---

2. Once again Mark's geography is vague and imprecise. Bethany is a village about two miles east of Jerusalem. In the last weeks of his life Jesus seems to have had a home base there to which he retreated from Jerusalem at night (11:11-12; 14:3-9). Bethphage seems to have been a village on the Mount of Olives between Bethany and Jerusalem.

3. The allusion to Zech 9:9, though not made explicit in Mark, as it is in the Matthean (21:4-5) and Johannine (12:14-15) parallels, is indicated by the stipulation that the colt is "unridden," picking up the "new colt" of Zech 9:9; cf. Taylor, *St. Mark,* 453–54.

4. In 1 Kgs 1:32-40 David ensures Solomon's accession to the throne by having him ride on the royal donkey.

5. Cf. Gnilka, *Markus* 2:117.

6. Moloney, *Gospel of Mark,* 220, argues that in Mark's account the disciples frustrate Jesus' attempt to make a humble entry by transforming it, contrary to his intention, into a messianic event. But when the disciples place their cloaks on the colt in what is an affirmation of kingship Jesus goes along with this by himself sitting on the colt (v. 7).

the colt and setting Jesus on it,[7] while people from the crowd strew their garments on the road before him and also leafy branches that they have cut for this purpose from the fields (vv. 7-8).[8] The crowd going before and after him hail him in the language of Psalm 118:26, as one "who comes in the name of the Lord" (v. 9), that is, as one who comes with the authority of the Lord to carry out the divine will.[9] They do not (as in Matt 21:9) hail him as "Son of David," but cry out "Blessed is the coming kingdom of our father David" (v. 10). The reservation lends the sense that Jesus is approaching the city as a messianic *candidate* whose royal installation is still to come. This leaves open the possibility for a redefinition of Davidic kingship on Jesus' part (12:35-37) and, above all, for his true "enthronement" to be seen, ironically, in his obedient death on the cross and in the exaltation to God's right hand that will follow his rising from the dead. It is presumably proximity to that radical "redefinition" of kingship that allows Jesus at this point, as also in the case of Bartimaeus just before ("Son of David" [10:47, 48]), to accept and go along with the recognition of him as Messiah that until now he had so vigorously resisted and tried to suppress.

Jesus enters the city and goes straight to the Temple (v. 11). The glance he casts around (*periblepsamenos;* cf. 10:23) before returning to Bethany with the Twelve gives notice of a task shortly to be carried out in its regard.

Fig Tree and Temple: 11:12-25

Between Jesus' reconnoitre of the Temple precinct and his dramatic action in it the following day there appears one of the strangest episodes in the gospel (11:12-14). On his way back to Jerusalem from Bethany, Jesus, feeling hungry, approaches a fig tree looking for figs. Finding no fruit but only leaves, he utters a strong curse against the tree—despite the fact that, as the evangelist notes (v. 13d), it was not the season *(kairos)* for figs. The following day, when Jesus and the disciples pass by again, Peter draws attention to the fact that the fig tree Jesus cursed the day before has withered (v. 21). This leads to a series of reflections on the efficacy of prayer made with a faith that does not doubt (vv. 22-25). Jesus' prophetic action in the

---

7. Cf. the attempt to install Jehu as king in 2 Kgs 9:13.

8. Palm branches accompanied the festive entry of Simon Maccabeus into the citadel of Jerusalem (1 Macc 13:51).

9. Originally a welcoming greeting to pilgrims approaching the Temple, the phrase may have obtained messianic overtones by the time of Jesus (cf. Matt 11:3 // Luke 7:19; John 1:15, 27; 6:14; 11:27); cf. Taylor, *St. Mark,* 457.

Temple (vv. 15-18) intervenes between these two "fig tree" episodes. This means that Mark has provided us with a "double sandwich":

Temple: v. 11

Fig tree: vv. 12-14

Temple: vv. 15-18

Fig tree: vv. 21-25

The careful arrangement indicates that both incidents are prophetic actions, meant to interpret each other.[10] This provides the clue to the interpretation of this singular "miracle," the only one in the gospel that Jesus does not work for the benefit of others and that, taken by itself, seems to be performed in an uncharacteristic—and unedifying—fit of pique.[11] Jesus performs a provocative act—akin, for example, to Jeremiah's action, under divine direction, with his loincloth in Jer 13:1-11—to draw attention to a divine judgment hovering over Israel, or in this case, more specifically, the Temple.[12]

When Jesus returns (v. 14) to the Temple he has briefly reconnoitred the previous day, he immediately takes action: driving out those who bought and sold there, overturning the tables of the money changers and the seats of those who sold doves (v. 15). The Greek verb *(ekballein)* is virtually a technical term in Mark for the driving out of demons (1:12, 34, 39; 3:15, 22, 23; 6:13; 7:26; 9:18, 28, 38; [16:9, 17]). This lends an exorcistic aura to

10. On the whole fig tree episode and its place in Mark's gospel see the excellent discussion by Meier, *Marginal Jew* 2:885–89.

11. To break my rule for once of not speculating about what "might have happened" at the level of the historical Jesus: readers may be comforted in regard to this odd miracle by John P. Meier's conclusion that the cursing of the fig tree does not go back to Jesus himself but was the creation of an early Christian author who took up the biblical tradition of punitive miracles to interpret Jesus' action in the Temple as a symbol of judgment (cf. *Marginal Jew* 2:896).

12. Mark's observation (11:13d) that "it was not the season for figs" does not, then, "explain" Jesus' action so much as point to its "prophetic" absurdity.

what he is doing. The specific activities he targets were those required for the maintenance of the Temple sacrifices with the required degree of cultic purity.[13] The additional information, peculiar to Mark's account, that Jesus would not permit the carriage of any "vessel" through the Temple (v. 16) suggests that most of this activity is being conducted in the court of the Gentiles, the large outer court that surrounded the inner Temple areas forbidden to non-Jews under pain of death.[14] This inference is supported by the composite scriptural text Jesus appeals to when he begins to "teach" in a comment on his action: "Shall not my house be called a house of prayer for all the nations? But you have made it a den of bandits" (v. 17). The first part of the quotation comes from Isaiah 56:7, the climax of a sequence in which the prophetic text forbids the separation from God's people of "the foreigners who join themselves to the Lord" and says of them:

> these I will bring to my holy mountain,
> and make them joyful in my house of prayer;
> their burnt offerings and their sacrifices
> will be accepted on my altar;
> for my house shall be called a house of prayer
> for all peoples.

The second part of the quotation in Mark 11:17 comes from Jeremiah 7:1-15, a sequence spelling out the utter incompatibility between the presence of God in the Temple and various forms of social injustice and idolatry practiced by the people; the Lord threatens to destroy "this house that is called by my name" but that has become "a den of bandits" (v. 11).[15] Jesus

13. The money changers exchanged foreign (Greek or Roman) coins for Tyrian or Jewish currency, which alone was acceptable payment in the Temple precinct—for both the Temple tax (the half-shekel: cf. Exod 30:11-16) and the purchase of animals or produce for sacrifice. The doves were sold as offerings for the poor (cf. Luke 2:22-24) or certain classes of people; cf. Donahue and Harrington, *Mark,* 327–28. Jesus' actions, as Mark describes them, probably signal the end of the cultic activity of the Temple (so, very strongly, Moloney, *Gospel of Mark,* 223–24; also Boring, *Mark,* 322), but the main point, in my opinion, is to expose and overthrow the exclusion of Gentiles from the "house of prayer."

14. Cf. Nineham, *Saint Mark,* 302 (following R. H. Lightfoot).

15. I have chosen to translate the Greek word *lēistēs* occurring in the phrase from Jeremiah in the sense it has throughout the gospel, where it refers not so much to thieves as to those who act violently, and specifically to armed revolutionaries—the kind of ultranationalist rebels ("Zealots") who held out against the Romans to the very end in the siege of 70 C.E. and brought upon themselves and the populace at large the ferocious reaction when the citadel fell, something that would have been well known to Mark's original readers. The phrase from Jeremiah, then, would not so much refer to dishonesty in the trading that was taking place in the Temple (so Donahue and Harrington, *Mark,* 328) as to the fact that the Temple was being

invokes the composite text to indicate, at first in a positive sense, God's intention for the Temple—that it should be a "house" where all peoples may have access to the Creator—and then, negatively, how the authorities in Israel ("you") have frustrated this divine intent.[16] They have frustrated it at one level by allowing trade and activity to ruin the court of the Gentiles as a place of prayer. At a deeper level, however, it is the very division of the house of God into an inner section for the "holy" (Israel) and an outer for the "unholy" (Gentiles) that frustrates the divine purpose. Elsewhere in the gospel we have seen Jesus' overcoming of the "holy/unholy" barrier running in parallel with his exorcistic activity, suggesting that the very division has in it something of the demonic. It is striking, then, that whereas the chief priests and scribes, when they hear what Jesus has done, are afraid and seek a way to destroy him (v. 18a), the people are astounded by his "teaching" (v. 18b)—exactly the same response as that recorded early in the gospel to his teaching and exorcism in the synagogue at Capernaum (1:21-28).

What, then, is the "teaching" Jesus is giving here (v. 17) that his expulsion of the traders has enacted? It surely has to do with creating, in connection with the onset of the Kingdom (cf. 1:15), a "house of prayer for all the nations." This "house" can hardly be the Temple as presently constituted, even if it is purged by Jesus' action. He will shortly foretell the destruction of that Temple (13:1-2).[17] As allusions later in the narrative confirm (12:10-11; 14:57-58), the "house of prayer for all the nations" will comprise the communities of believers from the nations of the world. They will be united in the belief that in the shedding of Jesus' blood on the cross God has reached out to them in their unholiness to make them through the cleansing power of the Spirit (1:8) members of a renewed holy people of God, the beachhead of the Kingdom in the world (cf. 15:39; 2 Cor 5:21).[18]

Next morning Peter points out that the fig tree Jesus had cursed has withered to its very roots (vv. 20-21). The withering completes the prophetic sign that "inclusively" surrounds his action in the Temple. The Temple will face a similar "withering" because it has not brought forth the "fruits" God intended. As presently controlled, it has not become a "house of prayer for all the nations".

---

rigorously divided along nationalistic grounds. I am indebted here to Watts, *Isaiah's New Exodus,* 330.

16. Cf. Gnilka, *Markus* 2:129.

17. Cf. also the negative comparison later made in regard to Temple sacrifice by the scribe characterized as "not far from the kingdom of God" (12:32-34).

18. Cf. Gnilka, *Markus* 2:129; Moloney, *Gospel of Mark,* 226.

Jesus' response to Peter (vv. 22-25) offers a series of instructions on faith and prayer that, by any reckoning, provide an odd commentary on the withering of the fig tree as a result of his curse.[19] It seems likely that in the tradition before Mark someone sought to transform the uncharacteristically harsh action of Jesus into a more edifying sequence by gathering together three unattached but relatable sayings in order to draw from the fig tree episode a short lesson on faith and prayer.[20] The saying on a faith that "moves mountains" (v. 23), albeit with prophetic exaggeration, goes along with the general sense in Mark that it is faith that channels God's power into the world. The second saying (v. 24), again with some measure of exaggeration, situates faith within the overall context of absolute trust in the goodness as well as the power of God. The final saying (v. 25) echoes a clause of the Lord's Prayer (cf. Matt 6.12, 14-15; Luke 11:4; also Matt 18:21-35; Luke 17:4). It teaches that, while human forgiveness does not motivate God to forgive, lack of it can block the flow of divine forgiveness that stands behind all life within the community of faith.[21] Odd though the series of sayings may be as a response to the withering of the fig tree, taken as a whole it is at home within a broader view that a community rich in faith, trusting prayer and forgiveness, is truly the "house of prayer" God promised to build "for all the nations."[22]

19. The sayings end at v. 25. The sentence appearing in some versions as v. 26 is generally regarded as a secondary import from Matt 6:15.

20. Nineham comments tartly: "Strictly speaking, the cursing of the tree was neither an act of faith, nor a prayer, and it hardly seems to exemplify the forgiving spirit demanded in v. 25" (*Saint Mark,* 299).

21. Cf. Boring: "If the Christian community is to be a 'house of prayer for all nations,' it must be a forgiving community, for only forgiveness makes it possible for people to live together" (*Mark,* 325).

22. Cf. Moloney, *Gospel of Mark,* 238.

The Contest for Authority in Jerusalem: 11:27–12:44

Through his messianic entry into the city and prophetic action in the Temple Jesus has thrown down the gauntlet as regards authority in Jerusalem. He has directly challenged the religious establishment currently clinging to whatever power they possessed through favor of the Roman occupying power and the assent of the populace at large. The gospel now presents a series of controversies in which representatives of four groups in the Jewish leadership confront Jesus over the course of a very long "day" in Jerusalem:

11:27–12:12:	The chief priests, the scribes, the elders
[12: 1-12:	Allegorical parable: the Murderous Tenants]
12:13-17:	Pharisees and Herodians (taxes)
12:18-27:	Sadducees (resurrection)
12:28-34:	Scribe (greatest commandment)

Jesus then goes on the offensive himself:

12:35-37:	The true nature of the Messiah (David's son or something more?)
12:38-40:	Warning against scribes
12:41-44:	Counterexample of a poor widow

The contests, which Jesus invariably wins, take place in public, with the result that the authorities see their authority slipping away in favor of the prophet from Galilee, whose victories over "the experts" the people view with delight (cf. 12:37). This intensifies the desire to destroy Jesus, a desire held in check only through fear of his hold on the people (11:18). The threat to Jesus' life, frustrated for the present but intensifying all the time, forms the dramatic backdrop to the series of controversies that now unfolds.

182

By What Authority . . . ?: 11:27-33

While Jesus is walking about in the Temple the chief priests, scribes, and elders of the people approach him and put to him the question that will dominate the entire sequence: "By what authority are you doing these things? Who gave you this authority to do them?" (vv. 27-28). The three groups named as putting the question collectively represent the peak of governance in the Jewish state, the ones responsible to the Roman occupation for keeping order in Jerusalem and its nerve center, the Temple.[1] The question they ask Jesus undoubtedly refers to his action in the Temple. Its second formulation ("*Who* gave you authority . . . ?") focuses the issue more personally. They pose the question in terms of human authority. As readers we have observed Jesus displaying authority *(exousia)* from the start and know its true source: his endowment with the Spirit (1:10). Now we watch him deal with this hostile challenge.

Jesus employs a rabbinic method of meeting a question by posing a counterquestion, in this case one concerning the origins of John's baptism: was it from heaven (that is, from God) or from human beings (vv. 29-30)? Rather than focusing simply on the rite (baptism), the question bears upon the validity of John's witness and ministry as a whole.[2] Hence the dilemma facing the adversaries (vv. 31-32). If they accept that John's ministry had heavenly validation they lay themselves open to the charge of not having believed his preaching, central to which was his witness to a "Stronger One" (Jesus) who would come after him and "baptize with the Spirit" (1:7-8); they will then have the answer to their original question ("By what authority . . . ?)—and be forced to confront its implications. If they deny the heavenly origin of John's ministry they risk losing authority with the people, who regard John as a prophet. The dilemma forces them into a humiliating backdown: "We do not know" (v. 33), allowing Jesus not only to escape from their inquisition (v. 34) but also to establish the source of his authority by implication rather than forced assertion. Despite his lonely death (6:16-29), John's witness continues.

---

1. The three groups are mentioned in the first Passion prediction (8:31) and will be the prime movers against Jesus. Collectively these groups make up the Sanhedrin, before which Jesus will appear before being handed over to the Romans; cf. Donahue and Harrington, *Mark,* 334.

2. Cf. Gnilka, *Markus* 2:139; Hooker, *Saint Mark,* 271–72.

The Murderous Tenants: 12:1-12

With the leaders reduced to silence, Jesus goes over to the offensive. He does so characteristically by telling a parable that has come to be known as the parable of the Wicked Tenants, though "wicked" sounds a bit lame in view of the behavior described. The parable as it appears in the text of Mark is clearly an allegory.[3] The description of the vineyard and its careful preparation by the owner (v. 1) echoes virtually word for word the beginning of the allegory in Isa 5:1-5, where the vineyard is Israel and the owner ("my friend") God. While these identifications remain, the Markan parable takes a different tack, basing itself on a situation in which the owner of the vineyard goes away, having leased it out to tenant farmers to manage in his absence.[4] The servants he sends at the appropriate time *(kairos)* to collect his share of its produce would be the prophets sent to Israel, and the ill-treatment the servants receive—in ever-increasing degree—at the hands of the tenants would represent the rejection Israel's leaders customarily mete out to prophets in the biblical tradition (vv. 2-5). In view of the divine address to Jesus following his baptism (1:11) and again at the transfiguration (9:7), the "only son, the beloved one" the owner sends as a last resort (v. 6) has to be Jesus, the Son of God, and the supreme ill-treatment he receives (vv. 7-8) would be a reference to his Passion and death as instigated by the leadership of Israel currently in power.

Up to a certain point—the rejection and murder of the son (vv. 7-8)—the parable brings out the extreme patience and long-suffering of God who, in the face of repeated rejection, reaches out to Israel again and again.[5] Over against the evil calculation of the tenants ("This is the heir; come, let us kill him . . ."),[6] the divine calculation, "They will respect my son" (v. 6), seems naïve in the extreme.[7] In the image of God implied in the parable it represents the foolishness of divine love. But this forbearance will not endure forever. The note of retribution comes in with the question Jesus raises and answers

3. I discuss the parable here as it appears in the Gospel of Mark. In some form (minus v. 5 and vv. 10-11) it goes back to Jesus himself. For an account of how the parable as told by Jesus is likely to have reached its present form see Hooker, *Saint Mark,* 274–75.

4. On the Palestinian situation behind the practice see Jeremias, *Parables,* 74–75; Boring, *Mark,* 329. A non-Israelite absentee landowner is likely in view. His foreignness and absence in a distant country might explain the otherwise foolish expectation of the tenants that they would get away with their murderous behavior.

5. Cf. Taylor, *St. Mark,* 472; Donahue, *Gospel in Parable,* 55.

6. The words echo those of the brothers of Joseph in Gen 37:20.

7. Some interpreters, however, make the point that the son could represent the authority of his father, the landowner, in a way that mere slaves could not; cf. Hooker, *Saint Mark,* 276.

in verse 9: the "lord of the vineyard" will destroy the murderous tenants and give the vineyard "to others." For the original readers of Mark's gospel the threat of dispossession and punishment would already be a reality in the destruction of the Jewish state in 70 C.E. and the transfer of the "inheritance" (the promise of the Kingdom) to the messianic community, Jewish and Gentile, gathered around faith in Jesus.

At this point the parable proper has come to an end, but as an allegorical survey of the history of salvation it is far from complete. Still outstanding is the truth that, as far as God was concerned, the rejection and brutal death of the Son was not the last word. With a change of image from vineyard to "building," a supplementary question (vv. 10-11) points to the divine following of the script marked out in Ps 118:22-23 (LXX) to make "the stone that the builders rejected" the "cornerstone"[8] of a new building (vv. 10-12). That is, God has raised the rejected Son and made him as risen Lord the foundation of a new building, a "temple not made by hands" (14:58) consisting of the community of believers (cf. 1 Cor 3:9-11, 16-17; 2 Cor 6:16b-18). It is to this community that the vineyard and its "produce," the pledge of the Kingdom, have been given (v. 9).[9]

Extended in this way (by the addition of the reference to Ps 118:22-23 in vv. 10-11), the parable has become an allegory of salvation history.[10] When the "beloved Son" is referred to Jesus it becomes in a sense a further Passion prediction, but one that sets the immediate fate of Jesus—his suffering, death, and resurrection—within the wider story of salvation: from God's original choice and nourishing of Israel ("the vineyard" [v. 1]) and the sending of the prophets, through the sending, death, and resurrection of the Son to the divided outcome at the end: the retribution visited on the leaders of Israel who rejected Jesus (seen in the destruction of 70 C.E.) and, more positively, the constitution of a renewed Israel built on the once-rejected, now raised Son of God. Seen within this total picture the overall message of the parable, while polemical in its function of challenge to the Jewish leaders, is not as negative as might at first appear. It shows how the divine love, while

8. The Greek phrase *kephalēn gonias* could refer to either the cornerstone of a building or, more likely, the capstone that holds up an arch.

9. It is important to point out that the parable does not target the people of Israel as a whole, but only the leaders responsible for the rejection of Jesus as Messiah (cf. Moloney, *Gospel of Mark*, 235), nor does the parable suggest the "replacement" of Israel by the Christian church. The "others" to whom the vineyard is given include Jewish as well as Gentile believers. Where this leaves the bulk of Israel, apart from the leaders, who have not come to faith in the crucified Messiah, is not a question Mark addresses. For that we have to look to Paul in Romans 9–11, especially the "mystery" of the inclusion of "all Israel" formulated in 11:25-32.

10. Cf. Gnilka, *Markus* 2:147.

it might seem foolish and naïve in the sending of the beloved Son in the face of so much earlier rejection, has in the end triumphed over human rejection to achieve what is "marvelous in our eyes" (Ps 118:23; Mark 12:11). In this sense it encapsulates the entire Markan gospel.

In the more immediate context of the narrative (v. 12), the leaders grasp all too well that the parable targets them, but they fail to accept it as containing a truth summoning them to repentance and conversion.[11] Manifesting the "hardness of heart" displayed by Jesus' adversaries in the gospel (3:5), they renew their determination to destroy him—a design once more held in check by his popularity with the bulk of the people.

Taxes to Caesar? 12:13-17

This short episode introduces the first of four issues, on each of which Jesus' response validates his authority in the face of challenge from the Jewish leaders (11:27-33). These leaders (the chief priests, the scribes, and the elders of the people [11:27]) are presumably behind the delegation of Pharisees and Herodians who have been sent to entrap him (v. 13).[12] Frustrated in their direct challenge to Jesus, the leaders employ this combined group as a front for their own malevolent intent. This would explain the long-winded flattery with which the delegation makes its approach (v. 14a), doubtless designed to convey an impression of deference before catching him off guard with a pointed question.[13]

The question about the lawfulness of paying the tax to Caesar is indeed deadly. The Romans imposed the highly unpopular tax, a poll tax, when they took over the administration of Judea, Samaria, and Peraea after the deposition of Herod Archelaus in 6 C.E. For the Jews it was a deeply resented reminder of their subject status, aggravated by the fact that it had to be paid in the form of the Roman denarius coin bearing the emperor's image.[14] If Jesus supports payment of the unpopular tax he will lose standing with the

---

11. Cf. Watts, *Isaiah's New Exodus,* 346–47.

12. The (historically unlikely) combination of these two groups featured in an earlier conspiracy to destroy Jesus (3:6), and they were the subject of Jesus' warning in 8:15. Along with most interpreters, I take the unnamed senders of this delegation—"they sent"—to be the same as the subject of the preceding two episodes.

13. Mark likely wants us to see the irony in their assurance: "we know . . . you teach the way *(hodos)* of God in truth": Jesus from the start has been following the "way of God" (1:3), a way they will not recognize; cf. Hooker, *Saint Mark,* 280.

14. Its imposition immediately led to a revolt under Judas the Galilean in 6 C.E. (cf. Acts 5:37) and, according to the Jewish historian Josephus (*Antiquities* 18.1, 2, 6), eventually led to the rise of the Zealot faction, the leading players in the revolt of 66–70 C.E.

people—the one thing that is protecting him at the moment from the designs of his enemies (11:18, 22). If he rejects payment, his ruling will be conveyed to the Roman governor, exposing him to the highly dangerous charge of sedition.

As in his handling of the earlier challenge (11:27-33), Jesus does not give a direct answer. Well aware of the "hypocrisy" lurking behind the flattery of his questioners (v. 15a), he throws the issue back to them, demanding first of all that they produce the hated coin (the denarius) in which the tax had to be paid (v. 15b). In the ancient world all coinage was commonly understood to be the property of the ruler under whose authority it was issued and whose image and inscription it bore. When the adversaries are compelled to acknowledge that the coin bears Caesar's image, the way is clear for Jesus to say: "Give back to Caesar what belongs to Caesar" (v. 17a). But he immediately expands the issue in a whole new direction by adding "and to God what belongs to God" (v. 17b). The tax is to be paid, but only in the context of a far more significant obligation to God.

This short episode and, in particular, Jesus' enigmatic ruling in verse 17 has had to bear a very heavy weight of interpretation in regard to the relationship between Christianity and the state. In his response Jesus does not define the separation of church and state in the modern sense. That was a much later task and one still evolving today. The response does lay the foundation for such developments by recognizing the legitimacy of the civil sphere and its claims, while setting them within the overarching framework of obedience to God.[15] In an extended sense Jesus' words summon believers to constant discernment, within the changing patterns of civil society, about how they are to carry out their civic obligations within the higher claim of God. That is, he bequeaths to later generations of believers an ethical task rather than a legal prescription.

The Resurrection of the Dead: 12:18-27

The next challenge to Jesus' authority comes from a group of Sadducees, members for the most part of the priestly aristocracy, conservative in both politics and religion. They tackle Jesus on one issue characteristic of their

---

15. The Markan text would then be adopting an attitude to the state similar to that found in Rom 13:1-7 and 1 Pet 2:13-14 (contrast Rev 13 and 17). For some interpreters the second clause renders Jesus' response ambiguous since it could suggest that one's obligations to God override obligations to the civil ruler. Jesus could then be seen as siding with those who refused to pay the emperor's tax (cf. Donahue and Harrington, *Mark,* 346). This seems to me to downplay the sense of the first clause.

refusal to go beyond basic biblical belief: the resurrection of the dead.[16] Addressing Jesus as "Teacher," they put before him a biblical prescription that, taken to its logical extreme, would seem to render the concept of life after death ridiculous. Deuteronomy 25:5-10 (quoted in v. 19 with some influence from Gen 38:8) lays down that if a man dies childless his brother should take his widow in marriage in order to raise up offspring for him so that his name would not be blotted out. That, for the Sadducees, is the way—a purely this-worldly way—in which Moses envisaged that a person would achieve some measure of immortality. Introduce the notion of resurrection and then, on the highly unlikely but not impossible supposition that a woman could be widowed seven times without providing any of her husbands with a child, the question arises (vv. 20-23): whose wife will she be in the resurrection existence—since she has had seven husbands? In this construction, the biblical law makes belief in the resurrection both unnecessary and impossible to imagine.

Jesus makes a two-pronged response, accusing the Sadducees of knowing neither the Scriptures (to which they are appealing) nor the power of God (v. 24). He tackles the "presenting issue" first: the nature of risen existence (v. 25). The problem the Sadducees have posed arises because they can only conceive of life after death as something continuous with the present existence, in which—to take the relevant example—people marry and are given in marriage for the purpose of continuing the race. But in the resurrection existence marriage is no longer necessary since the just share the eternal, deathless existence of angels.[17] The Sadducees do not "know the power of God" (v. 24) because they do not countenance the power of the Creator to bring about a mode of human existence in which personal continuity, albeit with radical transformation, transcends the barrier of death.[18]

---

16. Belief in life after death (apart from a shadowy, lingering existence in Sheol for a time) makes a very late appearance in the Old Testament: Dan 12:1-2; Isa 26:19. It became a characteristic tenet of the Pharisees—and, of course, of the movement founded by Jesus.

17. Postbiblical Jewish literature frequently describes the life of the just as *akin* to that of angels; see Byrne, *"Sons of God"—"Seed of Abraham,"* 64–67; Donahue and Harrington, *Mark,* 350. Jesus' words do not mean that human beings will be transformed into angels. The point is that in the resurrection existence they will enjoy the angelic privilege of immediate vision of God and the immunity to death that goes along with it.

18. Cf. John P. Meier, *A Marginal Jew.* Vol. 3: *Companions and Competitors* (New York: Doubleday, 2001) 423. Paul addresses the same issue—the difficulty of conceiving of resurrection existence—when responding to the Corinthians' denial of the resurrection in 1 Cor 15:35-49. Significantly, he prefaces his instruction with a similar accusation that those who deny the resurrection exhibit "ignorance of God" (1 Cor 15:34b; cf. Mark 12:24); see further Brendan Byrne, "Eschatologies of Resurrection and Destruction: the Ethical Significance of Paul's Dispute with the Corinthians," *Downside Review* 104, no. 357 (October 1986) 288–98.

Having cleared up this general question, Jesus is free to move beyond the narrow terms in which the Sadducees had set the issue in their pedantic argument from a highly particular and minor item of the Law (vv. 26-27). He shows up their ignorance of the Scriptures (v. 24a) by going to a far more central biblical text: the episode of the burning bush in which God, calling Moses to be the instrument of Israel's rescue from Egyptian slavery, makes a self-identification as "the God of Abraham and the God of Isaac and the God of Jacob" (Exod 3:1-6, 15). Since God is not the God of the dead but of the living (v. 27a) this means that those patriarchal figures, though they died, must be considered as living beyond death in a life of continuing relationship and communion with God.

Jesus' argument may not seem entirely persuasive in terms of modern exegetical technique.[19] In a broader sense it goes to the heart of the matter, and especially to the Judaeo-Christian understanding of God. If the relationship God forges with human beings is one that death simply snuffs out—death that comes in such a variety of ways: slowly or suddenly, after a long life or a short one, at times violently or capriciously—is that relationship one that can be regarded as truly personal? Christian theology and spirituality have jibbed at the notion that denial of life after death is compatible with the nature of God revealed in the teaching, the ministry, the death, and, above all, the resurrection of Jesus. For Jesus, as for Paul, such a denial betrays "ignorance of God" (1 Cor 15:24). Those who maintain it are "very much in error" (Mark 12:27b).

Love—the Greatest Commandment: 12:28-34

Scribes are usually hostile figures in the gospel—one group among the triple array of antagonists plotting Jesus' downfall (11:27; 12:12; 14:1). This makes all the more remarkable the friendly exchange between Jesus and a scribe who asks him about which commandment (of the Jewish law) is "first of all" (v. 28).[20] The friendly tone may explain why Jesus, instead of

19. For one thing, it does not strictly demonstrate the reality of bodily resurrection, but simply of some kind of immortality. But the argument proceeds from a more holistic Jewish anthropology in which the notions of the immortality of the soul and resurrection of the body were not so sharply distinguished as in philosophical discourse under Greek influence. For an outstanding discussion of this passage and the tradition behind it see Meier, *Marginal Jew* 3:411–44, 468–87 (Notes).

20. The friendliness of the Markan account contrasts with the Matthean (22:34-40) and Lukan (10:25-28) parallels in which those who put the question are said to be testing Jesus. The Markan account is more in the nature of a scholastic dialogue than a controversy.

responding with a counterquestion as in the earlier controversies, provides an answer himself (vv. 29-30). He does so by citing the opening phrases of the *Shema,* the text from Deuteronomy 6:4b-5 recited morning and evening by observant Jews then and now:

> The first is, "Hear, O Israel: the Lord our God, the Lord is one; you shall love the Lord your God with all your heart, and with all your soul, and with all your mind, and with all your strength."[21]

The scribe had asked for one commandment. Jesus goes on to lay alongside it a second, taken this time from Leviticus 19:18: "You shall love your neighbor as yourself."[22]

Jesus does not reduce both commandments to a single "first" or "greatest" commandment. Though inextricably bound together, they remain "first" and "second." This signals that God is worthy of love and worship in an absolute sense: God is to be loved for Godself alone. Love of God, though finding necessary expression in love of neighbor, cannot simply be reduced to loving action on behalf of the neighbor.[23] Moreover, by prefacing the command to love God with the opening phrases of the *Shema* ("Hear, O Israel . . ."), Jesus is placing himself firmly within the biblical tradition, according to which God's free choice of Israel (election) comes before any requirement God makes of Israel.[24] All Israelites are summoned each day to "Listen" *(shema)* because Israel is a people that enjoys the supreme privilege of being addressed by God, addressed in words of promise and love. Hence Jewish—and Christian—love of God is always a response to the God who has first loved us and whose continuing gestures of love we are daily urged to note. The entire ministry of Jesus represents a divine attempt to set human beings free to love by drawing them into the communion of love that is the Trinity (cf. Mark 1:10-11).

---

21. The quotation follows the LXX exactly except for the substitution of a pair, "mind" *(dianoia)* and "strength" *(ischys),* in place of a single word, *dynamis* (power) in the Greek. The addition of "mind" may add an "intellectual" aspect considered appropriate in the Hellenistic milieu in which the Gospel was preached. The intention, however, is not to distinguish separate faculties but to underline the completeness of the response required; cf. Taylor, *St. Mark,* 486.

22. Bringing the two commandments together seems to have been something distinctive of Jesus' ministry—though Jewish parallels are not lacking from a later period; see Nineham, *Saint Mark,* 324; Moloney, *Gospel of Mark,* 270.

23. See Edward V. Vacek, "The Eclipse of Love for God," *America* 174/8 (March 1996) 13–16; reprinted in Paul Jersild et al., eds., *Moral Issues and Christian Response* (7th ed. New York: Harcourt Brace College Publications, 2002) 6–10.

24. Cf. Gnilka, *Markus* 2:164.

Loving one's neighbor "as oneself" may not, at first sight, seem all that demanding. One is not being asked to put the interests of the neighbor before oneself, but simply to put them on an equal level. The commandment certainly presupposes a healthy love and valuing of oneself. But what it also asks is, on closer inspection, quite radical, an act of imagination in high degree: to ask myself: What do I really want from another person?—understanding, tolerance, respect, loyalty, compassion?—and then to make sure that all my actions in their regard enact rather than neglect those qualities. Fundamentally, what is being required when this second commandment is placed alongside the first is that the divine love I have received be returned not only directly to God but also through another "channel," that of the neighbor in whom, as Jesus has already pointed out, not only he himself but the One who sent him is "received" (9:37).

Unique to the Markan version of this episode is the continuation of the friendly interaction (vv. 32-34a). The scribe commends Jesus' response, recalls the opening words of the *Shema*,[25] and then repeats virtually word for word Jesus' formulation of the two commandments. When he adds a further comment to the effect that all this is "much more important than burnt offerings or sacrifices" (v. 33b), Jesus assures him that he is not far from the Kingdom of God (v. 34a). The prophets of Israel had stressed the insufficiency of the sacrificial cult when more radical obedience to God and social justice were lacking (1 Sam 15:22; Isa 1:11; Jer 7:22-23; Hos 6:6; Ps 40:7; etc.). The scribe's statement seems to go beyond this critique in the direction of the new reality to which Jesus' recent action in the Temple has pointed: the replacement of the Temple and its ritual with a new temple that, with Jesus as its cornerstone, will be a "house of prayer for all the nations" (11:17; 12:10). In that "house of prayer" the community of the Kingdom will live by the twin commandment of love in place of the detailed prescriptions of the Law (cf. Paul in Rom 8:3-4; 13:9-10; Gal 5:14).[26] Because the scribe has come close to recognizing this, he is "not far from the kingdom of God";[27] all that would seem to be required for him to enter the community of the Kingdom is to "repent and believe the good news" (1:15). Whether or not he takes this step we do not know. But his positive response shows up the obduracy of his fellow scribes who remain hostile. The notice that after this no one dared to ask Jesus any more questions (v. 34b) wraps up

25. The scribe further stresses the oneness of God by incorporating a phrase from Isa 45:21 ("and besides him there is no other").

26. Cf. Moloney, *Gospel of Mark,* 241.

27. Cf. what is said later in the gospel of another sympathetic Jewish leader, Joseph of Arimathea: that he was waiting expectantly for the Kingdom of God (15:43).

the sequence of challenges posed to Jesus. In all four cases his responses have ensured that his authority stands (11:28).

How Can the Messiah Be David's Son?: 12:35-37

As if to press home his advantage further, Jesus now poses a question himself. He does so while teaching the crowds in the Temple. They are his audience but, despite the friendly encounter just recorded, the scribes remain the principal target.

These experts in religious law maintain, in line with conventional view, that the Messiah is to be "Son of David."[28] How can this be, says Jesus (v. 35-36), citing a biblical text, Ps 110:1, where David, as inspired author of the Psalms, refers to the Messiah as "my Lord" ("The Lord [*kyrios* = YHWH] said to my Lord [*kyriōi mou*]")? How could a father address his son in this exalted way? Must he not be referring to someone superior to himself and therefore not his son? Hence, on an understanding of Psalm 110 as messianic in the sense that the second "lord" addressed by "the Lord" (= YHWH) is the Messiah,[29] the latter cannot be David's son.

While at first sight the argument may seem to deny the title "Son of David" to Jesus[30]—a title elsewhere ascribed to him in the New Testament— it would be wrong to press the logic too rigorously. Jesus does not say "it is, then, impossible for him (= the Messiah) to be David's son," but leaves a question hanging in the air: "How then (literally "whence" [*pothen*]) is he his (= David's) son?" (v. 37b). The pedagogical and rhetorical effect of this is not necessarily to rule out the Messiah's being son of David, but to make the point that, as the psalm suggests, the messianic notion has to be radically extended in the direction implied by the title "Lord." Far beyond the purely human status attaching to "Son of David," even in a messianic sense, the Messiah will bear and wield the authority of "the Name above all other names" (Phil 2:9-11).[31]

---

28. On the conventional understanding of "Messiah" in the Judaism of Jesus' day see the introductory chapter above on the worldview presupposed in Mark's gospel.

29. The argument presupposes a messianic understanding of the psalm—though whether such an interpretation was current in pre-Christian Judaism is not clear. Applied to the post-resurrection exaltation and enthronement of Jesus as messianic Lord, Ps 110:1b is the Old Testament text most cited and alluded to in the New Testament; cf. Boring, *Mark,* 348.

30. So Moloney, *Gospel of Mark,* 243–44; Boring, *Mark,* 348–49.

31. The comment made by Henry B. Swete over a century ago remains apt: "Jesus does not on the one hand dispute the inference (that is, that the Messiah is Son of David), or, on the other, press the identification; He contents Himself with pointing out a difficulty, in the

"How" this will come about remains for the present unsaid. Jesus is once again driving a wedge into the conventional understanding of messiahship in order to clear the way for a messianic "installation" destined to come about in a way totally unforeseen in that understanding: namely, through his own obedient death, resurrection, and exaltation as "Lord" to the right hand of God (cf. "whence?"). It is this future scenario that David, under the inspiration of the Holy Spirit, foresaw when he heard the Lord (= YHWH) say to his "Lord" (= Messiah Jesus) "Sit on my right hand while I set your enemies under your feet" (Ps 110:1). David foresaw a Messiah who, as God's Son and bearer of the divine Name, would trample God's enemies under his feet and so claim human beings for the Kingdom. Jesus has already begun to do this, but the climax of the struggle is at hand in his coming death and resurrection. He is indeed the Messiah, but to contain all this within messianic understanding requires a radical broadening of that category.[32] This is what his assault on the Davidic interpretation the scribes have locked down is all about.

So much for the scribes. The wider populace, we are told (v. 37b), hears Jesus with joy. That popular esteem is both his protection and his greatest danger. It can only increase the "jealousy" of his power on the part of the leaders (cf. 15:10).

The Scribes and a Widow's Offering: 12:38-44

It is appropriate to discuss the final two episodes of Jesus' teaching in the Temple together. They form something of a diptych displaying two contrasting portraits of behavior inspired by religion.[33] In any case they are linked by the key word "widow" appearing in both.

Jesus has refuted the teaching of the scribes. Now, before the large crowd gathered in the Temple area, he criticizes their behavior.[34] In view of the sympathetic encounter that has just taken place between Jesus and one of their number (12:28-34), his blanket condemnation is surprising. But in

solution of which lay the key to the whole problem of His person and mission" (*The Gospel according to St. Mark,* 2nd ed. [London: Macmillan, 1909] 288).

32. The relativization without rejection of the Son of David title here has a parallel in the creedal formula cited by Paul at the beginning of Romans (1:3-4), which presents Christ as "of the seed of David according to the flesh," that is, as having the required human credentials to be Messiah, and then (from his resurrection) in a more transcendent sense as "Son of God in power according the Spirit of holiness"; cf. Gnilka, *Markus* 2:171.

33. Cf. Donahue and Harrington, *Mark,* 364.

34. Cf. Taylor, *St. Mark,* 493; Nineham, *Saint Mark,* 332. Historically there is no evidence that the scribes as such were more corrupt than other leaders.

the world of the gospel, which must of course be distinguished from the historical situation of Jesus, the scribes, along with the chief priests and elders of the people, represented the apex of the religious leadership now bent on his destruction. In a society in which the Law of Moses regulated all aspects of life their legal expertise gave them great power, prestige, and influence over others. It is as representative figures in this sense that they become targets of Jesus' critique.

Jesus attacks the scribes for making their expertise, which should be directed primarily to the honor and glory of God, a means of drawing attention and honor to themselves. The long robe they wear when performing official duties they continue to wear publicly at other times so as to attract respectful greetings in the marketplaces (v. 38b); in synagogue assemblies and banquets they contrive to have special places set aside for them as a mark of their leading role (v. 39).[35] Much more seriously, while making a pretence of religious piety (long-winded public prayer), they consume the property of widows (v. 40ab). That is, they dress up their legal expertise in a cloak of piety in order to win the trust of the most vulnerable in society, whose meager resources, once entrusted to them, they then proceed to plunder.[36] Their condemnation at the judgment (v. 40c) will be all the "more" severe because they work this injustice, in itself deserving of condemnation, under a cloak of hypocrisy.

In striking contrast to this picture of hypocrisy is the action of the widow in the following scene (vv. 41-44). Sitting opposite the Temple treasury,[37] Jesus observes many rich people making substantial contributions, while a poor widow throws in two pennies *(lepta duo)* only.[38] Summoning his disciples, he solemnly makes the point: this poor widow has given more than all the others who contributed to the treasury (v. 43). The reason is that

35. The scribes wore a particularly long version of the *tallith* or outer garment when engaged in official duties. The "first seats" in synagogues may refer to a row of elevated seats immediately in front of the ark containing the sacred scrolls and facing the rest of the congregation; cf. Hooker, *Saint Mark,* 295; Moloney, *Gospel of Mark,* 245.

36. In view of the vulnerable position of widows (along with orphans and the stranger in the land) biblical law laid down provisions for their sustenance and protection (Exod 22:22; Deut 24:19-21; 27:19), while the prophets spoke powerfully for their care (Isa 1:17; Jer 7:6; 22:3; Ezek 22:7; Zech 7:10; Mal 3:5; etc.). Jesus' complaint here is in the line of the prophetic insistence that God upholds the widow's cause.

37. The reference may be to the Temple treasury in a general sense, or more particularly to a number of large trumpet-shaped containers that, according to later reports, stood in the Court of the Women, for the purpose of collecting monetary offerings.

38. The *lepton* coin, which Mark translates for his wider readership as equivalent to half a Roman *quadrans* (Greek *kodrantes*), was the smallest coin in circulation, the equivalent of one sixty-fourth of a denarius, a day's wages; cf. Moloney, *Gospel of Mark,* 247, n. 168.

they gave from their superfluity whereas, out of her very want, she gave everything she possessed, all that she had to live on (v. 44). While her action contrasts with that of other contributors to the treasury, the contrast with the behavior of the scribes that Jesus has just condemned is all the stronger. Their practice of religion was all external show, designed not to give honor to God but to attract it to themselves. In terms of monetary value her gift is paltry, yet in the eyes of God who sees the heart she has put in "more" than all the rest because her offering represents total trust and abandonment of herself to God, the protector of widows and orphans (Ps 146:9). She exemplifies the attitude of surrender to God in perfect trust that Jesus has been commending to his disciples and that he himself will supremely show as he moves now toward his Passion and death, giving up his "life as a ransom for many" (10:45) In place of the Temple cult, which Jesus has effectively brought to an end, the community of the Kingdom will truly worship God when the "two pennies" of each one's outward contribution represent the totality of surrender and trust.[39]

39. It is possible to interpret the widow's offering in a totally different way, as something Jesus deplores rather than commends. Following immediately upon a reference to the scribes' consuming the property of widows (v. 40a), the widow's action can be interpreted as an instance of the way in which religious authorities, specifically the Temple administration, prey upon the piety of the vulnerable to exact tribute from them far beyond what they can afford. This paves the way for the prophecy of the coming destruction of the Temple that Jesus is very soon to utter (13:2). For this interpretation see G. Addison Wright, "The Widow's Mites: Praise or Lament?—A Matter of Context," *Catholic Biblical Quarterly* 44 (1982) 256–65; Myers, *Binding the Strong Man,* 320–22; also Donahue and Harrington, *Mark,* 365 (a possible alternative). Giving particular weight to the context in which the widow's offering is described, there is much to be said for this interpretation. My sense is that it is more appropriate as an interpretation of the Lukan parallel (21:1-4; see Brendan Byrne, *Hospitality of God,* 160–61), which lacks the detail of Jesus' summoning the disciples for instruction, which in the Markan version seems to support the exemplary rather than the prophetic denunciation sense. On the widow as an example to the disciples see Moloney, *Gospel of Mark,* 247–48.

The Challenge and Hope of the Future: 13:1-37

The thirteenth chapter of Mark's gospel, after some introductory sentences setting the scene (vv. 1-4), consists entirely of a long discourse of Jesus on the future facing his disciples. Taken as a whole it represents the most difficult part of the gospel for interpretation—even though, precisely because it looks beyond the time span of the gospel, it most directly addresses the situation of its audience, past and present. The difficulty stems from the content of the discourse (couched for the most part in the language and imagery of Jewish apocalyptic), from the obscurity of several of the allusions, and perhaps most of all because it seems to send mixed messages to the faithful, oscillating in a rather disturbing way between reassurance and warning. Before we take the plunge into its turbulent waters it will help to be aware of some considerations of a more general and introductory nature. These bear upon the nature and purpose of apocalyptic, the literary genre of the discourse, its overall structure, and the sequence of "messages" it purports to convey.

Since Mark's gospel as a whole presupposes the worldview of Jewish apocalypticism, in approaching this long discourse in chapter 13 we are not encountering apocalyptic for the first time, but only in greater concentration. As I explained in the introductory chapter dealing with the worldview of the gospel, the purpose of apocalyptic discourse is to give encouragement to the faithful now suffering the evils of the present age. It does so by imparting prior and privileged information concerning the divine plan and program whereby God or God's agent(s) will soon intervene. A moment of reckoning and judgment will shortly arrive, which will mean exposure and condemnation for the wicked, vindication and reward for the faithful, who will then share the final triumph of God's rule (the "Kingdom of God"). This is essentially what Jesus is doing in the discourse in Mark 13, which comes to a climax with the description of the advent of the Son of Man (Story 3) in verses 24-27.

Though the discourse has long been referred to as "the Markan Apocalypse," this is not a fully accurate description since its content is not revealed from heaven (as is the case with apocalypses, such as the book of Revelation) but proceeds from the mouth of Jesus on earth. While "apocalyptic" in its language and imagery, and also in the eschatological "program" of the end it presupposes, the discourse is more akin to another literary genre found in the Bible, that of a farewell testament: an address or instruction that a significant teacher or leader gives to his or her disciples just prior to death.[1] In such testaments the revered figure looks beyond his or her own death to the future awaiting the disciples, foreseeing the troubles and temptations that will inevitably arise, and offering appropriate warning and encouragement.

This is very much the case with the discourse we are considering. It assures the community that Jesus had accurately foreseen the trials they are experiencing or have just experienced in the recent past. They are to draw comfort and encouragement from the fact that he has foreseen these trials and has located them within an unfolding divine "program" leading inexorably to the final triumph of God. The discourse also has to dampen down false hopes and expectations arising out of events that might reasonably have been seen as signs that the final days were at hand, leading to disillusionment and loss of faith when these expectations were not met. Within the community such misleading events could include the appearance of persons claiming to be the returned Messiah Jesus (those who come in his name saying: "I am he!" [13:6]). On a wider scale, events such as wars, famines, earthquakes, and other calamities could be taken as indications that the final cosmic upheaval was under way (vv. 7-8). Above all, the catastrophe represented by the fall of Jerusalem and destruction of the Temple (70 C.E.) was surely an occasion, appropriate as no other, for the return of Jesus to complete his messianic work.

One of the difficulties the discourse presents for interpretation stems from the fact that it proceeds from a question about the timing of the destruction of the Temple in Jerusalem (v. 4), but this soon morphs into the

---

1. The entire book of Deuteronomy is a farewell discourse pronounced by Moses just before he dies on the threshold of entering the Promised Land; so also Jesus' discourse at the Last Supper in John 13–17 and Paul's address to the elders of Ephesus in Acts 20:18-35. See further the very clear discussion provided by Nineham, *Saint Mark*, 339–42. This is also the conclusion of Keith D. Dyer after a thorough critical review of recent interpretation: *The Prophecy on the Mount: Mark 13 and the Gathering of the New Community* (Bern, etc.: Peter Lang, 1998) 233–66, 268–69.

much broader question concerning the timing of "the End," that is, the end of the present world order as such, heralded by the arrival of the Son of Man. It is necessary, then, to realize that the main "horizon" in view throughout the discourse is really not the destruction of the Temple or of Jerusalem but the fate of the present world itself. The discourse, in fact, seems to presuppose the destruction of the Temple in 70 C.E. and addresses the issue, doubtless crucial for the immediate audience of the gospel, of whether this cataclysmic event heralds the imminent arrival of "the End" in the more fundamental sense described.

In regard to all this the discourse communicates a two-pronged message: (1) Maintain your hope. Do not be dismayed that the Son of Man has not yet arrived, or even if he delays a little longer. All these things—the calamities that have occurred, and even worse—must take place before "the End" (the coming of the Son of Man: vv. 24-27; cf. v. 7). (2) But come he will—not only as deliverer, but also as the One to whom an account must be given: so be vigilant and watchful in your pattern of life.[2]

This oscillation between reassurance and warning is clearly reflected in the structure of the discourse. Passages dealing with community warning and exhortation alternate with passages of more apocalyptic tone dealing with the program of the End. The former group all begin (or in one case [vv. 21-23] conclude) with the phrase: "Take heed" *(blepete).*

2. Cf. Hooker, *Saint Mark,* 300–301.

Introduction: Setting: vv. 1-2

Introductory Questions ("When . . . ? What sign . . . ?"): vv. 3-4

Community Warning/Exhortation   **Apocalyptic Program of the End**

Warning against false prophets:
vv. 5-6
"Take heed . . ."

Prelude to the "Affliction": vv. 7-8

Trials/Persecutions: vv. 9-13
"Take heed . . ."

The Great "Affliction": vv. 14-20

Warning against false Christs:
vv. 21-23
"Take heed . . ." (v. 23)

The End: the Son of Man:
vv. 24-27

The Parable of the Fig Tree:
vv. 28-32

Exhortation: "Watch!" : vv. 33-37
"Take heed . . ."

Finally, a word about the eschatological "program" the discourse seems to presuppose: in general it reflects the conviction, widespread in apocalyptic Judaism at the time, that "the End," that is, the final transformation of the world through the intervention of God, would be preceded by a period of intensified suffering for the elect: a time when evil would "boil over," as it were, as the powers opposed to God run riot before succumbing to divine judgment and destruction. This is the time of the "Great Affliction" or the "birthpangs of the Messiah" preceding the full arrival of the Kingdom. Again we can set out schematically the four "stages" that seem to be featured in the discourse.

> The **Present** time

> The "**Beginning** of the Birthpangs"

> The **Birthpangs** proper (**"The Affliction"**)

> The **"End"**: The arrival of the Son of Man
> The Gathering of the Elect
> The Establishment of the Kingdom

Appreciation of these more general features of the discourse will, I hope, render it more accessible and obviate the need to go into all its details in depth. For most Christians today the expectation of Christ's return in glory ("Second Coming"), though still proclaimed in liturgy and creeds, is hardly a daily preoccupation. We "look back" to his life, death, and resurrection as the chief elements of his saving work. For the early generations, however, the emphasis was the other way around. It was as the Son of Man returning in glory that Christ would perform his principal messianic role: be the agent of the final victory of God. Cohabiting with a lively faith in the risen Lord was a strong sense of "unfinished business." Because they believed that the messianic age had "dawned" in the ministry and resurrection of Jesus there was impatience—and doubtless increasing dismay—that the conditions of the pre-messianic era (sinfulness, suffering, and death) lingered on. When would the Lord return to deal with all these things and finally institute the rule of God?[3] The same concerns—and not a few more—linger on for us today and raise the same issues about the faithfulness and power of God. Both in its original context and as it can be read today, the discourse has about it a large aspect of theodicy: in the face of all the evidence, is it still possible to believe in God—and cling to the promise of Jesus?

The Setting of the Discourse: 13:1-4

Victorious in the struggle for authority (cf. 11:28), Jesus now leaves the Temple, whose continuing function as a place of worship he has symbolically brought to an end by his action earlier in the week (11:15-17). As he does so, one of the disciples, speaking like a Galilean "hayseed" on his first visit to the "big smoke,"[4] remarks on the size of the Temple foundations and buildings (v. 1). This leads Jesus, in vividly evocative language, to prophesy the Temple's utter ruin (v. 2). The scene now (vv. 3-4) shifts to the Mount of Olives, a site looking directly across at the Temple and one associated through the prophecy of Zechariah 14 with the definitive victory of God's rule. Jesus adopts the sitting posture of a teacher, and Peter, approaching with James, John, and Andrew—the original four disciples called at the beginning (1:16-20)—asks him the double question that sparks the discourse: "When will this be, and what will be the sign that all these things are about to be accomplished?"[5]

False Interpretation of Dismaying External Events: 13:5-8; Community Trials and Persecutions: 13:9-13

As the discourse gets under way the "when" question tends to recede from view for a time[6] while Jesus addresses all the phenomena that could be interpreted—falsely—as "signs." In the first of the community warning sequences (vv. 5-6) Jesus warns the disciples about prophetic figures who

3. Paul addresses the very same issue in Rom 5–8; cf. Byrne, *Romans,* 163.

4. Cf. Donahue and Harrington, *Mark,* 368.

5. Some interpreters (e.g., Moloney, *Gospel of Mark,* 253) find three questions in Mark's formulation: (1) When will the destruction of Jerusalem ("these things") occur? What will be (2) the signs and (3) the timing of "all these things," that is, the wider end of the world (told from v. 24 on)? If this is Mark's meaning he has been more than usually cryptic. I think it is better to understand that for Mark the question about the destruction of the Temple, which had already been answered by history, shades immediately into that concerning "the End" in a more cosmic sense, and so there are only two basic questions.

6. It reappears toward the end of the discourse (vv. 24-37)—but only to be characterized by Jesus as ultimately unanswerable since the time is known only to the Father (v. 32).

will claim to speak in the name of the risen Lord ("I am he" [v. 6]) and lead the faithful astray through misinterpretation of what is going on around them.[7] They may interpret dismaying external events—wars and rumors of wars, earthquakes and famine, occurring on such a scale as to suggest the collapse of the entire world order[8]—as pointing to the imminent return of the Son of Man. But they would be wrong: all this will not be "the End," but only the beginning of the messianic woes that are to intensify before its arrival (vv. 7-8).

Closer to home for the community are the trials and persecutions it has to endure (vv. 9-13). Some of this trouble will come from outside in the shape of being given up to councils and beaten in synagogues, and being put on trial before governors and kings (v. 9).[9] As John the Baptist preached and "was given up" (1:9), and as Jesus has preached and will be "given up" (9:30; 10:33), on the same pattern—you preach and you get "given up"—the disciples will also "be given up" as a consequence of proclaiming the Gospel. In this sense the discourse foresees the "passion of the disciples," the cost of discipleship. Since the persecution will come about for the sake of Jesus' name it will serve as "a witness to them" (the persecutors) and hence be itself a proclamation of the Gospel. Moreover, they will not even have to mount their defense since what they are to say will be given them through the Holy Spirit (v. 11).[10] Much more poignant, however, will be the suffering caused by intrafamily betrayal, sometimes leading to death (v. 12), and the overwhelming sense of being an object of universal hatred because of bearing Christ's name (v. 13a). The steadfast endurance of all these trials, which may last for a long period, will result in "salvation" (v. 13b)—not necessarily in the sense of being rescued from physical death but salvation in the eschatological sense of sharing in the resurrection of the Lord.

---

7. In seeing a reference here to Christian prophets who spoke in Jesus' name I am indebted to Boring, *Mark,* 362-63, who points out the difficulties in finding here a warning against false messianic claimants outside the community or against people within the community claiming to be the returning Jesus.

8. Instances of the phenomena listed—particularly the civil strife within the Roman Empire (the sole superpower of the time) following the death of Nero in 68 C.E.—are attested for the decade culminating in the fall of Jerusalem in 70 C.E. On the other hand, the events as described are prominent in prophetic and apocalyptic literature, implying a stock, more general reference. For details see Taylor, *St. Mark,* 505.

9. "Councils" and "synagogues" refer to bodies exercising authority over Jews; "governors" and "kings" more likely refer to Roman officials and perhaps rulers such as the Herods; cf. Donahue and Harrington, *Mark,* 370.

10. The Spirit is here performing the role of "Paraclete," as in the Fourth Gospel (John 14:16, 26; 15:26; 16:7; cf. 1 John 2:1).

Somewhat intrusively in the midst of all this there appears the statement that really reflects the principal theme: "First the Gospel must be preached to all the nations" (v. 10). The "End," the appearance of the Son of Man, will not occur before a mighty task has been completed: the worldwide proclamation of the Good News of the Kingdom so that all nations will have a chance to respond in conversion and faith (1:15). The duration of that task has been extended beyond anything Mark or any of the early believers would have imagined, but the inclusion of this note about the necessity of the Gospel's proclamation to all nations before the coming of the "End" inserts into the discourse a kind of wedge that, in retrospect at least, frees it from its original narrow time span and gives it a flexible and potentially indeterminate application. Here is the point at which the discourse reaches out to and includes within its scope believers of all subsequent ages, down to our own. What Jesus foresees will apply as long as the Gospel is still to be proclaimed—up to our time and indefinitely beyond.

The "Great Affliction": 13:14-20; A Further Warning: 13:21-23

At this point we arrive at a section of the discourse that offers perhaps more difficulty to interpreters than any other part of the gospel. Despite the warning just issued to dampen down intense expectation of the End in view of dismaying events such as wars and rumors of war, and despite the insistence that a space of time has to be allowed for the preaching of the Gospel to the nations ("the wedge" [v. 10]), the discourse now seems to speak of a phenomenon that will function as a sign that the time of intensified suffering that is to precede the End is at hand: "the abomination that desolates standing where he ought not be" (v. 14a). It goes on to give quite specific instructions about action to be taken as soon as the sign is perceived (vv. 14c-18): flight to the mountains, not delaying to fetch an outer garment or return from the field, along with warnings about the hardship that will bear upon women who are pregnant or nursing infants, and recommending prayer that the flight not have to take place in winter. These instructions seem to envisage quite concretely a situation brought about by warfare. But the sign itself, presumably equally historical, is cloaked in language taken from the book of Daniel ("abomination that desolates") that the evangelist, in a unique aside (v. 14b), calls on the reader of the gospel to understand.[11] Presumably

---

11. The "desolating sacrilege" (v. 15a) refers in Dan 9:27; 11:31; 12:11 to a pagan image set up in the Temple in 167 B.C.E. by the Seleucid Greek king Antiochus IV Epiphanes. Later tradition seems to have related the Danielic phrase to subsequent sacrileges both actual and

Mark's original readers were able to grasp what dismaying event was being alluded to in this reference.[12] We are no longer in that position. Mark is pointing to some deplorable event that, perhaps for political reasons,[13] he does not want to name openly, but that for him is or will be the sign that the time of great affliction that is to precede the final transformation is at hand.

The following verses (19-20), again in language taken from Daniel (12:1), linger on the horrors of that time. The forces of evil that are to be let loose in the world will be so great that their conquest will involve a re-enactment of the process of creation, when God overcame the original chaos to bring forth the ordered world (v. 19).[14] The only thing guaranteeing the survival of human beings throughout this time will be God's gracious "shortening" of the time of turmoil "for the sake of the elect," that is, the community of the Kingdom (v. 20).[15]

What is in view is an apocalyptic scenario that has left historical events behind, even if, in words that Mark shrouds in mystery, some historical circumstance we cannot identify is to be the sign of its arrival. Rendering the passage even more mysterious is the fact that the advice given here about taking vigorous action when the sign appears seems to exist in very considerable tension with the attempt in the preceding section to dampen premature expectation of the End, despite the onset of cataclysmic events that might signal its onset, and even more in tension with the space of time required for the proclamation of the Gospel "to all the nations" (v. 10). We subsequent believers, who still occupy that space and carry out that mission,

---

foreseen, including—perhaps relevantly for the tradition behind Mark 13—the attempt by the emperor Caligula in 40 C.E. to have his image set up and venerated in the Temple.

12. The most obvious identification would be the destruction of the Temple by the Romans in 70 C.E. However, the phrase suggests desecration rather than destruction, and in Mark (contrast Matt 24:15) the qualifying participle ("standing . . .") is masculine rather than neuter (as strictly required by the word it qualifies: "abomination" *[bdelygma]*); this suggests a more personal reference—perhaps to the acclamation of the Roman general Titus in the Temple precinct following the conquest of Jerusalem; cf. Moloney, *Gospel of Mark,* 258–60. Alternatively and more likely in view of the fact that from the perspective of the discourse the sign is still in the future, the reference could be to the appearance of an antichrist figure along the lines of "the lawless one" in 2 Thess 2:3-10; cf. Taylor, *St. Mark,* 511; Gnilka, *Markus* 2:195–96.

13. Cf. Taylor, *St. Mark,* 511.

14. Cf. Hooker, *Saint Mark,* 315.

15. For the apocalyptic motif of the "shortening of the time of affliction" see Donahue and Harrington, *Mark,* 373. The final petition of the Lord's Prayer ("Deliver us from evil [or 'the evil one']," Matt 6:13; cf. Luke 11:4b) is a prayer for preservation in view of the same time of affliction preceding the full arrival of the Kingdom.

are perhaps well advised not to be on the lookout for an "abomination that desolates," nor, of course, can we follow the very particular instructions addressed originally to a community of believers in Judea (vv. 14c-18). This is a section of Mark's gospel so anchored in its original context as to resist contemporary actualization We can perhaps only allow to wash over us its firm conviction that all remains in the hands of God, who shaped the original chaos into order and continues to do so no matter how great a distress should come upon the world.[16]

This "boiling over" of evil will be, according to the apocalyptic program presupposed in the discourse, the prelude to the arrival of the Son of Man to institute the great judgment and finally establish the Kingdom. Before describing that moment the discourse turns aside, in inclusive fashion (cf. vv. 5-6), to warn once again (vv. 21-23) against prophetic figures who will make premature and hence false claims about the appearance of Jesus returned to complete his messianic work.[17] The warning rather brings us down to earth after the apocalyptic descriptions of the "affliction." But in the desperation of the times these false prophets will work the kinds of "signs and omens" that may induce "the elect" to believe that they do have heavenly credentials. Forewarned by Jesus, the community must be on the watch against them and give no credence to their claims (v. 23).[18] As we are only too well aware, the danger of extreme times overstimulating the religious imagination has not been confined to the church's first century.

The Appearing of the Son of Man: 13:24-27

This short, evocative passage forms the climax of the entire discourse, and in many ways the climax of Mark's gospel as a whole since it describes the moment of divine vindication (Story 3) that completes the resolution of the tension between the identity of Jesus as Messiah and God's beloved Son (Story 1), and his destiny to suffer and die for the "ransom of many" (10:45: Story 2). The event it describes is beyond history and indeed beyond the explicit narrative of the gospel, and yet what it depicts is what alone gives

---

16. Cf. Gnilka, *Markus* 2:199.

17. Here again (cf. n. 7 above in reference to vv. 5-6) I follow Boring, *Mark,* 269–71, in seeing a reference here to false prophets within the community rather than to messianic claimants within or without. The phrase "false christs" (*pseudochristoi* [v. 22]) is a difficulty, but it may not be original: it is lacking in a significant manuscript (D).

18. A very similar warning against false rumors suggesting that the Day of the Lord has arrived is to be found in 2 Thess 2:2—where also the "antichrist" figure is accompanied by false signs and wonders (vv. 9-10); cf. Hooker, *Saint Mark,* 317.

meaning to both the historical life of Jesus and the lives of those who follow him in discipleship and suffering, and who in that constitute the community of the Kingdom, the final establishment of which this scene proclaims.

The text falls into two parts. (1) After a time marker (v. 24a) indicating that what is about to be described follows "after that affliction" (that is, after the time of intensified suffering described in vv. 19-20), a composite quotation of biblical texts[19] indicates, in highly apocalyptic mode, the collapse of the heavenly bodies that give light to the world (vv. 24b-25). This terrifying chain of phenomena, which really amounts to the end of the world as presently constituted, is the sign pointing to (2) the imminent arrival and glory-clad appearance of the Son of Man (vv. 26-27) to institute judgment and bring in the final establishment of God's Rule.[20]

In contrast to the false messianic rumors, about which the preceding section gave warnings (vv. 21-22), the One who is now "seen" *(opsontai)* is the true Messiah, Jesus, coming to bring to completion the messianic task of quashing all opposition to God's Rule on earth. Throughout his earthly ministry, as described in the gospel, Jesus' identity as Messiah, though *felt* in his "works of power" (exorcisms), had to be suppressed ("messianic secret") lest it be swamped in public imagination by the conventional understanding of the role, in which destiny to suffering and death did not feature. Now that Jesus has broken the grip of evil through his obedience "unto death" (Phil 2:8) and has been raised and exalted to the right hand of God, his messianic status can be displayed in the truly transcendent sense in which it applies to him, vastly outstripping mere conventional expectation (cf. 12:35-37). Thus it is that in a vision evoking Dan 7:13 ("coming on clouds, with great power and glory" [v. 26b])[21] Jesus will appear, clad with divine authority and power, to bring in the Kingdom at last.

Central to that task will be sending out the divine messengers, the angels, to "gather the elect" from the entire universe (v. 27).[22] "The elect" are the community of the Kingdom, all those who have responded through repentance and faith to the good news (1:15). The need to gather them from far and wide reflects the preaching of the Gospel to all the nations of the

---

19. The basic text seems to be Isa 13:10; cf. also Isa 34:4; Joel 2:10.

20. Cf. Donahue and Harrington, *Mark,* 374.

21. Clouds are associated with divinity in the biblical tradition; cf. Hooker, *Saint Mark,* 319; Gnilka, *Markus* 2:201.

22. Literally "from the four winds (= points of the compass: north, south, east, west), from the end of the earth to the end of heaven," a phrase embracing Deut 13:7 and 30:4, to denote the entire universe; cf. Donahue and Harrington, *Mark,* 375.

world (13:10),[23] a task that, in the perspective of this vision, has already been accomplished. They have followed the way of discipleship, sharing in Jesus' sufferings, some even to the point of death (10:38). Now, since they have not been "ashamed" of him, he will not be "ashamed" of them (8:38; cf. 14:62). On the contrary, they are to enter with him into the fullness of the Kingdom.

What is described here in highly apocalyptic language is not, of course, to be taken literally. But this does not mean that it has no relationship to reality. The gospel is attempting to describe a transcendent reality—the establishment of God's Rule on earth—and employing the only language suitable for expressing that reality: the language of symbol and myth.[24] As myth, it is told as a "story," an event that takes place in the future. Yet precisely as myth it gives assurance of what is already happening. This is because Jesus, as risen and exalted Lord, is not sitting passively at the right hand of God, but, through the Spirit, is actively exerting his messianic rule throughout the cosmos.[25] The vision of the Son of Man this passage puts before the faithful is an assurance that, despite the cost of their discipleship and the remaining prevalence of evil, the divine victory already seen in the resurrection of Jesus is currently being extended on earth and will soon be seen to be definitively and universally in place.[26]

Watchfulness: 13:28-37

In some respects it would have been fitting had the discourse on the future ended with the magnificent description of the Son of Man's arrival in glory. Instead, in something of an anticlimax, we have a number of sayings strung together, along with two parables, around the basic theme of watchfulness in view of the End. This final section of the discourse is necessary in the sense that here Jesus moves to respond to the "when?"

---

23. Cf. Moloney, *Gospel of Mark,* 267.

24. Cf. Donahue and Harrington, *Mark,* 381.

25. Other passages in the New Testament express this present aspect of Christ's messianic rule: cf. especially the final stanza of the Christ-hymn in Phil 2:9-11; also 1 Cor 15:23-28; Eph 2:20-23.

26. How that victory will embrace those who have already "fallen asleep" is a problem that began to exercise believers from the earliest times—when death became a phenomenon in the community of the Kingdom. Paul led the charge in insisting that those who had "fallen asleep" would not lack participation in the Kingdom (1 Thess 4:13-18). Hence hope for the resurrection of believers became integral to Christian faith in the resurrection of Jesus (1 Corinthians 15). The Kingdom is a transcendent reality, but not one totally discontinuous with the present life on earth.

question asked by the disciples (v. 4a), whereas up till now he had been more, though by no means exclusively, attending to the question: "what sign?" (v. 4b). Paradoxically, however, the answer he gives is no answer at all: he stresses that the timing of "that day and hour" (v. 32) is known to the Father alone. Moreover, in considerable tension with the early part of the discourse, where his aim had been to dampen down over-keen expectation of the End, here the general tendency is to stress its imminence and demand watchfulness in that regard.

In short, the "mixed messages" aspect of the discourse appears here in high concentration. We modern readers of the gospel have to reckon with the fact that the ancient mindset was less concerned than we tend to be to eliminate inconsistency; it happily allowed a variety of voices to be gathered and heard—now one, now the other—as occasion required. So the short "parable"—really just an extended image—of the fig tree[27] reinforces the sense that the heavenly portents described in verses 24b-25, dismaying though they may be, really are the signs of the imminent arrival of the Son of Man (vv. 26-27).[28] This is confirmed by Jesus' solemn assurance that "these things"[29] will occur in the lifetime of the present "generation" (v. 30; cf. 9:1)—something that patently has not taken place. The early church tradition has preserved the saying and bolstered it by affirming even more strongly the permanence of Jesus' words (v. 31)[30] because it introduces the sense of the nearness of the end that will be a key consideration in the exhortation to watchfulness that follows (vv. 33-37).[31] No sooner are these

27. Unlike most trees in Palestine, the fig tree is deciduous and puts out new leaves only at the very end of spring. The appearance of the foliage of this very common tree is, then, a quite clear and familiar indicator of the onset of summer.

28. This is to take "these things" in v. 29 as referring to the portents mentioned in vv. 24b-25; cf. Moloney, *Gospel of Mark,* 268. A reference to events mentioned earlier in the discourse cannot, however, be ruled out.

29. Again, the reference must be to the cosmic events heralding the end of the world; cf. Moloney, *Gospel of Mark,* 268. A reference to such things as the destruction of the Temple or Jerusalem (70 C.E.) "saves" the veracity of Jesus' prediction at the cost of rather stretching the sense of "generation." However, at this point in the discourse the thought of those events has fallen away in favor of the eschatological reference.

30. In the Old Testament only God's word "abides forever" (Isa 40:8). There is a high christological claim in the statement that Jesus' assurance will remain the element of continuity and security for the faithful across the immense cosmic transformation described in vv. 24-27; cf. Moloney, *Gospel of Mark,* 269.

31. Just as the statements in vv. 29 and 30 are linked by the phrase "these things," so those in vv. 30 and 31 are linked by "pass away." The common terms are the "glue" that has brought these probably originally separately occurring statements together in the tradition; cf. the similarly linked string of sayings at the close of chapter 9 (vv. 47-50).

affirmations made, however, than a qualification washes over the sequence from another direction (v. 32): the end may be "near," but its timing is known to no one—not to the angels, or even to the Son—only to the Father. Whatever the problems this admission of ignorance on the part of Jesus may cause for christology,[32] it is best interpreted as a further expression of Jesus' complete surrender of his entire fate into the hands of the Father. As he goes obediently to his death, the time of his return in glory to claim the world for the Kingdom, no less than his being raised from the dead, rests entirely with the Father.[33]

The discourse ends with an exhortation to watchfulness based around a parable (vv. 34-36) that aptly picks up this sense of living in keen expectation of the end yet remaining in ignorance as to its precise timing. Like many of the parables of Jesus it has become something of an allegory in the tradition. The "man who goes on a journey" is Jesus, shortly to go on a "journey" to the Father through death and resurrection. The servants are the faithful. They are not simply to lie about idly awaiting his return. Each one has his or her "work" to do, but it is the one who must watch the door, the gatekeeper, who particularly illustrates the watchfulness required of all. The master does not want to be pinned down to a preannounced time of arrival.[34] In line with master-slave relationships of the time, he has no scruple in expecting his slaves to be awake and ready to receive him when he arrives, and will be greatly displeased to find them asleep. Hence their only proper course is to stay awake through all the watches of the night.[35] The events of Jesus' final meal, arrest, and trials will occur across these watches, providing a significant narrative link between this conclusion to the discourse and the Passion story that follows.[36] In particular, three of the disciples who are the immediate audience of the discourse will, during Jesus' prayer in Gethsemane,

---

32. Whether the statement goes back to the historical Jesus is a matter of dispute. The absolute use of "the Son" suggests that it does not, but, on the other hand, many think it unlikely that the early tradition would have created a saying attributing ignorance to Jesus. My sense is that the early church may simply have formulated the saying to communicate the sense that, *pace* the statement in v. 30, it did not have from Jesus definite information about the time of the end. The tension with the saying in v. 30 is eased when one considers that "it is possible to be confident that an event will occur within a certain space of time without being certain of precise day or hour" (Hooker, *Saint Mark,* 323).

33. Cf. Kelly, *Eschatology and Hope,* 183.

34. Though the parable speaks of the man as having gone away on a journey (v. 34), the application (vv. 35-36), with its presumption that he will arrive home at some stage during the night, is more consonant with his having gone out to a banquet or wedding feast; cf. Hooker, *Saint Mark,* 323–24.

35. The four times listed—evening, midnight, cockcrow, morning—are those of the Roman military watches; cf. Moloney, *Gospel of Mark,* 271.

36. Cf. Moloney, *Gospel of Mark,* 271.

provide a counterexample of inability to keep watch (14:34, 37-38, 40, 41).

Though the discourse has been addressed to them, along with Andrew (13:3), Jesus makes clear in a final command that what he has said to them applies to all: "Watch!" (v. 37). The original Markan audience and all subsequent readers of the gospel live as servants "waiting" on the return of their Lord. The discourse has looked out at this time and, as we have remarked several times, communicated mixed messages in its regard. While to some degree disconcerting, the variety addresses the multifaceted character of Christian life in which at times enthusiasm needs to be dampened, while other times and seasons call for encouragement, hope, and reassurance.

VI
JESUS' PASSION AND DEATH
14:1–15:47

Passion 1:
Jesus Confronts His Death: 14:1-52

Across the four gospels Mark's account of Jesus' Passion is by far the most stark and unrelieved. Certainly I have found composing the three chapters of this book that deal with it by far the most difficult, and there is no way that an interpreter can—or should—protect the reader from its challenge. That Jesus is about to suffer and die is not, however, a prospect that takes the reader by surprise. Threats to his life begin very early in the gospel. The arrest of John the Baptist following his preaching (1:14) sets an ominous precedent. Shortly after Jesus begins his own ministry there is a dangerous accusation of blasphemy when Jesus forgives sins (2:7), followed by mention of a time for fasting when "the Bridegroom" (Jesus) would be "taken away" (2:20). The early cycle of controversy stories ends with an explicit notice of a conspiracy to "destroy" him (3:6a). The execution of John foreshadows that of Jesus (6:14-29). Eventually Jesus makes clear in the sequence of Passion predictions his disciples find so challenging (8:31-33; 9:30-32; 10:32-34; cf. 10:35-45) that his destiny is to suffer and die in Jerusalem. After he arrives in Jerusalem, a desire on the part of the authorities to do away with him forms a dramatic backdrop to his ministry in the Temple and the challenge to their authority it represents (11:18; 12:12). The only thing protecting him is his popularity with the common people (12:12, 37b). This leads his adversaries to look for a way of getting hold of him in private, away from the crowds that, as the Passion story gets under way, are beginning to throng Jerusalem for the Passover feast (14:1).

The account, then, of Jesus' arrest, condemnation, and execution is something toward which the narrative has been driving from the start. It marks the point at which the tension between the two "stories" with which the disciples in particular have been wrestling—that Jesus is Messiah and

Son of God (Story 1), and that he is destined to suffer and die (Story 2)—comes to a high point of concentration and then finds some measure of resolution in the centurion's confession following Jesus' death on the cross (15:39).[1] In the Passion, as Mark describes it, Jesus' conflict with the demonic comes to a climax as, in the utter loneliness of his death, he plumbs human alienation from God to its depth. In contrast to the other evangelists, Mark does not hesitate to portray Jesus' "obedience unto death" (Phil 2:8) in all its unrelieved starkness. Jesus, whose authority had shone out from the start of the gospel, confounding demons and human adversaries with equal force, now surrenders himself to violence and abuse. As humanly he shrinks from the "cup" that now stands before him (14:35-36), he will seek comfort and companionship from his closest friends and find them wanting. Most poignant of all, as human violence is wreaked upon him in ever-increasing intensity, is the sense of silence "from heaven" that will culminate in his cry of abandonment just before he dies on the cross (15:34).

At one level, then, there is a terrible "absence" of God in the Passion according to Mark. But this is not the whole story. Jesus goes to his death deliberately, following a divine "script" set forth in the Scriptures (14:27, 49). Hints of this surface in certain details that echo Psalms 22 and 69, showing that David, prophetic author of the Psalms, foresaw the suffering of his messianic "son" and "Lord" (cf. 12:35-37). Moreover, the attempt to portray Jesus (falsely) as a messianic pretender ("King of the Jews") and to mock him as such, even to the extent of clothing him with the insignia of kingship, *ironically* communicates the truth: that he is in fact the King Messiah, though in a sense far transcending conventional messianic pretension. Abandoned by his followers, Jesus dies between two bandits in the most godless, abhorrent place in Jerusalem, the place of execution. Yet, the moment his obedience has run its full course, there *is* a response "from heaven" (the rending of the Temple curtain) that shows, as the centurion goes on to avow, that this "truly was the Son of God" (15:39), and that in his dying the divine presence and power was striking the decisive blow in reclaiming humanity for the Kingdom.

By telling the story in this way the early Christian community addressed the first of two immense issues that confronted it in its proclamation of the Gospel of the Crucified: how was it that Israel's Messiah, who was also God's beloved Son, was allowed to suffer and die at the hands of the Gentiles

---

1. As I have argued from the start, full resolution of the "stories" awaits the completion of the divine action through Story 3: Jesus' advent as Son of Man, as described in the discourse on the future (13:24-27).

(Romans) through the connivance of Israel's leaders? In its preaching and catechesis the community told the story of Jesus' death in a way that brought out that it was God's express design that Israel's Messiah should accomplish his saving work through suffering and death, and that details of his suffering were inscribed in the Scriptures to indicate that divine intent.[2] On the surface Jesus goes to his death the passive victim of the human authorities who had become his enemies. At a deeper level his submission to violence and condemnation fulfills a divine design to strike the decisive blow against the rule of Satan in the world and establish once and for all in its stead the liberating rule of God. It is to this deeper subtext that the scriptural allusions call our attention, even as Jesus dies a human death devoid of "supernatural" alleviation.

This means that there are really two levels of "causality" operating throughout the Passion. At one level *human* agents (the chief priests, Judas, Pilate) are bringing Jesus to arrest, trial, and execution, while his closest followers betray (Judas), deny (Peter), and desert him. At another *(divine)* level all this malign and treacherous human agency is actually working a divine purpose. Despite the overt "absence" of God right up to and including the moment of death, Jesus enters into his Passion with complete foreknowledge of all that will take place and refers all that is happening to the "script" laid down for him on the divine level (14:21, 27, 49).

The second issue the early community had to address was an "apologetic" one vis-à-vis the Greco-Roman world that had become the milieu for the preaching of the Gospel. The early believers were proclaiming as Savior one who had been condemned in a Roman judicial process to a most degrading and abhorrent form of execution, one reserved for rebels and runaway slaves. Effective proclamation of the Gospel required establishing Jesus' complete innocence of the charges brought against him and the acceptance that his condemnation had been accomplished through betrayal, false accusation, and malicious pressure applied to the Roman governor who, while recognizing his innocence and anxious to set him free, acted against his own better judgment. Mark's account of Jesus' Passion reflects this concern with Jesus' innocence, culminating in the acknowledgment given by the Roman centurion immediately after Jesus' death (14:39).

The mode of Jesus' death shows that the Roman authorities had concluded or had been led to conclude that he was a danger to the preservation

---

2. In telling the story of Jesus' Passion, Matthew brings out the "fulfillment of Scripture" motif much more explicitly than Mark (cf. Matt 26:54, 56; 27:9, 34). Luke does so retrospectively, as it were, in the resurrection appearances (24:25-27, 44-47; but cf. 22:37).

of peace and order in Palestine, especially at the fraught time of Passover. To what extent, from a historical point of view, Jewish authorities were complicit in this is debated, but as far as the gospels are concerned we can see already in Mark a tendency to shift responsibility for Jesus' death away from the Romans and back upon the Jewish authorities. This tendency, accentuated in the later gospels, clearly served the interests of the proclamation of the Gospel in the wider world. It has led, however, to the Passion stories becoming "texts of terror" in regard to Christian attitudes to Jews and Judaism down the ages.[3] While the problem is not so acute in regard to the interpretation of Mark's gospel as it is in the case of Matthew or John, it is a matter that interpreters of Mark have to take very seriously if interpretation is to proceed with ethical integrity today. Jesus died as a victim of violence in which religion played a central role. His death showed the extent to which religion is open to demonic infestation as much as any other sphere of human life. It has been a tragic irony that religious violence, carried out in his name and with appeal to the gospels, has borne so heavily against the people who were and remain his "brothers (and sisters) according to the flesh" (cf. Rom 9:3, 5).

Amid Hostility and Threat to Jesus an Unnamed Woman Anoints Him for Burial: 14:1-11

The action of the Passion story gets under way with a further reminder (vv. 1-2) of the intense desire of the authorities (the chief priests and scribes) to lay hands on Jesus and bring about his death. The approach of the feast of Passover, with the increased danger of riot it entails, accentuates the one factor blocking the gaining of their objective: the esteem Jesus enjoys among the people. Consequently, any move against him has to be put off for the present. Shortly, as we shall learn (vv. 10-11), one of his companions, Judas Iscariot, will solve the problem for them.

Between these two notices of hostility and treachery Mark inserts a narrative going in a totally opposite direction: an unnamed woman braves misunderstanding and criticism to perform for Jesus an action replete with love and appreciation of what he is about to undergo.[4]

The incident takes place at Bethany, Jesus' base during his Jerusalem ministry (11:11-12, 19). As so often in Mark, it happens in a house—one belonging to Simon the Leper. It is unlikely that Simon could have offered

---

3. The phrase "texts of terror" comes from Phyllis Trible, *Texts of Terror: Literary-Feminist Readings of Biblical Narratives* (Philadelphia: Fortress Press, 1984).

4. The placement is, of course, a classic example of Mark's "sandwich" technique.

hospitality on the scale implied in the narrative were he suffering from leprosy at the time. Perhaps we are to think of him as someone whom Jesus had cured and who had become a disciple or at least a friend. Nonetheless, the epithet "Leper" reminds us of Jesus' association with the outcasts of society and willingness to cross boundaries set up by the purity ("clean"/ "unclean") laws.[5] An unnamed woman invades this (presumably all male) space, breaks open an alabaster jar of pure and costly nard, and pours its contents over Jesus' head (v. 3). The extravagance of her gesture provokes an angry response from those present (vv. 4-5),[6] who complain: "Why this waste?" The jar's contents could have been sold for a sum amounting to a year's wages[7] and the proceeds spent on relief of the poor. The criticism serves as a perfect foil for Jesus, speaking in defense of the woman, to interpret the true meaning of her act (vv. 6-9).

The protest about waste and the higher claim of the poor reflects the continuing inability of the disciples to "hear" what Jesus has been saying over and over: his destiny is to suffer and die in Jerusalem (Story 2). The woman, on the other hand, has performed for him an action that is not only "beautiful," but truly fitting *(kalon)*[8] because it reflects a true understanding of what Jesus is about to undergo and responds in kind to the cost of that undertaking. Jesus' remark about "having the poor always with you" (v. 7a) does not endorse poverty as a permanent factor in human society.[9] Rather, in an echo of the social justice prescription of Deut 15:11,[10] it sets up a contrast between the factual prevalence of poor people in society and the ongoing opportunity to relieve them that this provides, on the one hand, and the absolute impermanence of his own presence, on the other (cf. the "taking away" of the bridegroom in 2:20), something they have consistently failed to grasp. Appreciating both the imminence and the costliness of his coming absence, the woman "has done what she could" (v. 8) in the sense of spending all her resources on the precious ointment and pouring it out entirely. Like the widow who contributed to the Temple treasury (12:44), she is giving

5. Cf. Boring, *Mark,* 382.

6. In contrast to the Matthean parallel (26:8) they are not described as "disciples," which is curious, given Mark's tendency to stress the disciples' failings.

7. Literally "more than three hundred denarii," a denarius being equivalent to a day's wages.

8. It is hard to convey all the nuances of the Greek adjective *kalos,* with its resonances of "beautiful" and "honorable" as well as "appropriate"; cf. Donahue and Harrington, *Mark,* 387.

9. Cf. Taylor, *St. Mark,* 532.

10. "Since there will never cease to be some in need on the earth . . . 'Open your hand to the poor and needy neighbor in your land.'"

her all because she knows that Jesus is giving his all. At a deeper level, because he is going to his death, her gesture can be interpreted as an anointing of his body for burial—something that will not in fact take place when Jesus' body is taken down from the cross and buried by a stranger (15:46).[11]

Jesus concludes his defense with a solemn pronouncement: "Wherever the gospel is proclaimed, in all the world, what she has done will be told in memory of her" (v. 9). This majestic statement binds the woman's action into the essence of the Gospel, the proclamation of which will be incomplete if the Passion story is told without it. This is because what she has done represents the truly "fitting" *(kalon)* response to the self-offering of Jesus. She has recognized the cost to him of the "service" he is performing for all (10:45) and has responded in love, gratitude, and generosity to her utmost capacity. In so doing she "models" the true response of a disciple—both now (in contrast to the calculating coldness of the male disciples) and in the time to come when the Gospel is proclaimed throughout the world.[12] This may explain, too, the most puzzling feature of the final comment: why, if the story is to be told in her memory, is she not named at any stage? It is perhaps her very anonymity that allows her to be a point of insertion into the story for all, women and men alike, who seek to respond appropriately to Jesus' giving up of his life as a ransom "for many" (10:45).

There is a kind of chilling continuity between the disciples' concern for money, albeit in a good cause (relief of the poor), and Judas' acceptance of the promise of money from the chief priests in return for handing Jesus over (vv. 10-11). One of Jesus' closest companions has now gone over completely to the side of his adversaries, while inability to appreciate what Jesus is about to do places the remaining eleven in a situation of dangerous ambiguity. In stark contrast, the woman's loving service shines out all the more.

---

11. I do not share the widely held view that the woman's anointing of Jesus at this point represents an anointing of him as king; cf. Hooker, *Saint Mark,* 238; Moloney, *Gospel of Mark,* 281; Donahue and Harrington, *Mark,* 390. While the "kingship" theme develops as the Passion story unfolds, it is something that has to be "read back" into the text at this point—in contrast to the "burial" aspect about which Jesus is so explicit; cf. Gnilka, *Markus* 2:224; Boring, *Mark,* 383, n. 81.

12. For a moving interpretation of the anointing as an act of healing—and a paradigm of women's healing ministry—see Elaine Wainwright, "The Pouring Out of Healing Ointment: Rereading Mark 14:3-9," in Fernando Segovia, ed., *Towards a New Heaven and a New Earth: Essays in Honor of Elisabeth Schüssler Fiorenza* (Maryknoll, NY: Orbis, 2003) 157–78.

Jesus Celebrates a Eucharistic Passover with His Disciples: 14:12-25

As the time for celebrating the Passover meal draws near,[13] the disciples approach Jesus seeking instructions concerning the preparations for the celebration (v. 12). In a way that closely parallels the arrangements before his entry into the city (11:1-6), Jesus sends two of them there with instructions concerning what they will find (a man carrying a jar of water) and how they are then to proceed (follow him to a house where the householder has a large room ready for "the Teacher's" use at Passover). The exact correspondence between the instructions given and what the disciples find (vv. 13-16) communicates the sense that Jesus is solemnly entering into a process he has foreseen and is following with calm deliberation.

The same sense of foreknowledge emerges from the announcement that Jesus makes as, with the Twelve,[14] he reclines that evening at supper (vv. 17-21): one of them, one who now is eating with him, is about to betray him. The fact (twice mentioned) that the betrayer is one who shares his table heightens the sense of treachery. But precisely as victim of such treachery from within his closest group, Jesus is following the "script" laid out for him in the Scriptures (Ps 41:9, quoted in vv. 18 and 21). In obedience to divine will the Son of Man is going toward a supremely costly confrontation with human evil just when that evil has penetrated his inmost circle and made one of his own its key accomplice. In the mysterious interplay of divine and human causality that appears in biblical thought,[15] Judas is the willing perpetrator of evil and yet an instrument of the wider divine purpose that will encompass its defeat—even if, for him personally, it would have been "better had he never been born" (v. 21c).[16]

13. Mark's time indication is obscure. "(T)he first day of Unleavened Bread" is the first day of the feast of Passover when the lambs were eaten rather than the preceding day of preparation when they were slaughtered; cf. Donahue and Harrington, *Mark,* 392. Mark clearly regards the coming meal as the Passover celebration even though his description has no reference to key elements in that meal, such as the eating of the lamb and the herbs, etc. On the vexed question as to the actual day of the week on which the Last Supper took place see Hooker, *Saint Mark,* 332–34; thorough discussion in John P. Meier, *A Marginal Jew: Rethinking the Historical Jesus.* Vol. 1: *The Roots of the Problem and the Person* (New York: Doubleday, 1991) 386–401.

14. In vv. 12-16 there is reference to "the disciples," in vv. 17-21 to "the Twelve." While the variation may simply reflect the use of separate sources, Mark may also be indicating that others besides the Twelve were present at the supper; cf. Donahue and Harrington, *Mark,* 392.

15. The interplay comes out in the use of the verb *paradidonai,* which, as we have seen, has both the more neutral sense of "give up" as well as the pejorative meanings "betray," "hand over" (to enemies); cf. Hooker, *Saint Mark,* 337.

16. This prophetic statement and the "Woe" that precedes it is not so much a curse or a threat but a cry of sorrow and anguish; cf. Taylor, *St. Mark,* 542. It need not imply Judas' eternal damnation; cf. Gnilka, *Markus* 2:238.

It is in this context of betrayal in his innermost circle that Jesus begins the gestures that transform the Passover ritual into the Christian Eucharist. He does so to specify the meaning of the death he is about to undergo and to draw the disciples and the audience of the gospel into the saving effects of that death. He takes a loaf of bread and, following Jewish custom before eating in company, blesses God for the gift of food it represents. He then breaks the loaf into pieces, gives a piece to each of those present, saying "Take," and adds in explanation, "this is my body" (v. 22). By designating the broken bread as "his body," that is, his very person,[17] Jesus indicates that eating the bread forges a most profound union with himself (cf. 1 Cor 10:16-17).

The actions and words over the cup (vv. 23-24) follow in parallel.[18] This time, however, there is a significant extension in Jesus' words of explanation: "This is my blood of the covenant, which is poured out for many" (v. 24). "Blood of the covenant" alludes to a ritual act recorded in Exod 24:4-8, when Moses sealed the Sinai covenant by sprinkling the blood of sacrificial animals on the Israelites, saying: "See the blood of the covenant that the Lord has made with you in accordance with all these words" (Exod 24:8; cf. Zech 9:11). The added phrase "for many" does not have a restrictive sense ("many" = "some," as distinct from "all") but, in a Semitic idiom, indicates an action of an individual that confers benefits on others ("many" = "more than one").[19] Taken as a whole, the words of Jesus over the cup reflect the early Christian tradition (cf. also Rom 3:25; 5:9; Heb 9:11-14) that interpreted the shedding of his blood on Calvary as the inauguration of a new covenant for a renewed people of God.[20] When disciples partake of the cup blessed by Jesus they sacramentally lay hold of the saving benefits conferred by his death. On the model of the liberation of Israel from Egyptian slavery commemorated at Passover, they become the nucleus of a covenant people set free by this saving action of God. By reenacting these eucharistic gestures they will draw new generations into the freedom and promise of that saving act.

---

17. Cf. Gnilka, *Markus* 2.244.

18. A difference is that all drink from the cup before Jesus' words of explanation (v. 23c). Some interpreters think this is to avoid any suggestion that Jesus drank his own blood.

19. Cf. Rom 5:15, 19, where "many" is interchangeable with "all."

20. In contrast to the eucharistic narratives recorded by Paul (1 Cor 11:23-25) and Luke (22:20), Mark, followed by Matthew (26:28), does not mention "new covenant" (cf. Jer 31:33), but the motif of a new covenant is implicit in the new sprinkling of blood (that of Christ on Calvary), which has a similar function (covenant sealing) to the sprinkling performed by Moses.

Unlike the Matthean parallel (26:28), the words over the cup in Mark do not specify that Jesus' blood is to be poured out "for the remission of sins." Nor is an allusion to the Servant figure of Isa 53:10, 12 who bears the sins "of many" as clear as in the Matthean text.[21] This raises the question as to whether the shorter explanation over the cup in Mark includes the remission of sin among the saving effects of Jesus' death[22] or whether it should not, rather, be taken as referring to the liberation in a more general sense achieved by Jesus' victory over the demonic world and the forces opposed to the Kingdom.[23] It is true that Jesus' declaration of forgiveness early in the gospel (2:5) has no explicit connection with the prospect of his death.[24] But "repentance" is an essential element of response to the Kingdom from the start (1:15; cf. John's preaching of a baptism of repentance "for the forgiveness of sins" [1:4]). Moreover, the implication that Jesus, in the shedding of his blood, replaces the atoning function of the Temple, now rendered obsolete (11:15-17), suggests that Matthew may be making explicit something that is implicit in Mark and part of his overall understanding.[25] Those who become members of the new covenant people of God do so as cleansed and purified by the blood of Jesus.

Jesus closes his words and gestures at the supper with a solemn pronouncement that he will no longer drink of the fruit of the vine until the day when he drinks it new in the Kingdom of God (v. 25). The statement makes clear that his death will intervene before the full implementation of the Kingdom. It also makes this supper and every subsequent eucharistic celebration during the time after he has been "taken away" (2:20) a continuation of the union with him the disciples have experienced till now, and an anticipation and pledge of the full fellowship they will experience in the banquet of the Kingdom.

In this way the supper touches no less than five "moments" in the story of salvation. Looking "backward," so to speak, it (1) recalls and renews the covenant made with the original people of God following their liberation from slavery in Egypt, and (2) less remotely, it recalls the meals in which

---

21. Matthew secures the allusion to the Servant by changing the preposition in the phrase "for many" (*peri pollōn* instead of *hyper pollōn,* as in Mark 14:24) to make it conform exactly to the LXX of Isa 53:4, 10.

22. So many older interpreters: e.g., Taylor, *St. Mark,* 546; also Gnilka, *Markus* 2:245–46; Watts, *Isaiah's New Exodus,* 356–62.

23. So especially Dowd and Malbon, "Significance of Jesus' Death," 292–94.

24. As I noted in that connection, the declaration is not given without cost, since it leads immediately to the accusation of blasphemy, the charge on which Jesus will later be formally condemned (14:63).

25. Cf. Taylor, *St. Mark,* 546.

Jesus celebrated the mercy of God with sinners (2:15), especially the two occasions when, with the same gestures ("taking," "blessing" ["giving thanks"], "breaking," "giving"), he multiplied the loaves to ensure that the people did not go away faint and hungry (6:35-44; 8:1-9). (3) Now, on the eve of his death, he transforms the Passover celebration in order that (4) during the time following his being "taken away" (2:20), the disciples may sacramentally experience union with him and the benefits of his redemptive act, as a foretaste and anticipation of (5) union with him in the banquet of the Kingdom.

Eating the bread, then, that is his broken body and drinking the cup that is his blood poured out for many forges a union with Jesus that will transcend his mortal existence now coming to an end. Moreover, precisely as a union with One whose body is to be broken and his lifeblood poured out for many, it is a union that not only confers benefits on those who partake but also catches them up, in an ethical sense, in the rhythm of his self-giving life. They will become not merely passive beneficiaries but active participants in the mission of the One who came not to be served but to serve, and to give his life as a ransom for many (10:45).[26]

To the Mount of Olives:
Jesus Foretells the Disciples' Desertion and Peter's Denial: 14:26-31

Having sung a hymn (one of the Hallel psalms [113–18]) to conclude the Passover celebration, Jesus and his disciples return to the Mount of Olives (v. 26). Just as, immediately before the supper, he had foretold the betrayal of Judas and related that to the divine purpose (vv. 18, 20-21), so now—in a way that completes a narrative "frame" of failure in discipleship around his self-gift at the supper—he announces the desertion of the remaining Eleven. He encompasses this, too, within the divine plan by quoting a form of Zech 13:7: "I will strike the shepherd, and the sheep of the flock will be scattered" (v. 27).[27] Along with the betrayal, their impending desertion is part of the human failure and hostility that are bringing him to his death, but on the other, divine, level of "causality" it is a result of the Father's "strik-

---

26. In 1 Cor 11:17-34 Paul recalls the eucharistic tradition precisely to counter the selfish behavior that surrounds the celebration of the Lord's Supper at Corinth. The Corinthians should remember that when they eat the bread and drink the cup they "proclaim the death of the Lord until he comes" (11:26). How inappropriate, then, to indulge in behavior that runs clearly contrary to the self-sacrificing love displayed in that death.

27. The text as quoted by Mark has God as the agent ("I will strike . . ."), where the Hebrew and LXX have the imperative ("Strike . . .").

ing" of the Son that is the ultimate explanation of why he is going to his death. The gospel has portrayed him as compassionate Shepherd-King (6:34). Now the Shepherd himself will be struck and the flock (the disciples) scattered. But that will not be the end of the story. God will raise the Shepherd and, in the way that Palestinian shepherds lead their sheep, he will "go ahead" of them to Galilee (v. 28).[28] The Gospel of Mark will not give us a glimpse of the risen Lord. But here, as in the earlier Passion predictions, it makes clear that the Father who, for the rescue of the world from the demonic, will "strike" the Shepherd, will also raise him to gather the community for the Kingdom.

Peter's protestation (v. 29) that *he* at least will never be a deserter draws from Jesus (v. 30) a further prophecy, very specific as to time and circumstance: Peter will deny him three times this very night before the end of the third watch (cockcrow). Thus the series of denials from this leading disciple, when they do occur (14:66-72), will also be gathered into the wider picture of human hostility, treachery, and failure Jesus has foreseen and placed within his sense of the overall design of God. Peter reasserts his determination and the others join him (v. 31), but this will only serve to underline their failure, about to begin almost immediately.

It is easy to pass over the short exchange between Jesus and the disciples on the way to the Mount of Olives. In addressing the failure of the disciples that is to be so integral a part of the Passion story and setting that failure—even before it actually takes place—within the wider divine purpose, this dialogue addresses all human failure in respect to the demands of discipleship. As the disciples failed, we too fail—but that does not mean that Jesus ceases to be the Shepherd who will gather the scattered remnants of our loyalty and lead us to a new beginning in "Galilee."

Jesus in Gethsemane: 14:32-42

The anguished prayer of Jesus in Gethsemane when he shrinks before the prospect that lies before him and seeks the human support of his disciples is the most poignant episode in the gospel. Mark's account focuses first on Jesus and his prayer (vv. 33-36), then on the failure of the three select disciples to watch and pray (vv. 37-41). For all their bold assurances so recently

---

28. The Greek verb *proagein* can mean both "go ahead of" in the sense of "precede" or, more actively, "lead." The first sense appears in 16:7. Since Palestinian shepherds "lead" their flock by "going ahead" of them, both nuances can be operative here; cf. Hooker, *Saint Mark,* 345. Jesus' "going ahead" of them as risen Lord will repeat his "going ahead" of them to Jerusalem (10:32), when the disciples hung back in fear and dismay.

given, their complete failure to be "with him" (cf. 3:14) at this suffering time now begins.

The depiction of Jesus himself in this scene represents a tremendous change. Until now, though he has demonstrated strong emotion, he has never ceased to be a figure of striking power and authority before whom the demons, in particular, quaked (1:23-24; 3:11; 5:6-9). Again and again he has made clear his destiny to suffer and die, and has given the impression of striding to that fate with unflinching determination. Now, as the Passion proper begins, we see him go to pieces before our eyes, torn between the desire to escape what lies before him and faithfulness to the mission given him by the Father. Nowhere else in the gospel do we see Jesus so humanly presented,[29] and yet nowhere else are we given such intimate access to his relationship with the Father.

The three disciples Jesus chooses to support him in his prayer—Peter, James, and John (14:32-33a)—had seen him summon back to life the daughter of Jairus (5:37-43). As privileged witnesses of his transfiguration on the mountain (9:2-9), the same trio had heard him addressed by the Father as "Beloved Son, in whom I am well pleased" (9:7). Now they hear him crying out to God in the most intimate of filial addresses ("*Abba,* Father")[30] and

---

29. Mark first (v. 33b) describes Jesus' emotional distress with two strong verbs, *ekthambeisthai* and *adēmonein,* expressing "the strongest and deepest feeling" (Taylor, *St. Mark,* 552). Jesus confirms this (v. 34a) with a statement echoing Ps 41 (LXX 42):6: "My soul is deeply grieved *(perilypos)* even to the point of death"; the sense is that of being burdened with a sorrow so intense as to be life-threatening; cf. Donahue and Harrington, *Mark,* 407. Mark then (v. 35a) describes Jesus falling to the ground, and gives the content of his prayer to the Father in indirect speech (v. 35b) before going on to give it in direct quotation (v. 36).

30. The phrase "*Abba,* Father" is made up of the Aramaic familiar address to the male parent *(Abba)* followed by a Greek translation *(ho patēr). Abba* occurs only here in the gospels, but in two places (Rom 8:15 and Gal 4:6) Paul refers to the Spirit's prompting believers to address God in this way. The preservation of the address in Aramaic, together with the fact that both the Synoptic and the Johannine gospel traditions consistently portray Jesus' relationship to God in "Son-Father" terms, argues strongly for a recollection here of something characteristic of Jesus, expressing a relationship of intimacy with the Father that the post-Easter community later felt itself impelled to share under the impulse of the Spirit. Earlier scholarly claims (especially by Joachim Jeremias) for the uniqueness of such an intimate address to God on the lips of Jesus (in the sense of being without precedent in contemporary Judaism) now appear hazardous. Nonetheless, the significance of the address and its preservation in Aramaic should not be underestimated. See Raymond E. Brown, *The Death of the Messiah: From Gethsemane to the Grave: A Commentary on the Passion Narratives in the Four Gospels.* 2 vols. (New York: Doubleday, 1994) 1:172–74, who cites (p. 174) John P. Meier: "One is justified in claiming that Jesus' striking use of *Abba* did express his intimate experience of God as his own father and that this usage did make a lasting impression upon his disciples" ("Jesus" in Raymond E. Brown, Joseph A. Fitzmyer, and Roland E. Murphy,

receiving no response—a divine abandonment that will continue right up to the moment of his death (15:34). Jesus is left to struggle alone between the desire, on the one hand, that the "hour"[31] (v. 35) and the "cup"[32] (v. 36) might pass him by, and acceptance, on the other, that what must prevail is not his will but that of the Father. Humanly, he prays that divine power ("all things are possible to you" [v. 36b]) might find some other way to achieve the goal set before him. The "possibility" that this might be the case slips away as he aligns his will completely with the will of the Father,[33] which is that he should complete his mission by making the deepest possible entrance into humankind's sinful condition to overcome its evil by the power of divine love.[34]

What explains the tenacity of this scene's hold in the early Christian tradition (cf. Matt 26:36-46; Luke 22:40-46; John 12:27; Heb 5:7-8)[35] is the precious witness it gives to the costliness of Jesus' sufferings and hence to the extremity of love that lies behind them. Jesus goes to his death as obedient Son. But precisely because he is beloved Son the cost is borne also by the One who sent him. As Paul says, echoing Gen 22:16, "(God) . . . did not spare God's only Son but gave him up for us all" (Rom 8:32). What God did not in the end require of Abraham—the sacrifice of his only son, Isaac—God did in the end, for the rescue of humanity, require of Godself. While, then, this scene presents Jesus struggling with the will of the Father, we should not think of the Father as coldly indifferent or demanding his sufferings as a cost. In the person of the Son, the Father is paying the cost of human redemption to the extreme degree.

---

eds., *New Jerome Biblical Commentary* [Englewood Cliffs, NJ: Prentice Hall, 1990] 78:31 [p. 1323]).

31. The "hour" is, in the first instance, the moment of Jesus' Passion and death; biblical usage (cf. Dan 11:40; Mark 13:32) suggests also a broader eschatological connotation: the moment of the decisive cosmic struggle; cf. Donahue and Harrington, *Mark,* 408; Brown, *Death of the Messiah* 1:168; Moloney, *Gospel of Mark,* 292.

32. As in 10:38, "cup" has the biblical sense of the fate God is holding out before a person; see above, p. 167.

33. The words echo the third petition of the Lord's Prayer (Matt 6:10b), just as Jesus' later exhortation to the sleeping disciples (v. 38) will echo the sixth (6:13a). This, together with the address to God as "Father" *(Abba),* leads many scholars to conclude that the tradition appearing as the Lord's Prayer in Matt (6:9-13) and Luke (11:2-4) is hovering about Mark's account of Jesus' prayer before the disciples in Gethsemane (cf. also 11:25).

34. Cf. Paul in Rom 8:3-4; 2 Cor 5:18-21.

35. On the likely historicity of this tradition see the extended discussion in Brown, *Death of the Messiah* 1:216–34, especially the conclusion on p. 234; Gnilka, *Markus* 2:264; Moloney, *Gospel of Mark,* 291, n. 80.

Three times in the course of his prayer Jesus comes to his disciples and finds them asleep (vv. 37-38; v. 40; v. 41). He urges them to stay awake and pray that they may not enter into temptation (v. 38a).[36] Their sleep is physical, but also spiritual—a continuation of the "blindness" (cf. their "weighed down eyes" in v. 40) that had frustrated Jesus' attempts to instruct them "along the way" to Jerusalem. In their continual lapsing into sleep the disciples illustrate perfectly the attitude Jesus had warned against in the parable of the watchful servants that concluded his discourse on the future (13:33-37). For readers of the gospel their failure offers a negative model of discipleship and exacerbates the isolation of Jesus.

At the same time, since everyone does badly at suffering, the failure of Peter, James, and John is something with which most disciples, then and now, can identify, finding in it some grain of consolation. Discipleship involves taking up one's cross and following after Jesus (8:34). But there are many who find insupportable the cross they have been asked to bear. They may cry out with Jesus, "*Abba,* Father, all things are possible for you; take away this cup from me," and not be able to add with him, "not my will but yours" (v. 36bc).[37] The fact that Jesus' three most intimate disciples failed him in his hour of greatest need and heard from him not rebuke but simply a warning and a compassionate explanation ("The spirit is willing but the flesh is weak" [v. 38b]) and, further, that their failure was not the end of their companionship with him (14:28; 16:7), is an encouragement to hope and believe that what may appear impossible to human beings is possible to the One for whom all is possible (10:27). The fact, too, that God's beloved Son had to wrestle with the prospect of a terrible death, bereft of any comfort, human or divine (cf. 15:34), ensures the truth enshrined in another New Testament document (Heb 4:15; cf. 4:7-10), that we have a High Priest who can truly feel for us in our weakness because he has been "tested" as we are.

Jesus has three times approached his sleeping disciples (cf. v. 41). The number recalls the three Passion predictions, which they had failed to comprehend, and perhaps anticipates Peter's threefold denial yet to come.[38] But

---

36. What he is enduring is temptation *(peirasmos)* in the highest degree: a contest that goes to the heart of the final struggle with evil referred to in 13:19-20 as the "great affliction"; the disciples must pray not to "enter" it since they are showing themselves quite unprepared for the struggle; cf. Donahue and Harrington, *Mark,* 409.

37. Cf. Raymond Brown: "(Mark's) is a Passion Narrative that will have special meaning for those who have sought to follow Christ but find insupportable the cross that they are asked to bear in life, i.e., to those who at some time have been reduced to asking from the bottom of their hearts, 'My God, my God, for what reason have you forsaken me?'" (*Death of the Messiah* 1:28).

38. Cf. Hooker, *Saint Mark,* 349.

their sleeping on watch comes to an abrupt end as Jesus announces (vv. 41b-42) that the approach of the "betrayer" *(ho paradidous)* signals the "hour" when the Son of Man is to be "delivered up *(paradidotai)* into the hands of sinners."[39] John the Baptist had preached and been delivered up (1:14); Jesus had warned his disciples that they too, as preachers of the Gospel, would be delivered up (13:9-12). The centerpiece of this pattern is the experience of Jesus himself who, having completed his preaching of the good news of the Kingdom (1:15), is about to suffer the same fate (9:31; 10:33; 14:10-11, 41-42; 15:1, 10, 15).[40] Once again the gospel exploits the range of meanings in the Greek verb *(paradidonai).* At the most basic level it indicates the betrayal perpetrated by Judas, an act that initiates the process at the end of which Jesus will be "handed over" by the leaders of his people to "sinners" (15:1; cf. 9:31; 10:33), that is, to the Romans ("Gentile sinners"). But in submitting to being handed over to these human agents Jesus is handing himself over to the Father in obedience and perfect trust. It is knowledge of Jesus' vindication by the Father and future coming as Son of Man (Story 3) that gives hope to believers when they too, like John and like Jesus, are "given up" for preaching the Gospel (13:9-11) and seeking to promote the liberating values it enshrines.

Jesus is Taken Captive: 14:43-52

Jesus has wrestled with "the cup" (v. 36) that lies before him and in obedience to his Father's will accepted it. Now with calm dignity he allows himself to be taken into the physical power of those who will be its instruments. Facilitating their work, as we already know and Jesus himself has predicted, is Judas. The gospel underlines his treachery by reminding us that he is "one of the Twelve" (v. 43) and by describing how he turns a customary respectful and affectionate greeting into a way of identifying Jesus that will in the end be fatal.[41] Judas is now completely associated with a "crowd" from the chief adversaries (chief priests, scribes, and elders [cf. 11:27; 14:1])

---

39. The central part of v. 41 bristles with interpretive difficulties. Rather than telling the disciples to "sleep on and take their rest," Jesus is best interpreted as putting an admonitory question, "Are you still sleeping . . . ?" The following expression *apechei* defies explanation, but is best taken as an introduction ("Enough!") to the command to "wake up" in view of the approach of the arresting party. Cf. Taylor, *St. Mark,* 556–57; Hooker, *Saint Mark,* 349–50. For a lengthy discussion and unusual explanation (that it refers to Judas' being "paid off"), see Brown, *Death of the Messiah* 1:379–83.

40. Cf. Donahue and Harrington, *Mark,* 414.

41. The compound verb *kataphilein* has the enhanced sense of "kiss warmly"; cf. Donahue and Harrington, *Mark,* 415.

who have come out against Jesus with weapons of violence: swords and clubs. Without further ado these lay hands on him and arrest him (v. 46).

A number of responses follow (vv. 47-52). First (v. 48), "one of those standing by" strikes out with a sword, injuring the ear of one of the High Priest's men. Though Mark does not identify the striker,[42] it is likely that we are to understand this as a futile attempt on the part of one of the disciples to meet violence with violence.[43] The violence underlines the protest we then hear from Jesus (vv. 48-49). They have come out against him by stealth in the night as if they were arresting a man of violence *(lēistēs)*.[44] Yet they made no move against him when he was discharging in the Temple, in broad daylight,[45] his truly characteristic role: that of teacher. With these words Jesus unmasks the impotence of the authorities to counter his true authority (cf. 11:28-33 and 12:1-37) and their humiliating need, because of his popularity with the people, to have recourse to violence and stealth by night. He submits to their violence only because he is following an obedience traced out in the Scriptures (v. 49c).[46]

The remaining two responses have to do with desertion and flight: first (v. 50) that of the disciples—now simply "they . . . all of them"—then that of a young man who mysteriously appears in the scene, is arrested, but escapes leaving in the hands of the arresting party the linen garment that was all he was wearing (vv. 51-52). This final episode, which appears only in Mark, has mystified interpreters from the outset—beginning, it would seem, with Matthew and Luke.[47] My own suggestion would be that the young man is a symbolic figure representing believers who have followed Jesus and

---

42. John 18:10 attributes the action to Peter.

43. The attacker can hardly be one of the "crowd" (why would they be fighting among themselves?), and to introduce the suggestion of a "third party" is desperate. Moloney, *Gospel of Mark,* 297, convincingly argues that in Mark's view the companions of Jesus have, at least for the time being (cf. 16:7), forfeited the title "disciples" and become simply "bystanders."

44. The Greek word can refer to bandits and robbers as well as to revolutionaries, but in all cases implies armed violence; cf. Donahue and Harrington, *Mark,* 416. In 15:27 the two men crucified with Jesus are called *lēistai.* Only in John (18:40) is Barabbas called by this term—though the description of his criminal activity in Mark 15:7 would support its application to him.

45. This alternative interpretation of the Greek phrase *kath' hēmeran* suits the context better than "daily"; cf. Brown, *Death of the Messiah* 1:285; Donahue and Harrington, *Mark,* 416.

46. The scriptural passage is not specified. In view of the fact that Jesus is arrested as though he were a *lēistēs,* Isa 53:12d ("and he was numbered with the transgressors") comes particularly to mind (cf. 15:27).

47. For a thorough survey see Brown, *Death of the Messiah* 1:294–303; Boring, *Mark,* 403–404, n. 93.

received their baptismal robe[48] but who, when discipleship has meant arrest and the threat of death, have abandoned their baptismal allegiance and become deserters. They have fled "naked" in the sense of losing all the protection against the powers of darkness that their baptism and discipleship afforded them.[49] The appearance and behavior of the young man warn later readers of the gospel that this flight from faith and companionship is something they too can share.

48. The first recorded usage of the Greek word *sindōn* for a baptismal robe occurs in the *Acts of Thomas* (§121), dated to the early third century c.e. However, there is no good reason to doubt that the custom of reclothing baptismal initiates with a symbolic robe began much earlier. Such a custom may well lie behind the metaphorical references in Gal 3:27; Col 3:9-10; Eph 4:22-24.

49. I thus adopt a symbolic understanding of the young man. Brown's strictures against such an interpretation (*Death of the Messiah* 1:302–303) really only apply to views that see him playing a symbolic role that is *positive*. There is no need for him to function as a symbol of the *disciples'* failure (so Moloney, *Gospel of Mark,* 299–300); they are there and can represent themselves.

Passion 2:
Jesus on Trial: 14:53–15:20

The centerpiece of the Markan Passion is made up of the two trials Jesus undergoes: first the one before the Jewish authorities (14:53-72) and then the one before the Roman governor (15:2-15) that seals his fate. In each case description of what happens to Jesus is played off against information about another character, forming an ironic contrast. Thus while Jesus at the end of his interrogation proclaims his true identity (14:61-62), his closest associate, Peter, is outside denying his allegiance again and again (14:54, 66-72); while Jesus, the Son *(bar)* of the God he called *"Abba"* (hence "Bar Abba") is condemned as a political rebel, a genuine rebel, Barabbas, is released in his stead (15:6-15). After each trial Jesus is subjected to physical abuse and mockery that, again ironically, brings out a significant truth about him: that he is a prophet (14:65) and that he is a king (15:16-20). There is then a parallel between the two trial scenes, both in structure and in the use of irony to bring out the deeper truth running under the surface narrative of Jesus' suffering.

Before the Jewish Council: 14:53-65

Abandoned by all the disciples (v. 50), except for Peter who follows at a safe distance (v. 51), Jesus is brought by those who arrested him in Gethsemane to the house of the high priest,[1] where the full Council has gathered.[2]

---

1. Mark does not name the high priest. Matthew informs us that it is Caiaphas (Matt 26:57).
2. Historically it is most unlikely that a full meeting of the Jewish Council (Sanhedrin) to hear a capital charge would have been convoked (1) in the high priest's house, (2) at night, (3) on this particular night (Passover eve in Mark's reckoning), (4) with a verdict of guilt

230

Meanwhile (v. 54), in a characteristic "inclusion" ("sandwich"), Mark tells us of Peter's approach into the courtyard of the high priest's house. While Peter sits there among the servants warming himself, the trial of Jesus gets under way. The evangelist makes clear from the start that it is a "show" trial, the desired outcome already determined (v. 55). The aim is not to uncover the truth but to find a charge to pin on Jesus that will serve as grounds for demanding from the Roman governor that he be punished by death.

As far as achieving this aim is concerned, the trial does not get off to a good start. Many bear false witness against Jesus, but their witness is contradictory and hence ineffective (v. 56). Then two get up and accuse Jesus of maintaining that he would "destroy this sanctuary[3] made by human hands and in three days build up another not made by human hands" (vv. 57-58). Mark makes clear that he regards this testimony as false (*pseudomartyroun* [v. 57]) and inconsistent (v. 59). Jesus had prophesied the Temple's destruction (13:2) but this did not amount to a pledge to destroy it. Ironically, however, the charge has about it a certain ring of truth since Jesus' action in the Temple (11:15-17), coming between his prophetic cursing of the fig tree and its withering (11:12-14, 20-21), amounted to its symbolic destruction. And following his resurrection "on the third day" there will arise a new temple: not a material temple built by human hands but a temple consisting of the community of believers, constructed by God on the cornerstone of the rejected One (12:10-11).[4]

Throughout all this accusation Jesus retains a dignified silence; he simply allows the contradictory witness to be its own refutation.[5] Frustrated and unable to elicit a response (vv. 60-61a), the high priest puts to him the question that goes to the heart of what they really want to get from him: "Are you the Messiah, the Son of the Blessed One?" (v. 61b).[6] At this point

---

deserving of death pronounced at the end of the same hearing. What is described is more likely an informal arraignment designed to produce a charge against Jesus that would carry sufficient weight with the Roman authorities to lead to his execution. The scholarly literature on the historical and legal problems of the trial is vast; for a convenient summary of the issue see Hooker, *Saint Mark,* 354–57.

3. The word *naos* indicates the inner part of the Temple consisting of the Holy of Holies and the Holy Place.

4. Cf. Donald Senior, *The Passion of Jesus in the Gospel of Mark* (Collegeville, MN: Liturgical Press, 1984) 91; Brown, *Death of the Messiah* 1:453; Moloney, *Gospel of Mark,* 302–3.

5. Jesus' silence, here and later before Pilate (15:5), recalls that of the Servant figure in Isa 53:7; cf. Donahue and Harrington, *Mark,* 422.

6. The transition to the messianic issue is sudden, especially as there is no clear evidence of a Jewish expectation that the Messiah would rebuild the Temple (cf. Brown, *Death of the Messiah* 1:442–43). The fact that Pilate opens his interrogation by asking Jesus if he is "the

(v. 62) Jesus emerges from his silence with the majestic declaration "I am" *(egō eimi)*. The declaration puts aside a long reserve in regard to these titles ("Messiah" and "Son of God") from the beginning of the ministry. Messianic acclamation was something to be suppressed so long as it was in danger of being pinned on him in purely conventional terms, in which suffering and giving up his life in service as a ransom for many (10:45) played no part. In the context of his present captivity and the direction in which it is all too clearly heading, there is no longer any need for that reserve. As he stands here on trial, "Story 1" (that he is Messiah and Son of God) and "Story 2" (that he is destined to suffer and die) now inevitably mingle together.

This does not mean that the titles "Christ" and "Son of God" (literally "Son of the Blessed One") mean the same thing on the lips of Jesus and those of the high priest. There is no need to hear in the titles coming from the high priest anything beyond conventional messianic expectation.[7] Jesus' acceptance of the titles, however, presupposes the very significant christological enhancement these titles have received in the course of the gospel. In addition to being blended with the nuances stemming from Story 2 (8:30-31), "Messiah" has moved beyond mere "Son of David" in the direction of the far more mysterious "David's Lord" (12:35-37). We readers of the gospel who have been made aware of the divine voice both after Jesus' baptism (1:11) and at the transfiguration (9:7), and who have heard Jesus cry out "*Abba,* Father" in Gethsemane (14:36), know that he is God's "Beloved Son" in a unique, transcendent sense.

A further extension of the titles occurs when Jesus in this same response to the high priest adds to "I am" yet another statement of high christological content: "And you will see the Son of Man seated on the right of the Power and coming with the clouds of heaven" (v. 62b). Couched in language from Psalm 110:1 and Daniel 7:13, the statement points to his coming in judgment at the end of the age (Story 3). Those before whom he is now on trial may not see him presently in a state that reveals his messianic status, but one day they will: they will see him enthroned as Messiah—not on an earthly throne

---

King of the Jews" (15:2) suggests that the Jewish leaders have converted the claim to be the Jewish Messiah into language the Romans would understand—and hence that we are to understand that the "messianic" claim was the central charge the leaders wanted to pin on Jesus from the start.

7. This is true even of the second title ("Son of the Blessed One"). Even if there is no direct evidence from Jewish literature of the use of the title "son of God" itself in regard to the messianic King, the circumstantial evidence that the Messiah could be so designated is strong: see further Byrne, *"Sons of God"—"Seed of Abraham,"* 223–24. Moreover, the demonic confessions (3:10; 5:7) suggest that Mark certainly believed that the title could be used in this purely conventional way (3:11; 5:7).

but on a heavenly one, at the right hand of God. Furthermore, they will see him coming on the clouds of heaven as eschatological judge (cf. 8:38; 13:24-27).[8] At that moment the situation as regards judgment will be exactly the reverse: where he now stands on trial before them, *they* will find themselves standing before him.

Jesus' reference to himself and his future role here as "Son of Man" is of a piece, yet subtly different from his response to Peter's (correct) acknowledgment of him as Messiah at Caesarea Philippi (8:29: Story 1). Then Jesus had gone on to assert that the "Son of Man must undergo great suffering . . ." (8:31: Story 2). Now, following his acceptance of the title "Messiah," he likewise goes on to speak of himself as Son of Man, but this time as a Son of Man destined to come in glory on the clouds of heaven (Story 3). The response in terms of "Son of Man" in both cases is explained by its origins in the vision described in Daniel 7:13-14, 18. This text refers to the divine conferral of an eternal rule on "one like a son of man," who represents all those who have endured great suffering on account of their faithfulness to God. "Son of Man," then, indicates a role combining both suffering and glory—more accurately, a vindication (glory) that comes about as God's response to those who have remained faithful in great suffering. As such, the title most adequately embraces and holds together both Jesus' present situation (suffering) and what will arise out of it: vindication in both resurrection and glory at God's right hand.[9]

The immediate response of the high priest is to rend his garments and bring the trial to a close (v. 63).[10] They have no further need of witnesses because Jesus out of his own lips has convicted himself of blasphemy, a crime, they all concur, deserving of death (v. 64). According to biblical law blasphemy incurring the penalty of death involved use of the divine name in a curse (Lev 24:11-16). In his response to the high priest Jesus had in fact avoided speaking

8. Combining the two scriptural texts, the statement presents the Son of Man as both "sitting" and "coming" at the same time. But Jesus' sitting at God's right hand is meant to be taken not so much as a literal depiction but as a symbolic statement of his status following his resurrection and exaltation. It is as vindicated in this way that he comes as judge. See further Brown, *Death of the Messiah* 1:496–98; Hooker, *Saint Mark*, 362.

9. On the understanding of Jesus' use of the "Son of Man" title in this sense see especially Hooker, *Saint Mark*, 92–93. For a fuller survey of the likely origin and meaning of the title, see Brown, *Death of the Messiah* 1:497, 506–15.

10. In the biblical tradition rending garments is a sign of grief: Gen 37:34; Josh 7:6; 2 Sam 1:11-12. Later Jewish legislation prescribed rending of garments on the part of judges when a verdict of blasphemy was reached; cf. Donahue and Harrington, *Mark*, 423.

of "God," using the circumlocution "the Power."[11] Blasphemy in this case must be taken in an extended sense to refer not simply to his acceptance of the titles "Messiah" and "Son of God" (v. 62a) but to the far more transcendent christological claim implied in what they will "see" in regard to the Son of Man (v. 62b). It is the same charge he had provoked early in the gospel by his claim to the divine power to forgive sins (2:1-12).

Following the general condemnation on this charge, the physical suffering of Jesus begins as he endures mockery and taunting from the members of the Council and blows from the servants of the high priest (v. 65).[12] Covering his face, they invite him to "prophesy," that is, to identify the one who has struck him. Ironically, what they are doing reveals him to be a prophet since it follows exactly what he has predicted long before (10:34).

Peter's Denial of Jesus: 14:66-72

Meanwhile, out in the courtyard, another scene has been taking place that again reveals all too well Jesus' prophetic power. While he has been solemnly acknowledging his identity before the high priest and the whole Council, his leading disciple, under far less threatening interrogation, has denied him three times, exactly as predicted (14:30; cf. v. 72b). Challenged twice by a maidservant (vv. 66-67) and then by bystanders she brings in (vv. 69, 70), Peter first feigns ignorance, then denies association with Jesus before bringing his crescendo of denial to an end with a solemn oath. The second crowing of a cock at this point reminds him of Jesus' prophecy, whereupon he burst into tears (v. 72c).

The preservation of this tradition describing the failure of Jesus' leading disciple in the Passion accounts of all four gospels is truly remarkable, given Peter's status in the early Christian community.[13] To be sure, the accuracy of Jesus' prophecy provides further evidence of the deeper divine story accomplishing its purpose through the suffering inflicted on him. But for the original Markan audience, many of whose members had no doubt failed under persecution and perhaps even betrayed fellow believers (cf. 13:12),

---

11. On this circumlocution for the divine name cf. Brown, *Death of the Messiah* 1:496–97, who argues that the usage may call attention to the source of the authority Jesus, as Son of Man, will wield over his enemies.

12. The curious final sentence, "they received *(elabon)* him with blows," like Jesus' silence (vv. 60-61), recalls the treatment of the Isaianic Servant (Isa 53:6). Brown, *Death of the Messiah* 1:609–10, with characteristic thoroughness, surveys various possibilities for interpreting the statement.

13. Cf. Hengel, *Der unterschätze Petrus,* 68–73.

the tradition of Peter's threefold failure, his repentance, and his restoration (cf. 16:7) would convey warning but also hope. If the one who despite his brave assurances (14:29, 31) had denied the Lord three times subsequently not only found forgiveness but went on to give heroic witness (cf. John 21:15-19), then others too could have a second chance and, under God's grace, finally prevail.[14] Human failure may be part of the story, but it is not the end of the story in the divine scheme.

The Roman Trial: Jesus Before Pilate: 14:1-15

The chief instigators of the case against Jesus have decided that he is deserving of death (14:64). Now they must persuade the Roman governor Pontius Pilate to carry out the sentence. The Jewish crime of blasphemy will not cut much ice with Pilate.[15] Meeting early in the morning (15:1), they form a plan to dress up Jesus' admission that he is the Messiah (14:62) in suitably political terms to make it appear a threat to Roman rule.[16] Their strategy decided, they bind Jesus and "hand him over" to Pilate, further fulfilling the Passion predictions (9:31; especially 10:33).

Like the scene before the Jewish Council, Jesus' appearance before Pilate is hardly a formal trial.[17] There is simply an interrogation, which leaves the governor unconvinced of Jesus' guilt (vv. 2-5). The rest of the proceeding (vv. 6-15) amounts to an unsuccessful attempt on his part to find a way of setting Jesus free without alienating the crowd that has gathered and that the chief priests have stirred up to demand his execution.

When Pilate asks Jesus whether he is "the King of the Jews," his reply is noncommittal: "You say so" (v. 2).[18] Jesus does not deny that he is a king. In the sense of his positive yet qualified acceptance of the title "Messiah"

---

14. Cf. Nineham, *Saint Mark,* 399–400; Brown, *Death of the Messiah* 1:624–25; Donahue and Harrington, *Mark,* 428–29.

15. On the extent to which the portrayal of Pilate in the Passion narratives of the gospels conforms to the impression gained from nonbiblical literature (Philo and Josephus), see Brown, *Death of the Messiah* 1:693–705, 722.

16. This way of presenting the case against Jesus is clearly implied by Pilate's opening question: "Are you the King of the Jews?" (15:2b); cf. Gnilka, *Markus* 2:300; Senior, *Passion of Jesus in Mark,* 109. In the New Testament, where Jews would tend to speak of "King of Israel" (as in Mark 15:32), "King of the Jews" is the way non-Jews refer to a Jewish ruler (including the Messiah); cf. Brown, *Death of the Messiah* 1:731.

17. On the legal status of the trial in the light of Roman jurisprudence see Brown, *Death of the Messiah* 1:710–22.

18. "It is an affirmation which implies that the speaker would put things differently" (Taylor, *St. Mark,* 579).

before the high priest (14:62), he is a King. But he is not a King in the highly political—and hence threatening to Rome—sense implied by the title "King of the Jews."[19] After his simple reply, Jesus lapses into silence—a silence he will maintain until his final cry on the cross (15:34). His continual silence before multiple and highly compromising accusations has about it a hint of the divine that leads Pilate to "wonder" (v. 5; cf. later 15:44), the same effect caused by the "Servant" figure according to Isa 52:15.[20]

A custom of releasing a prisoner on the occasion of the feast (v. 6) seems to provide a way out for Pilate: both to save Jesus and to satisfy the crowd.[21] When they arrive to ask for the customary release (v. 8), Pilate seizes the opportunity to offer them the release of "the King of the Jews" (v. 9). He does so, we are told (v. 10), because of his awareness of what is really motivating the leaders who have brought Jesus before him: not zeal to protect civil order and Roman rule from one genuinely posing a threat to it, but "jealousy" *(phthonos)* of the hold he has over the people, a challenge to their own leadership.

The stratagem backfires. Pilate is also holding "a certain Barabbas," a man caught with a group of "rebels who had committed murder during the insurrection" (v. 7). This gives the chief priests, when Pilate makes his offer, the opportunity to stir up the crowd to ask instead for the release of Barabbas (v. 11). When Pilate—pathetically—asks them what, then, he should do with the one they call "the King of the Jews" (v. 12), they respond with the fateful cry "Crucify him!" (v. 13). A final plaintive protest about Jesus' innocence (v. 14a) simply elicits, still more strongly, the same response (v. 14b). Pilate's resistance in the name of Jesus' innocence collapses. To satisfy the crowd he releases to them Barabbas and hands over Jesus for the mode of execution customary for rebels: crucifixion preceded by scourging (v. 15).

In the overall action of the Passion story the failed stratagem with Barabbas may seem fairly incidental, but at the deeper level running through the account it is truly significant. The name "Barabbas" means "son of the father."[22] The primary identity of Jesus in the Gospel of Mark is that of God's beloved Son, a God whom, uniquely in this gospel, he addresses as *"Abba"* (14:36).

---

19. Cf. Moloney, *Gospel of Mark,* 311.

20. Cf. Gnilka, *Markus* 2:300.

21. Brown, after a thorough review of the evidence in both Roman and Jewish practice (*Death of the Messiah* 1:814–18) concludes (p. 818) that there is no historical precedent for the custom in Judea of regularly releasing a prisoner at a feast. This conclusion need not be incompatible with a genuine reminiscence that a prisoner named Barabbas was released by Pilate at the same feast at which Jesus was condemned and executed (ibid., 819–20).

22. Cf. Gnilka, *Markus* 2:301.

Jesus is, then, "Bar Abba," the son of *Abba*. The leaders of Israel, like the wicked tenants in the parable (12:6-8), have brought about that the crowd should choose for themselves a Barabbas implicated in rebellion and bloodshed and, by the same token, reject "Bar Abba," the One who is the beloved Son of their God.[23] They have not "respected" the Son (12:6). Instead of what he had to bring—the Rule of God—they have made a choice foreshadowing a later choice for rebellion and violence that will lead to the destruction of their city and complete submission to the rule of Rome (70 C.E.).

As for Barabbas, he is totally passive throughout the transactions leading to his unforeseen release. Man of violence though he is, as first beneficiary of the "giving up" of Jesus he is also symbol of the "many" (sinners) whom the Son of Man came to serve and for whom he is giving up his own life as a ransom (10:45; cf. 2 Cor 5:21). There is a sense in which all believers can say that the action of Jesus has led them from being "Barabbas" to being sons and daughters of *Abba* within the family of God.

Though the chief priests and scribes are the prime movers in bringing about Jesus' condemnation, Pilate cannot escape responsibility. Like Herod in the case of John the Baptist (6:17-29),[24] he has been led, against his own better judgment, for fear of offending a gathered crowd (6:26; 14:15), to perpetrate a monstrous injustice against one whom he not only knew to be innocent but who also held for him a certain quasi-religious fascination (15:5). Pilate's failure through human pride to implement the justice that Rome at its best could deliver has gained for him an unending creedal notoriety: "suffered under Pontius Pilate."

The Mockery of the King: 15:16-20

Jesus had undergone mockery and physical abuse following his condemnation at his appearance before the Jewish Council (14:65). Now a similar, though more formal mockery takes place following his "handing over" by Pilate. The members of the Jewish Council had mocked him as "prophet," thereby ironically bringing out a truth that his accurate prediction of Peter's denial confirmed. Now, in close parallel, the Roman soldiers, taking up the chief accusation on which he had been brought before Pilate—"King of the Jews" (15:2)—enact a ritual that mocks him as a king.[25]

---

23. Cf. Donahue and Harrington, *Mark,* 432, 439; Dowd and Malbon, "The Significance of Jesus' Death," 295.

24. Cf. Moloney, *Gospel of Mark,* 315; Donahue and Harrington, *Mark,* 439.

25. Cf. Senior, *Passion of Jesus in Mark,* 113; Donahue and Harrington, *Mark,* 435.

The formality of the ritual is signaled by the gathering of the entire cohort: that is, all the soldiers present in the governor's quarters (v. 16). Jesus is clothed with a "purple robe" (v. 17a)—perhaps a soldier's faded red cloak[26]—and crowned with a wreath of thorns (v. 17b).[27] He is then saluted—"Hail, King of the Jews"— with what corresponds to the acclamation given to the emperor: "Hail, Caesar" (v. 18). The charade becomes more vicious as Jesus is beaten with a reed and spat upon (cf. 10:34; cf. 14:65). It culminates in the soldiers' bending the knee before him in imitation of the worship given to oriental rulers. The mockery, the immediate prelude to his being led out for execution (v. 20b), makes clear, again ironically, that all through the degradation and suffering that is to come, Jesus is and remains king. His enemies cannot help but unwittingly proclaim this truth.[28]

26. Cf. Taylor, *St. Mark,* 585.

27. This detail is probably not to be interpreted as an instrument of torture (thorns facing inward) but as a caricature of crowns with spikes radiating outward as in depictions of ancient-world rulers in imitation of the sungod; cf. Hooker, *Saint Mark,* 370; Brown, *Death of the Messiah* 1:866–67.

28. Cf. Hooker, *Saint Mark,* 370.

Passion 3:
Jesus Crucified and Buried: 15:21-47

Mark's story of Jesus comes to its climax with the account of his crucifixion, death, and burial. What Jesus endures in these last hours of his life
is a horrific ending for any human being. What Mark describes, however, is
the infliction of such a death on One portrayed throughout the gospel as
God's beloved Son, one whose belonging to the heavenly as well as to the
human world has shone through many episodes and scenes. Faced by this
stupendous mystery, Mark has chosen to give a simple recital of the facts,
refraining from any attempt to soften the stark reality or embroider it with
pious reflection or emotion. The all-too-familiar details of crucifixion he
can leave to his readers' imagination. Unlike the later evangelists, he does
not allow the underlying "divine" story to emerge explicitly. He simply re-
counts the outward events, confident that the alert reader or hearer will pick
up, through the echoes of Scripture (especially Psalm 22) and the continuing
thread of irony, the deeper, divine story being told. At one level there is a
terrible absence of God, culminating in Jesus' cry of desolation just before
he expires (15:34). At a deeper level all is proceeding according to a pre-
ordained divine scheme. Jesus has been "given up" totally into the hands of
his Gentile executioners, but that is simply an outward expression of his
more fundamental giving up of himself into the hands of the Father.

The main sequence falls into three parts: verses 20b-26 describe the
crucifixion; verses 27-32 describe what happens as Jesus hangs for six hours
on the cross—especially the mockery (vv. 29-32); verses 33-39 describe the
death of Jesus and its immediate aftermath (the rending of the Temple curtain
[v. 38] and the response of the centurion [v. 39]). The Passion concludes
with a notice about the presence of women disciples (vv. 40-41) and an account of Jesus' burial (vv. 42-47).

The Crucifixion of Jesus: 15:20b-26

Finished with their ritual mocking of Jesus as "king" (vv. 16-20a), the Roman soldiers lead him out of the praetorium to crucify him (v. 20b). On the way they compel a man coming into the city from the country, Simon of Cyrene, to carry his cross—more precisely, to bear the crossbeam. This was contrary to custom; normally criminals were made to carry their own cross to the place of crucifixion. The exception suggests that Jesus was already too weakened, by the scourging and ill treatment, to carry it himself. For Mark, however, there is in this detail a precious reminiscence and connection. He identifies Simon as "the father of Alexander and Rufus," a pair evidently familiar to the original readers of the gospel, since they are otherwise unexplained.[1] Through this relationship the Markan audience is placed in personal connection with the central event told in the gospel: the death of Jesus. The gospel does not speculate on Simon's feelings when confronted with this task, but the mention of his sons suggests that his family and the wider community of faith came to see it in the light of faith. In assisting Jesus in this way Simon was, in fact, modeling what Jesus had earlier described as the way of true discipleship: taking up one's cross and following after him (8:34).[2] Where the principal "Simon" (Simon Peter) is glaringly absent, another Simon has appeared to be a point of entry into the story for all subsequent disciples.

Arrived at Golgotha, the "Place of the Skull"— a cranial-shaped knoll outside the city wall[3]—they (presumably the soldiers) offer Jesus a drink of wine mixed with myrrh (v. 23). This narcotic potion, designed to have some anesthetic effect at the extremely painful moment of crucifixion, Jesus refuses: he will drain to the full the "cup" set before him (14:36; cf. 10:38).[4] Then (v. 24a) we are simply told: "they crucified him"—Mark sees no reason to elaborate on a horrific procedure sufficiently familiar to his readers.

Only three further details are mentioned: the casting of lots for Jesus' clothing (v. 24b), the time when he was crucified (v. 25), and the inscription stating the charge against him (v. 26). The casting of lots for his clothing is a first indication that what is happening to Jesus fulfills the pattern set out for the righteous sufferer in Psalm 22 (v. 19). The information that "it was

---

1. Interestingly, a certain "Rufus" (along with his mother) is among those in Rome to whom Paul sends greetings in Romans: "Greet Rufus, chosen in the Lord; and greet his mother—a mother to me also" (16:13).

2. Cf. Moloney, *Gospel of Mark,* 318–19.

3. For the topographical discussion see Brown, *Death of the Messiah* 2:936–40.

4. Ibid. 2:941–42.

at the third hour (nine a.m.) that they crucified him" (v. 25) initiates a three-hour pattern (cf. v. 33 ["sixth hour"]; v. 37 ["ninth hour"]) serving to indicate that "in a mysterious way, God's design is being worked out in this brutal murder (cf. 10:45; 14:36)."[5] Finally, the inscription "the King of the Jews," outwardly a sarcastic warning on the part of the Roman authorities that this is how messianic pretenders end their days, ironically proclaims the profound truth: in the obedient "service" (10:45) that has brought him to this "enthronement," Jesus really is the Messiah King whom God intended for Israel.

Jesus Mocked as He Hangs on the Cross: 15:27-32

The description of the mockery that Jesus has to endure as he hangs on the cross begins (v. 27) and ends (v. 32b)[6] with a reference to the two bandits *(lēistai)* who were crucified alongside him, one on his right and one on his left. The description eerily recalls the request of the sons of Zebedee to sit one on Jesus' right, one on his left, when he should come into his glory (10:37). We now understand why, in response, Jesus asked them whether they were prepared to drink the "cup" he had to drink preparatory to that entry (10:38). At his arrest Jesus had protested that the arresting party had come out against him as though he were a bandit (14:48). Now that view of him shines forth in the company he is forced to keep on his cross.[7]

Meanwhile, Jesus endures mockery from three parties. Passersby, wagging their heads—a further echo of Psalm 22 (v. 7 [LXX 21:8]; cf. Lam 2:15)—rail at him (vv. 29-30), repeating a charge that had been brought up unsuccessfully at his first trial. Let him who would destroy the Temple and rebuild it in three days save himself by descending from the cross. Once again the mockery unwittingly discloses the truth. Jesus has in effect destroyed the Temple, and following his obedient *remaining* on the cross until death, in three days' time (cf. 10:34) he will be raised as the foundation stone of a new Temple "not built by hands" (14:58) that will genuinely be a "house of prayer for all the nations" (11:17).[8] An attempt to "save himself" by descending from the cross would, on a principle Jesus had already taught

---

5. Moloney, *Gospel of Mark,* 321.

6. Thus forming an "inclusion."

7. In some late manuscripts an additional verse (v. 28) appears at this point indicating the fulfillment here of Isa 53:12: "He was reckoned with the transgressors" (cf. Luke 22:37, from which the verse seems to have been derived).

8. Cf. Moloney, *Gospel of Mark,* 322.

his disciples (8:35), run counter to the entire direction of his mission.[9] The path to salvation lies in remaining, through obedience, in the hands of the Father (cf. Phil 2:8-9).

A second party consisting of his archadversaries, the chief priests and scribes, takes the notion of "save" in a different direction. Jesus saved *others;* he cannot save himself (vv. 31-32a). If the one who purports to be "the Christ, the King of Israel" descends from the cross, then they will see and believe.[10] Again beneath the mockery lies a genuine truth. Jesus' whole mission has been about the rescue of "others" from the grip of Satan; he has come not to be served but to serve, and to give his life "as a ransom for many" (10:45). It is precisely through his remaining faithful to that mission that his own salvation and that of the "others" will be assured through the fidelity of the Father. What they are demanding as the kind of "sign" that would induce them to "see" and "believe" (cf. 8:11-12)[11] simply reveals the falsity of their messianic notion and their lack of faith. It is by staying on the cross that Jesus establishes himself as Israel's true king and savior.[12] As a final mocking party, even the bandits crucified with him join in the chorus (v. 32b).

Jesus Dies upon the Cross: 15:33-39

The focus on the isolation and seeming helplessness of Jesus should not lead us to forget that the mockery he undergoes is ultimately human mockery of God. Jesus remains what the gospel from the start has portrayed him to be: the Father's beloved Son (1:1, 11; 9:7) in whom the divine is manifest to the world ("I am he" [6:50]). There is, then, a chilling threat of divine response and judgment in the darkness that comes down upon the whole earth at the sixth hour (noon) and remains until the ninth (three p.m.). Almost certainly in view are words of the prophet Amos (8:9-10):

> On that day, says the Lord God,
> I will make the sun go down at noon,
> and darken the earth in broad daylight.
> I will turn your feasts into mourning,

9. Cf. Senior, *Passion of Jesus in Mark,* 119.

10. "King of Israel" is the intra-Jewish designation for the messianic king corresponding to "King of the Jews" on the lips of Gentiles and in the inscription (v. 26).

11. The demand to "see" is peculiar to Mark (contrast Matt 27:42). It may reflect Mark's symbolic sense of faith as sight and lack of it as "blindness"; cf. Senior, *Passion of Jesus in Mark,* 121; Moloney, *Gospel of Mark,* 324.

12. Cf. Hooker, *Saint Mark,* 374.

and all your songs into lamentation; . . .
I will make it like the mourning for an only son,
and the end of it like a bitter day.

The pervasive darkness recalls the primeval darkness out of which the Creator summoned light and life (Gen 1:3-5). We stand at a turning point. Is God, faced with the rejection and mockery of his Son, allowing creation to go into reverse, sliding back into chaos and destruction? Or are we here at the painful birth of a new age, a new creation?

After three hours of darkness, for the first time since his curt response to Pilate (15:2) we hear an utterance from Jesus: the terrible cry of dereliction: "My God, my God, why have you abandoned me?" (v. 34).[13] He has been rejected by his people, deserted by his companions; now he expresses a sense of abandonment by the God whose very will he is carrying out by hanging on the cross. Son of God though he is, he experiences at depth the terrible sense of divine absence that so often accompanies human suffering. The darkness without is matched by an intense darkness within. Jesus does not utter a cry of despair—he still is calling on God. But it is a cry of dereliction because no answer will come from God until he has shared to the full the lot of all human beings in death. The gospel has at this point brought us face to face with a mystery before which we can only stand dumb. The Father is letting the Son die, plumbing, it would seem, the depths of human alienation from God not because of personal sinfulness but because he bears the weight of all human sinfulness, having become a "ransom for many" (10:45; cf. 14:24). In the words of Paul, the Father has not spared the beloved Son but "given him up for us all" (Rom 8:32) or, in the most daring phrase of all: "(God) has made him who knew no sin into sin, so that in him we might become the righteousness of God" (2 Cor 5:21; cf. Rom 8:3-4; Gal 3:13; also Heb 5:7).

Jesus' cry, expressed by Mark in Aramaic followed by a Greek translation, prompts some of the bystanders to remark that he is calling upon Elijah (v. 35).[14] At this one of them runs up, soaks a sponge in sour wine and,

13. The plaintive question forms the opening of Psalm 22, a lament that concludes on a note of thanksgiving for rescue and restoration brought about by God (vv. 21b-31). Awareness of this conclusion should not, however, be allowed to soften or mask the sense of desolation and abandonment by God conveyed by the part of the text that Jesus does cry out with a loud voice: so, e.g., Nineham, *Saint Mark,* 428; Donahue and Harrington, *Mark,* 451–52; also, to some extent, Senior, *Passion of Jesus in Mark,* 123–24. Against this tendency see Hooker, *Saint Mark,* 375; Brown, *Death of the Messiah* 2:1044–51; Moloney, *Gospel of Mark,* 326–27; Boring, *Mark,* 430.

14. It is not altogether clear how the Aramaic invocation (transliterated as *Elōi*) could be heard as a calling to Elijah. Matthew (27:46), apparently perceiving this difficulty, puts the

placing it on a reed, gives Jesus a drink of the vinegary wine, exclaiming, "Do let us see whether Elijah will come to take him down" (v. 36).[15] Behind the action seems to lie a Jewish tradition of Elijah as the rescuer of those in extreme distress[16] or, more likely in the context of the mockery Jesus has endured, the expectation that Elijah would come before the advent of the Messiah (cf. 9:11). The offerer of the sponge attempts to prolong Jesus' life—and of course thereby his suffering—in order to give Elijah a chance to arrive in time to save him and thus validate his messianic claim. The stratagem reflects the misunderstanding about messianism that Jesus has been countering throughout the gospel. Elijah has already come in the shape of John the Baptist (9:12-13; cf. 1:2-4, 6), whose fate, following his preaching (6:17-29), has all too closely prefigured what is now happening to Jesus.

Whatever about Elijah, the moment of Jesus' death has arrived (v. 37). Uttering once again a loud cry—this time wordless—he expires.[17] Immediately the curtain of the Temple is rent in two from top to bottom (v. 38)[18] and the centurion, standing opposite Jesus and seeing how he died, makes his remarkable confession: "Truly, this man was the Son of God" (v. 39).[19]

---

opening invocation in Hebrew: *"Ēli . . . ,"* which makes the identification a little more understandable.

15. "Do let us see" is an attempt to translate the Greek phrase *aphete idōmen,* which might more naturally be rendered: "Wait, let us see . . ."; cf. Taylor, *St. Mark,* 595. Struck by the incongruity of the person who performs the action saying "Wait, . . . ," as if to hold it back, Matthew distinguishes the offerer of the sponge from others who cry "Wait" (Matt 27:48-49).

16. Cf. Hooker, *Saint Mark,* 376.

17. Literally "He expired [*exepneusen*]." Whether there is a suggestion in Mark of Jesus' giving out his "spirit" to the Father, as is more explicit in the other three gospels (Matt 27:50; Luke 23:46; John 19:30) is not clear; cf. Donahue and Harrington, *Mark,* 448.

18. One or other of two curtains in the Temple precinct could be meant: either the innermost curtain that screened the Holy of Holies from the Holy Place or the outer one dividing the Holy Place from the outer courts; for a discussion of the curtains in the Herodian Temple see Brown, *Death of the Messiah* 2:1109–13. The use of the term *naos* ("sanctuary"), which refers to an especially holy place, favors a reference to the inner curtain; cf. Carl Schneider, art. *"katapetasma"* in Gerhard Kittel and Gerhard Friedrich, eds., *Theological Dictionary of the New Testament.* 10 vols. (Grand Rapids: Eerdmans, 1964–76) 3:628–30; see p. 629; also Moloney, *Gospel of Mark,* 329.

19. The confession lacks the definite article "the" in the Greek, leaving open the possibility that the centurion was simply saying that the one who had just died the death of a criminal was in fact "a son of God" in the sense of an innocent or upright person (cf. Luke 23:47). In view of the significance of the "Son of God" title from the start of the gospel (1:1, 11; 9:7), there is widespread agreement among interpreters that at this climactic point in the gospel (the third of the "pillars" in terms of "Son of God") the phrase bears its full christological content; cf. the extensive discussion in Brown, *Death of the Messiah* 2:1146–52; Moloney,

What is striking here is the *order* of these events as told by Mark. If the centurion reacts to the way Jesus died,[20] why is this reaction not described immediately? Why is the detail about the Temple curtain (v. 38) interposed between the descriptions of the other two events (vv. 37 and 39)?[21]

First of all, we have to ask what it is about the manner of Jesus' death that prompts the centurion to react in the way he does. He responds to the fact that, in a manner totally unprecedented in a death by crucifixion, a loud cry preceded death. There is something awe-inspiringly different about this death by crucifixion.

But what is the narrative attempting to convey to the reader by the interposed information concerning the Temple curtain? The passive construction—"was rent"—indicates the action of God. The divine silence that has prevailed right up to and including the moment of Jesus' death is at last broken.[22] Moreover, the tearing apart *(eschisthē)* of the curtain at this moment of Jesus' death (15:38) corresponds to the tearing apart *(schizomenous)* of the heavens at the beginning of the story immediately following his baptism at the hands of John (1:10). In both cases, at the beginning and toward the end of the narrative, the rending signals a divine response to the obedient association of Jesus with sinful humankind: submission to baptism along with the repentant mass of Israelites who approached John at the Jordan; being crucified along with two bandits in fulfillment of the deeper "baptism" with which he "had to be baptized" (10:38d). In the first instance the rending of the heavens was followed by the Father's assurance, "You are my Son, the Beloved; with you I am well pleased" (1:11), an assurance repeated for the benefit of three privileged disciples at the transfiguration (9:7b). In the final instance of rending (15:38) there is no accompanying divine voice acknowledging Jesus as "beloved Son." In startling paradox the acknowledg-

---

Gospel of Mark, 330, n. 282; Donahue and Harrington, *Mark,* 449. For a very negative interpretation (the last hostile "triumphal gloat of Rome") see Myers, *Binding the Strong Man,* 384, 393–94.

20. This is made clear by the phrase "seeing that in this way he died (. . . *hoti houtôs exepneusen)* that catches up the *exepneusen* of v. 37. It was not the sight of the curtain being rent that prompted the centurion's reaction.

21. Matthew and Luke both seem to have sensed a narrative problem here and dealt with it each in his own way: Matthew postpones the indication of the curtain's tearing until after the centurion's reaction and then makes it the first of a series of apocalyptic events (earthquake; splitting of rocks; opening of tombs and appearances of the dead) that seem to presage the resurrection (27:51-53). Luke omits the Elijah reference entirely and goes in the opposite direction from Matthew, mentioning the rending of the curtain before the description of Jesus' death and his single loud cry (23:45-46).

22. Cf. Moloney, *Gospel of Mark,* 328.

ment comes from the opposite direction entirely: from the stained human lips of the centurion who has supervised the execution. In acknowledging the crucified One to be "in truth the Son of God," the Gentile centurion gives utterance to the foundational tenet of the Christian Gospel (Mark 1:1; cf. Rom 1:1-4; Gal 1:16; cf. John 20:31; 1 John 5:5, 10, 13). In making this act of faith he becomes the paradigmatic recipient of God's saving outreach to the nations of the world, among whom the readers of Mark's gospel are clearly to be numbered.

In this light the rending of the curtain has both negative and positive aspects.[23] Negatively it signals an end to the mode of atonement in force until now: the sacrificial system of the Jerusalem Temple. The rending of the curtain foreshadows the destruction of the Temple, which will occur, as Jesus has himself predicted (13:1-2), a generation later in 70 C.E. (in all likelihood an event of the recent past for Mark's original readers). But long before this physical destruction the expiatory system conducted in the Temple had been replaced and rendered void by God's action on Golgotha. In his earlier cleansing action in the Temple (11:15-17) Jesus justified what he was doing by appeal to Scripture: "My house shall be called a house of prayer for all the nations" (v. 17, citing Isa 56:7). Viewed retrospectively from Golgotha, that action gains full prophetic force: the rending of the Temple curtain signals, now in more positive vein, that Jesus' obedient death is bringing about a new "house of prayer for all the nations" (Gentiles). Ironically, as we have seen, the charges laid against him at his trial before the Council—the claim that he would destroy "this temple made with hands, and in three days build another not made with hands" (14:58)—contained a kernel of truth: his death has brought about a "house of faith" where believers of all nations have unrestricted access to the reconciling presence of God.[24] Those who, in the steps of the Roman centurion, respond in faith to the preaching of the Gospel and participate in the eucharistic rite instituted by Jesus on the night before he died bring themselves under the scope of a culminating Day of Atonement worked by God on Calvary.[25] Though Jesus'

---

23. Cf. Gnilka, *Markus* 2:323–24; Moloney, *Gospel of Mark,* 329, n. 279; Moloney makes this point against Brown's wholly negative interpretation of the rending—as a divine judgment on the Temple and those who administer it (cf. *Death of the Messiah* 2:1099–1106, 1113–18).

24. Cf. Harry L. Chronis, "The Torn Veil: Cultus and Christology in Mark 15:37-39," *Journal of Biblical Literature* 101 (1982) 97–114, especially 107–14.

25. Mark does not make explicit a reference to the Day of Atonement ritual. However, references to the curtain are so prominent in the prescriptions for the setting up of the Holy of Holies in Exodus 25–26 and in those for the Day of Atonement in Leviticus 16 as to make an allusion to the expiatory rite performed on that day virtually certain; see further Brendan

blood has been "sprinkled" once and for all, its saving effects linger on for those who consume the broken bread and drink the cup, which "is the blood of the covenant, poured out for many" (Mark 14:22-24).

The supreme paradox is that Golgotha, the horrible God-forsaken (15:34) place of execution, has been rendered, through the obedience of the Son, the locale of God's saving presence. After Jesus' obedient submission to baptism the "rending" of the heavens had signaled the breaking down of the barrier between the divine and human world (1:10). So now, following his obedience unto death (Phil 2:8), the rending of the Temple curtain signals the "break out" of the divine saving presence from the Jerusalem Temple to the world. Indeed, if God can be present in this way at Golgotha, then there is no corner of the globe so evil, so totally under the control of the demonic, as to be immune to the outreach of divine grace. Correspondingly, if the supervisor of Jesus' execution, one who had doubtless participated in and possibly led the Roman mockery (15:16-20), could have access to that grace, then there is no captivity to evil so great as to render impossible conversion and faith. In this perspective the "great cry" Jesus utters just before he dies, echoing the similar cry of the first demon he drove out (1:26), may signal the climactic exorcism of the world.[26] God's Rule may not yet be finally established on earth, but in his obedience unto death Jesus has dealt the opposing rule of Satan a decisive and ultimately fatal blow. As Paul would say: "Where sin abounded, grace has abounded all the more" (Rom 5:20b).

As I have maintained from the start, at this moment of Jesus' death, followed by the rending of the curtain and the centurion's act of faith, what I have called "Story 1" (that Jesus is Messiah and Son of God) finds resolution with "Story 2" (his destiny to suffer and die). Jesus does not suffer *despite* being God's Son but *as* the beloved Son sent on saving mission to the world. The "stories," however, are not complete. A remaining "Story 3" (Jesus' coming in glory as Son of Man to judge the world [13:24-27]) has yet to run its course. For Jesus personally it has already done so through his resurrection and exaltation to God's right hand. For the faithful it remains a matter of hope and expectation. When it is realized, all aspects of the costly divine action to liberate the world will come together in a final integration.

Byrne, "Paul and Mark before the Cross: Common Echoes of the Day of Atonement Ritual," in Rekha M. Chennattu and Mary L. Coloe, eds., *Transcending Boundaries: Contemporary Readings of the New Testament: Essays in Honor of Francis J. Moloney.* Bibliotheca di Scienze Religiose 187 (Roma: Libreria Ateneo Salesiano, 2005) 217–29; cf. also Hooker, *Saint Mark,* 378.

26. Cf. Brown, *Death of the Messiah* 2:1045, n. 37.

Women Disciples Witness the Burial of Jesus
by Joseph of Arimathea: 15:40-47

Jesus does not die totally bereft of human company. A group of women, three of whom are named—Mary Magdalene, Mary the mother of James the Little and Joses, and Salome[27]—are present. They, of course, are constrained to watch the proceedings "from afar" (v. 40) but at least, in contrast to the male disciples, they "watch with him" (cf. 14:37). At the beginning of the Passion (14:3-9) an unnamed woman performed for Jesus a "beautiful act" (14:6) showing that, again in contrast to the male disciples, she had understood Jesus' words about his imminent death and responded appropriately. Anointing his body beforehand for burial, she had "done what she could" (14:8a). Now, at the close of the Passion, these women do what *they* can: be present as silent witnesses to the "cost" of the "service" he is rendering "as a ransom for many" (10:45). Along with a number of other women they had followed him and served him in Galilee; now, having journeyed with him to Jerusalem, they complete that following and "service" by their faithful presence to his suffering.[28] All they can do is "watch from afar," but their witness is precious. The same three named women who witness Jesus' death and burial (v. 47) will also discover the emptiness of his tomb and be the recipients of its heavenly explanation (16:1-8). Their witness constitutes the vital principle of continuity across Jesus' death and burial and the discovery of his empty tomb.

The account of John the Baptist's lonely death at the hands of Herod (6:14-29) had concluded at least on a positive note with the information that his disciples had come and taken his body and laid it in a tomb (v. 29). Jesus, by contrast, is denied this posthumous care from his own. A stranger, Joseph of Arimathea, described as an influential member of the Sanhedrin and

---

27. This trio of named women disciples forms something of a faithful foil in the Passion/Resurrection story to the inner male trio—Peter, James, and John—now conspicuous by their absence; cf. Gnilka, *Markus* 2:326. Mary Magdalene is, of course, prominent in the Passion narratives of all four gospels. Though a James and a Joses occur among the list of Jesus' "brothers" given in Mark 6:3, this does not mean that the second Mary listed here as the mother of James the Little and Joses is the mother of Jesus, since, were she present (cf. John 19:25), she would hardly be identified other than by reference to him. Boring, however (*Mark,* 437–38), entertains the possibility that Mark may be obliquely indicating her presence as corrective to the unfavorable picture given in 3:31-35. James the Little may be the second James, "James the son of Alphaeus," listed among the Twelve in 3:18. Mark seems to presuppose that James and Joses, and also Salome, are known to his readers; cf. Taylor, *St. Mark,* 598.

28. Cf. Senior, *Passion of Jesus in Mark,* 131. We may recall here too the "service" performed by Peter's mother-in-law, when at the beginning of his ministry in Galilee he had "raised her up" from illness (1:29-31).

concerned lest, contrary to the Law, the body of Jesus remain unburied before the onset of the Sabbath, takes on himself the task of seeing to its burial.[29] He boldly approaches Pilate and requests the body of Jesus, an act requiring courage since it exposes him to the risk of being seen as sympathetic to the cause of one whom the Roman authorities had crucified as pretended "King of the Jews."[30] Pilate, who had already "wondered" *(thaumazein)* at Jesus' silence before his accusers (15:5), now "wonders" again (15:44) at the report that he is already dead. On having this confirmed (v. 45) by the centurion, Pilate grants the body of Jesus to Joseph. Having obtained the body, Joseph moves swiftly to complete his task (v. 46): he buys a linen sheet *(sindōn),*[31] removes the body from the cross, wraps it in the sheet, and lays it in a tomb he had hollowed out of rock—presumably with a view eventually to his own burial. Finally, he rolls a stone over the entrance of the tomb to seal it. Mary Magdalene and the other Mary take no part in the burial, but continue their watch from afar, observing where the body is laid (v. 47).[32]

Jesus, then, receives a hasty burial. His body is not washed or anointed in accordance with custom—that will have to wait till after the Sabbath (cf. 16:1). He is buried by a stranger—indeed, by a member of the very Council that had condemned him and handed him over to the Romans (14:64; 15:1). But Joseph is not just a stranger. He is described as "himself waiting expectantly for the kingdom of God" (v. 43), a description recalling Jesus' commendation of the scribe who questioned him about the first commandment of the Law (14:34).[33] As that scribe stood apart from the members of a group otherwise invariably portrayed as hostile, so Joseph stands apart from the rest of the Jewish Council. The Christian Gospel has preserved and treasured the memory of this courageous and observant Jew whose action sheds a ray of decency on the otherwise unrelieved cruelty that surrounded the events

29. Mark (15:42) tells us that it was already the time of "preparation" *(paraskeuē)* for the Sabbath, that is, the time for accomplishing tasks not permitted on the Sabbath; cf. Donahue and Harrington, *Mark,* 453. Joseph had to move fast in order to fulfill the legal prescription that bodies of criminals "hanged on a tree" should be buried on the day of execution lest a curse pollute the land (Deut 21:22-23); cf. Hooker, *Saint Mark,* 381.

30. Cf. Gnilka, *Markus* 2:333.

31. A *sindōn* was not a garment, but simply a large piece of linen cloth; cf. Donahue and Harrington, *Mark,* 455. To tie Jesus' corpse up in a *sindōn* was perhaps the absolute minimum one could do for the dead (cf. Brown, *Death of the Messiah* 2:1046), but this does not mean (contrary to Brown) that Jesus was given a dishonorable burial. Joseph is portrayed as doing "what he could" (cf. 14:8a) in the circumstances.

32. The two women in this sense serve the function of the two or more witnesses to an event required by the Law: Deut 19:15; cf. Gnilka, *Markus* 2:334.

33. Cf. Brown, *Death of the Messiah* 2:1215.

of the Passion. Matthew and John see him as a disciple (Matt 27:57; John 19:38)—perhaps recording in anticipation an eventual conversion on his part. Whatever the case may have been, "[i]n any assessment of Mark's attitudes towards Judaism the figure of Joseph of Arimathea needs to be taken into account."[34]

34. Donahue and Harrington, *Mark,* 456.

VII
EPILOGUE
16:1-8

The Empty Tomb ("He has been raised"):
16:1-8

The short passage describing the experience of the three women who visited the tomb of Jesus on the third day is the last section of the gospel written by the evangelist Mark. The summary of appearances of the risen Lord to Mary Magdalene and other disciples that appears in texts of Mark as 16:9-20 is very different in style. It is also missing in significant early manuscripts. It is universally judged to be a digest of the resurrection traditions of the remaining three gospels added early in the second century C.E. to address the problem created by ending the narrative at verse 8, an ending that leaves readers with no account of the disciples meeting with the risen Jesus as promised in verse 7, and that makes the gospel conclude simply with the report of the women's fearful flight from the tomb and their failure to report anything to anybody "because they were afraid" (v. 8).

Recognition of the secondary nature of verses 9-20 leaves us with a series of questions concerning the authentic Markan narrative 1:1–16:8. Mark either intended to conclude his narrative at 16:8 or he did not. If the latter is the case—and the absence of a narrative follow-up to the promise that the disciples would see Jesus in Galilee (v. 7) is admittedly puzzling—then we have to ask why the ending is missing. Did Mark die or become otherwise incapable of concluding his story beyond this point? Did the scroll he was using run out of space at 16:8? Was a final leaf of the gospel in codex form mutilated very early through usage or torn off and lost?

Answers to these questions can only be speculative at best. Most scholars today incline to the view that Mark did intend to end his story at this point; they then ponder the implications of this strange ending for the overall interpretation of the gospel. We cannot, of course, discover now what Mark's intention was. What we have is the text of the gospel concluding at verse 8. We have to work with this text and unlock its interpretive possibilities for our time.

The Women at the Tomb: 16:1-4

According to Mark's time scale, Jesus died on the day preceding the Sabbath, that is, a Friday (15:42); it was the beginning of the Sabbath on the Friday evening that impelled his hasty burial. Now (16:1), when the Sabbath rest is over, that is, on the Saturday evening, the same three women who had observed his death (Mary Magdalene, Mary the mother of James [and of Joses],[1] and Salome) buy spices in order to perform the anointing of Jesus' body they were unable to carry out before he was buried. It was customary to prepare bodies for burial by anointing them with aromatic spices to ward off the odor of death. To seek to achieve this effect thirty-six hours after death had occurred was pointless; after this lapse of time the gesture could only be a final act of loving devotion.[2] It also shows that these women, like the male disciples, had failed to grasp Jesus' repeated insistence that he would be put to death, yes, but that would not be where the story would end; after three days he would be raised (8:31; 9:31; 10:34).

Be that as it may, the women set out for the tomb very early the following day "as the sun was rising" (v. 2).[3] A pervasive darkness recalling the primeval darkness of creation (Gen 1:2) had attended the death of Jesus (15:33). Now the reference to the rising of the sun hints at a more-than-ordinary dawn ripe with promise of renewed creation. On the way (16:3) the women worry about how they will roll back the stone that has been placed over the entrance to the tomb (15:46). From a realistic point of view this is something they might well have thought of before setting out on their errand. As the story is told, however, the belated mention of the problem serves to heighten the drama of their discovery when they arrive (v. 4): looking up, they see that the stone, which was "very great," has been rolled

---

1. The second Mary in this trio receives three different designations: 15:40 ("mother of James the Little and Joses"), 15:47 ("mother [or possibly daughter] of Joses"), 16:1 ("mother [or possibly daughter] of James"). Salome does not feature in the account of the burial (15:47), but reappears in the visit to the tomb (16:1).

2. Cf. Hooker, *Saint Mark,* 383.

3. Scholars worry about Mark's double and somewhat conflictual time marker in v. 2: "very early" (that is, between 3 and 6 a.m.) and "as the sun was rising"; cf. Taylor, *St. Mark,* 604–5. Fascination with this minor problem leads to neglect of the highly evocative allusion to the rising of the sun.

away—the impersonal passive construction offering a first hint that a more-than-human force has been at work.[4]

The Young Man (Angel) and His Message: 16:5-7

The entrance laid open, the way is clear for the women to enter into the tomb (v. 5), into the realm of death. What they then see makes clear that in entering the tomb they are also entering into another world, a heavenly world signaled by the sight of a young man "sitting on the right side" (presumably on the shelf on which the body had lain) clad in a white garment. The young man's apparel identifies him as an angel, a bringer of messages from the divine to the human sphere;[5] his posture (seated) and position (on the right) signify authority.[6] Previously in Mark's narrative the barrier between the divine and human worlds had fallen away momentarily just after Jesus' baptism (1:10) and at his transfiguration (9:7). Where the first had involved a communication to Jesus alone (1:11), the second had been experienced also by the three chosen disciples and had left them utterly at a loss (9:6). Now, confronted by a similar manifestation of the heavenly where they had expected to find death, the women react with extreme alarm.[7] They are grappling on earth with a reality of a new world, a new creation breaking in—something that the otherwise sober narrative of Mark can only describe by having recourse here, for the first time, to the biblical symbolism of angels.[8]

As in similar epiphanies (manifestations of the divine) in Scripture, the heavenly figure first seeks to calm the women ("Do not be alarmed"). He then addresses their concern for the body of Jesus (v. 6): Jesus of Nazareth, the crucified One, whom they are seeking, has been raised. He is not here—see the emptiness of the place where "they" (Joseph of Arimathea) had laid him. In terms of strict logic the sequence of explanations might well have run: he is not here (because) he has been raised. But the existing order

4. Mark's characteristically delayed explanatory comment about the size of the stone underlines the sense that a mighty force has rolled it away. The use of the perfect passive tense *(kekylistai)* in the Greek conveys the sense of a rolling away, the triumphant effect of which lingers on forever.

5. Matthew explicitly identifies him as an angel (28:2); for similar descriptions of angels as young men cf. 2 Macc 3:26, 33.

6. Cf. Boring, *Mark,* 445.

7. The Greek expression *exethambēthēsan* expresses intense emotion (cf. also 9:15; 14:33 [Jesus' distress in the garden]); cf. Donahue and Harrington, *Mark,* 458.

8. Cf. Taylor: "Mark's description is imaginative; he picturesquely describes what he believes happened" (*St. Mark,* 607).

creates a powerful effect. Placing "He has been raised" immediately after "the crucified One" reinforces the sense that it is as the Son obedient unto death, even death on the cross (Phil 2:8), that Jesus has been raised by the Father;[9] even as risen Lord he will never cease to be the Crucified One, who in Paul's words "loved me and gave himself up for me" (Gal 2:20). And the closing indication of his "absence" in the tomb—specifically in the "place where they (= human agency) had laid him"—suggests a presence elsewhere: a divinely wrought presence as "Lord" at the right hand of the Father in fulfillment of the messianic promise to David (12:35-37; cf. 14:62). The tension between "Story 1" (that Jesus is Messiah and Son of God) and "Story 2" (that he has been "given up" to suffering and death) is finding resolution in this hint of "Story 3" (Jesus' vindication through resurrection and exaltation to the right hand of God).

Beyond this wonderful explanation of the emptiness of the tomb, the heavenly figure sends the women on mission (v. 7): they are to go and say to Jesus' disciples "and to Peter" that he is going before them to Galilee where they will see him, as he had told them. The last phrase recalls the reassurance Jesus had given the disciples en route to Gethsemane. In the face of their vigorous protestations he had foretold their imminent desertion and scattering, but had gone on to say that after his resurrection he would go before them to Galilee (14:34).[10] Their desertion was, then, something he had foreseen, something indeed foretold in Scripture (cf. 14:27, quoting Zech 13:7), and hence gathered up into the wider saving design of God. The instructions that the women are now to pass on to "his disciples" show that, despite their failure, they are still called to discipleship. When he had "gone before" them to Jerusalem they had hung back dismayed and fearful (10:34), a reluctance to follow that had culminated in their wholesale desertion (14:50). Though they have all in this sense "been ashamed" of him, he has not carried out his threat to be ashamed of them (cf. 8:38).[11] He is still "going before" them, this time to Galilee, and they are once again being summoned to "follow" him there to make a new start on discipleship back where it all

---

9. The Greek aorist passive *egerthē* could have the active sense "he has risen," but is more suitably translated here as a genuine passive referring to the action of the Father; cf. Hooker, *Saint Mark*, 385. The change to the aorist after the perfect passive ("the crucified") conveys the sense that the resurrection has just occurred; cf. Taylor, *St. Mark*, 607.

10. Strictly speaking, Jesus' assurance in 14:34 had not mentioned seeing him—though this is perhaps implied. The phrase "as he told you" has to be understood, then, in a loose sense; cf. Taylor, *St. Mark*, 608.

11. Cf. Hooker, *Saint Mark*, 385.

began.[12] This will inaugurate the second and final stage of the overcoming of their "blindness" on the pattern of the two-stage enlightenment of the blind man Jesus had cured at Bethsaida (8:22-26).

Peter, as so often in the narrative, is singled out ("and to Peter"). The addition suggests that the women are meant to take him aside and pass on the message personally and privately. He who had stood apart from the remaining disciples in following a little longer "from afar" (14:54) and who had ended up denying all association with Jesus (14:66-72) now receives assurance of forgiveness and reinstatement.[13] Peter, the first named and first called disciple (1:16) retains that primacy in the new phase of discipleship that Jesus' resurrection is opening up for the community of the Kingdom.[14]

The Women's Reaction: 16:8

The final verse of Mark's gospel (16:8) is also perhaps the most puzzling in the entire narrative—even apart from the additional problem created by its forming the conclusion of the narrative as we now have it. The verse speaks of the women's flight from the tomb, overcome by "trembling and astonishment," and of their failure to communicate the message they had been given "because they were afraid." Trembling and astonishment represent a standard response to manifestations of the divine in biblical literature. This continuing reaction on the part of the women, despite the heavenly figure's reassurance (v. 6b), simply testifies to the overwhelming nature of what they had experienced: expecting to enter the realm of death, they had entered into and been told of the reality of the new creation. Their total inability to cope with the experience attests to the reader that here the narrative is entering and describing an exercise of divine power beyond the capacity of unaided human experience to grasp or even imagine (cf. 10:27; 11:22-24).

The "fear" *(ephobounto gar)* that prevented the women from saying anything to anyone may be of a slightly different order. Are we to understand that they failed to report what they had experienced simply because they remained paralyzed by fear? Or were they afraid of being disbelieved by the male disciples and regarded as "foolish women" (cf. Luke 24:10-11)? Were they afraid that the male disciples, in their guilt at having deserted Jesus,

---

12. Cf. ibid., 386.

13. Cf. Taylor: ". . . there can be little doubt that the denial is in mind" (*St. Mark*, 607).

14. The final reference to Peter (16:7) thus forms an overarching narrative "inclusion" with the call of the first disciples at the beginning (1:16). For Hengel, *Der unterschätze Petrus*, 67, it represents a kind of closing Petrine "signature" on the Markan gospel.

would react incredulously and negatively to the idea that women should be the chosen communicators of the divine turnaround and their own restoration? The Markan narrative simply leaves all these questions open. The account of the women at the tomb records the tradition concerning the emptiness of Jesus' tomb—a necessary, though by no means a sufficient cause for belief in his resurrection.[15] To arrive at that belief required "seeing" him, as the disciples were promised they would in Galilee (v. 7; cf. 14:34). The record of the women's failure to report may be intended to safeguard this complex of facts surrounding faith in the resurrection: the tomb was empty but the women, initially at least, failed to inform the disciples of that or of the heavenly figure's message. If the disciples came to believe in the resurrection, as indeed they eventually did, it was not on the basis of that emptiness or of the women's testimony. They came to believe because, as had been foretold (16:7), they saw the Lord (cf. 1 Cor 15:3-5).

The abiding mystery remains the failure of the Markan narrative to offer an account of that "seeing" of Jesus in Galilee that led the disciples to belief in the resurrection. If we take the gospel as it presently stands (that is, as concluding in 16:8), we may suppose that in the context of great suffering in his community and failure in discipleship Mark may have chosen to focus his audience's attention simply on Jesus' suffering and death, the stark reality unrelieved by any "backward glow" from his risen glory. The community was being called to live the "sorrowful" rather than the "glorious mysteries," the time when the Bridegroom had been "taken away" (2:20)— and they had, in all likelihood, been taken unawares and unprepared for the heroism required. They could identify in many ways with the disciples who found following Jesus to Jerusalem so challenging, and who had deserted him in the fateful hour. They could draw comfort from the indication that that failure was not the end of the story but simply part of the story, that there could be forgiveness, restoration, and the beginning of a new discipleship based on a more realistic sense of the cost of association with Jesus. Though the Son, who at the high point of his obedience cried out in a sense of abandonment, has been raised to sit at God's right hand, that exaltation remains the pledge of a victory over the rule of Satan still to run its course. Discipleship, for them, will mean taking up their cross and following after him, not now in the blindness that frustrated their acceptance of "Story 2" but in the hope stemming from awareness that "Story 3" is under way and will find completion when Jesus comes in glory to fully bring about the Kingdom (13:24-27).

15. Cf. Donahue and Harrington, *Mark*, 459.

We may think, as the three later evangelists certainly did, that a message intended to strengthen a persecuted church could better be served by concluding the narrative with scenes describing the "seeing" of the risen Lord promised in the angelic message. Be that as it may, Mark's gospel leaves such a "sight" of Jesus as a matter of promise, in the context of discipleship renewed. Firm in resurrection faith (not vision), the readers are urged to go to Galilee, to begin again the journey of discipleship. The mysterious, open-ended closure of the narrative thus lends a kind of "circular" structure to the gospel's grasp of the reader: having struggled with the failing disciples to the "end," readers must go with them back to Galilee, to set out again—and again—on the "way of the Lord" (1:2-3) with him.[16]

In this sense Mark leaves us with an unfinished story, the real end of which will only come with the advent of the Son of Man (13:24-27). The gospel addresses the present time of the church as it proclaims "Christ has died, Christ has risen," and then locates itself in the "in-between" time by adding "Christ will come again." Perhaps the odd ending of the gospel, the breaking off in midsentence, so to speak, is an invitation to allow our own lives to be written into the ongoing story—so that we too can be not only beneficiaries but also servants of God's costly outreach to the world.[17]

16. See the "Circular Reading of Mark" chart set out on p. 21 above.

17. Cf. Boring: ". . . with terrible restraint, the narrator breaks off the story and leaves the readers, who may have thought the story was about somebody else, with a decision to make . . ." (*Mark,* 449).

Appendix:
Appearances of the Risen Lord: 16:9-20

The second-century appendix to Mark's gospel appearing as 16:9-20 consists of an account of appearances of the risen Lord to Mary Magdalene (vv. 9-11), to two disciples journeying to the country (vv. 12-13), and to the Eleven as they reclined at table (vv. 14-18). It concludes with a statement of the Lord's ascension to God's right hand (v. 19) and an indication of the successful proclamation of the word throughout the world (v. 20). All in all it offers a rather colorless digest of several traditions appearing in the resurrection stories of the other three gospels. The description of Jesus' appearance to Mary Magdalene (vv. 9-11) stands closest to the account in John 20:1-18, though the information that she was the one out of whom he had driven seven devils echoes Luke 8:2.[1] The appearance "in another form"[2] to the two disciples going to the country is, of course "a distant echo"[3] of Luke's story of Jesus' appearance to the two disciples on the way to Emmaus (24:13-35).[4] The appearance to the Eleven as they reclined at table (vv. 14-18), along with Jesus' upbraiding them for their disbelief, recalls the similar traditions in Luke 24:36-43 and John 20:19-29, while the mission Jesus gives them (vv. 15-16) echoes the missioning of the disciples at the conclusion of Matthew (28:18-20).

1. The information that she went and told the disciples about the appearance of the Lord (v. 10) stands in contrast, of course, to Mark's strong insistence on the silence of the women, including Mary Magdalene (16:8).

2. This may refer to the fact that, according to Luke 24:16, their "eyes were held from recognizing" Jesus.

3. Taylor, *St. Mark,* 611.

4. It differs from that story in its insistence that the remaining disciples disbelieved their report: contrast Luke 24:33-35.

The account has a certain coherence and rises to an impressive climax. Its bald summaries lack the warmth and drama attending the resurrection stories in the remaining gospels, and Jesus' "upbraiding" the Eleven for their refusal to give credence to the first two reports (v. 14) lends a severe pedagogical tone to the whole, going well beyond the gentle remonstrations in Luke (24:25, 38-39). The command to go and preach the Gospel throughout the world to every creature does catch up the sense of universal mission foreshadowed in Mark's gospel by the rending of the Temple curtain and the centurion's confession of faith (15:39).

For most readers today the most distinctive features of the entire appendix will likely consist in the list of the "signs" that will "accompany"[5] believing response to the preaching. The opening reference to the expulsion of demons comes as no surprise in a Markan context, while speaking in tongues and healing of the sick through the laying on of hands are familiar across the New Testament traditions. More striking, however, and unparalleled are the references to handling snakes and drinking poisonous drafts without harm.[6]

Finally, as in the two Lukan accounts (Luke 24:50-53; Acts 1:9-11), Jesus at the close of his commissioning words ascends into heaven. The Appendix goes beyond the Lukan descriptions, however, in making explicit his messianic enthronement at the right hand of God, in fulfillment of Psalm 110:1 (cf. Mark 12:35-37 and 14:62)—a heavenly triumph that is having its effect on earth through the worldwide and successful proclamation of the word.

The Appendix, then, exists in some tension both with the resurrection traditions it summarizes and the Gospel of Mark it purports to supplement.[7] It has, however, its own integrity and concludes on this majestic vision of the Gospel sweeping throughout the world as an expression of the messianic triumph of the once-crucified, now risen Lord.

---

5. As in the gospel tradition generally, the "signs" accompany belief; they do not cause it but presuppose it.

6. Paul, of course, shakes off a snake that had attached itself to him soon after the shipwreck on the island of Malta (Acts 28:3-6).

7. It is a curious irony that the Lectionary of the Roman liturgy should feature this Appendix as the Gospel for the feast of St. Mark the Evangelist on April 25.

Concluding Reflection

At the start of this long journey with Mark I invited readers to enter into the worldview presupposed by the gospel. The risk is that interpreters and readers who make that entry will fail to emerge with any sense of its connection to our world today. Recent decades have seen several creative attempts to draw the connection between Mark and present reality fairly tightly.[1] Such interpretations, while stimulating and challenging for their time, inevitably date rather rapidly as sociopolitical conditions change and new challenges arise. As John P. Meier has wryly observed, ". . . nothing ages quicker [*sic*] than relevance."[2] That observation is a salutary warning against attempts to understand Mark and his world too readily in terms of our needs and issues today. Nonetheless, as I observed at the start, I think the apocalyptic perspective, in particular the conflict with the demonic, is so pervasive in Mark that unless we make some effort to relate that perspective to our world we shall not really come to terms with the gospel at any great depth.

My suggestion at the start was that the demonic is essentially about control: the control of human life by forces, frequently transpersonal and socioeconomic, that stunt human growth and freedom, alienating individuals from each other and from their own true humanity. The narrative of Mark unfolds in a series of scenes showing Jesus liberating people from such demonic control in the name of the coming Rule of God, which he proclaimed. In the course of the commentary I have not made too many suggestions about how the instances of the demonic control Jesus confronts

---

1. Notably Fernando Belo, *A Materialist Reading of the Gospel of Mark* (Maryknoll, NY: Orbis, 1981) and Ched Myers, *Binding the Strong Man: A Political Reading of Mark's Story of Jesus* (Maryknoll, NY: Orbis, 1988).
2. *A Marginal Jew* 2:677.

might be translated into corresponding conditions today. I have left it to readers to pose that question for themselves: to ask where in their personal, communal, and social living they feel "controlled" in this radical way.

As readers will also be aware, I have pointed out how, as the narrative proceeds, Jesus' conflict with the demonic is played out less and less in scenes of overt exorcism and more and more in the human heart: first in the "hardness of heart" displayed by the authorities whose hold over the people his mission is challenging; then, and particularly in the latter half of the gospel, in a similar "hardness" in the hearts of his disciples; they show themselves to be "blind" to the true direction of his messianic mission and seek to deflect him from it, earning in the person of Peter the severe rebuke "Get behind me, Satan" (8:33). All comes to a climax in the scene at Gethsemane (14:32-42) when the three closest disciples lapse into a dismayed sleep, leaving Jesus, bereft of human company, to confront the ultimate conflict with the demonic that lies before him.

Mark's gospel does not explain, as later Christian soteriology sought to do, how Jesus' "obedience unto death" in that conflict brought about the "ransom of many" (10:45), the fundamental act of human liberation. As I have attempted to show, however, in the three "pillar" moments when the veil between heaven and earth for a brief space falls away (Baptism; Transfiguration; Calvary) it makes clear the totality of the divine involvement in the costly liberating mission of the Son. The heart of its *theo*logy, in the strict sense, is a revelation of the God who reaches into the deepest recesses of human darkness to draw human beings to repentance and fullness of life.

The "favor" of the Father (1:11) and the power of the Spirit (1:10, 12) thus accompany the mission of Jesus from start to finish. But along with this "divine company," so to speak, there is also from beginning to end the human company he calls and seeks to make into "fishers of people" for the Kingdom (1:16-20). While I do not see the disciples as the primary focus of Mark's gospel, it is clear that their difficulties along the way and their failure at the end constitute a leading theme and a point of entry into the story for readers both ancient and new. The disciples who responded so enthusiastically to sharing the messianic mission of Jesus as they originally understood it (Story 1) start to hold back and display "blindness" when he begins to make known the cost of that mission—to himself and also to those called to be his followers along the way (Story 2). We who, like them, so often do badly when the cost emerges can take some comfort from the pledge of Jesus, at the high point of their failure (14:26-31), to go before them to Galilee where they can make a fresh start at following him along that "way."

Unlike its three fellows, Mark's gospel does not give us a glimpse of the risen Lord. It leaves that and the final vindication of those who have lost their lives for the sake of Jesus and the Gospel (8:35) as a matter of promise and final hope (Story 3). By sending us with the disciples "back to Galilee" (16:7) it invites us to go around the narrative again and again (circular reading) until the interplay of Mark's three "stories" becomes ever more deeply woven into the pattern of our lives.

Bibliography

Commentaries on Mark's Gospel

Belo, Fernando. *A Materialist Reading of the Gospel of Mark*. Maryknoll, NY: Orbis, 1981.

Boring, M. Eugene. *Mark: A Commentary*. NTL. Louisville and London: Westminster John Knox, 2006.

Donahue, John R., and Daniel J. Harrington. *The Gospel of Mark*. SP 2. Collegeville, MN: Liturgical Press, 2002.

Gnilka, Joachim. *Das Evangelium nach Markus*. 2 vols. *Vol 1: Mk 1:1–8:26; Vol 2: Mk 8:27–16:20*. Zürich: Benziger; Neukirchen-Vluyn: Neukirchener Verlag, 1978, 1979.

Guelich, Robert A. *Mark 1–8:26*. WBC 34A. Waco, TX: Word Books, 1989.

Hooker, Morna. *The Gospel according to Saint Mark*. London: Black, 1991.

Marcus, Joel. *Mark 1–8: A New Translation with Introduction and Commentary*. AB 27. New York: Doubleday, 2000.

Moloney, Francis J. *The Gospel of Mark: A Commentary*. Peabody, MA: Hendrickson, 2002.

Myers, Ched. *Binding the Strong Man: A Political Reading of Mark's Story of Jesus*. Maryknoll, NY: Orbis, 1988.

Nineham, Dennis E. *The Gospel of Saint Mark*. Harmondsworth: Pelican, 1963.

Perkins, Pheme. "The Gospel of Mark," in Leander E. Keck et al., eds., *The New Interpreter's Bible*. 12 vols. Nashville: Abingdon, (1994–2004) 8 (1995): 507–733.

Schweizer, Eduard. *The Good News According to Mark: A Commentary on the Gospel*. London: SPCK, 1970.

Swete, Henry B. *The Gospel According to St. Mark*. 3rd ed. London: Macmillan, 1913.

Taylor, Vincent. *The Gospel According to St. Mark: The Greek Text, with Introduction, Notes and Indexes*. London: Macmillan, 1957.

Studies on Mark

Byrne, Brendan. "Paul and Mark before the Cross: Common Echoes of the Day of Atonement Ritual," in Rekha M. Chennattu and Mary L. Coloe, eds., *Transcending Boundaries: Contemporary Readings of the New Testament: Essays in Honor of Francis J. Moloney.* Bibliotheca di Scienze Religiose 187. Rome: Libreria Ateneo Salesiano, 2005, 217–29.

Chronis, Harry L. "The Torn Veil: Cultus and Christology in Mark 15:37-39," *Journal of Biblical Literature* 101 (1982) 97–114.

Dewey, Joanna. "The Literary Structure of the Controversy Stories in Mark 2:1–3:6," in William R. Telford, ed., *The Interpretation of Mark.* Philadelphia: Fortress Press, 1985, 109–18.

―――. *Markan Public Debate: Literary Technique, Concentric Structure, and Theology in Mark 2:1–3:6.* SBLDS 48. Chico, CA: Scholars Press, 1980.

Dowd, Sharyn, and Elizabeth Struthers Malbon. "The Significance of Jesus' Death in Mark: Narrative Context and Authorial Audience," *Journal of Biblical Literature* 125 (2006) 271–97.

Dyer, Keith D. *The Prophecy on the Mount: Mark 13 and the Gathering of the New Community.* Bern, etc.: Peter Lang, 1998.

Heil, John P. "Jesus with the Wild Animals in Mark 1:13," *Catholic Biblical Quarterly* 68 (2006) 63–78.

Incigneri, Brian J. *The Gospel to the Romans: The Setting and Rhetoric of Mark's Gospel.* Biblical Interpretation 65. Leiden: Brill, 2003.

Loader, William. "Good News—for the Earth? Reflections on Mark 1:1-15," in Norman C. Habel and Vicky Balabanski, eds., *The Earth Story in the New Testament.* Earth Bible 5. London: Sheffield Academic Press; Cleveland, OH: Pilgrim Press, 2002, 28–43.

McVann, Mark. "Destroying Death: Jesus in Mark and Joseph in 'The Sin Eater,'" in Robert Detweiler and William G. Doty, eds., *The Daemonic Imagination: Biblical Text and Secular Story.* AARSR 60. Atlanta: Scholars Press, 1990, 123–35.

Senior, Donald M. *The Passion of Jesus in the Gospel of Mark.* Collegeville, MN: Liturgical Press, 1984.

Trainor, Michael J. *The Quest for Home: the Household in Mark's Community.* Collegeville, MN: Liturgical Press, 2001.

Wainwright, Elaine M. "The Pouring Out of Healing Ointment: Rereading Mark 14:3-9," in Fernando Segovia, ed., *Towards a New Heaven and a New Earth: Essays in Honor of Elisabeth Schüssler Fiorenza.* Maryknoll, NY: Orbis, 2003, 157–78.

Watts, Rikki E. *Isaiah's New Exodus in Mark.* Grand Rapids: Baker Academic, 1997.

Wright, G. Addison. "The Widow's Mites: Praise or Lament?—A Matter of Context," *Catholic Biblical Quarterly* 44 (1982) 256–65.

Other Literature

Brown, Raymond E. *The Death of the Messiah: From Gethsemane to the Grave: A Commentary on the Passion Narratives in the Four Gospels.* 2 vols. New York: Doubleday, 1994.

———. *An Introduction to the New Testament.* New York: Doubleday, 1997.

———. *The Semitic Background of the Term "Mystery" in the New Testament.* FBBS 21. Philadelphia: Fortress Press, 1968.

Byrne, Brendan. "Eschatologies of Resurrection and Destruction: the Ethical Significance of Paul's Dispute with the Corinthians," *Downside Review* 104/357 (October 1986) 288–98.

———. *The Hospitality of God: A Reading of Luke's Gospel.* Collegeville, MN: Liturgical Press, 2000.

———. "Jesus as Messiah in the Gospel of Luke: Discerning a Pattern of Correction," *Catholic Biblical Quarterly* 65 (2003) 80–95.

———. *Lazarus: A Contemporary Reading of John 11:1-46.* Zacchaeus Studies. Collegeville, MN: Liturgical Press, 1991.

———. *Lifting the Burden: Reading Matthew's Gospel in the Church Today.* Collegeville, MN: Liturgical Press, 2004.

———. *Romans.* SP 6. Collegeville, MN: Liturgical Press, 1996.

———. *"Sons of God"—"Seed of Abraham."* AnBib 83. Rome: Biblical Institute Press, 1979.

Charlesworth, James. H., ed. *The Old Testament Pseudepigrapha.* 2 vols. Garden City, NY: Doubleday, 1985.

Dodd, C. H. *The Parables of the Kingdom.* Rev ed. London: Fontana, 1961.

Donahue John R. *The Gospel in Parable: Metaphor, Narrative, and Theology in the Synoptic Gospels.* Philadelphia: Fortress Press, 1988.

García Martinez, Florentino. *The Dead Sea Scrolls Translated: The Qumran Texts in English.* Leiden: Brill, 1994.

Gathercole, Simon J. *The Preexistent Son: Recovering the Christologies of Matthew, Mark, and Luke.* Grand Rapids and London: Eerdmans, 2006.

Hengel, Martin. *Der unterschätze Petrus: Zwei Studien.* Tübingen: Mohr Siebeck, 2006.

Jeremias, Joachim. *The Parables of Jesus.* 3rd ed. London: SCM, 1972.

Kelly, Anthony. *Eschatology and Hope.* Maryknoll, NY: Orbis, 2006.

Lee. Dorothy. *Transfiguration.* New Century Theology. London and New York: Continuum, 2004.

Meier, John P. "Jesus," in Raymond E. Brown, Joseph A. Fitzmyer, and Roland E. Murphy, eds., *New Jerome Biblical Commentary.* Englewood Cliffs, NJ: Prentice Hall, 1990, 78, pp. 1316–28.

———. *A Marginal Jew: Rethinking the Historical Jesus.* 3 vols. to date. Vol. 1: *The Roots of the Problem and the Person.* Vol. 2: *Mentor, Message and Miracles.* Vol. 3: *Companions and Competitors.* New York: Doubleday, 1991, 1994, 2001.

Perrin, Norman. *Jesus and the Language of the Kingdom: Symbol and Metaphor in New Testament Interpretation.* Philadelphia: Fortress Press, 1976.

Schneider, Carl. Art. *"katapetasma,"* in Gerhard Kittel and Gerhard Friedrich, eds., *Theological Dictionary of the New Testament.* 10 vols. Grand Rapids: Eerdmans, 1964–76, 3:628–30.

Throckmorton, Burton H. *Gospel Parallels: A Comparison of the Synoptic Gospels.* 5th ed. Nashville: Nelson, 1992.

Trible, Phyllis. *Texts of Terror: Literary-Feminist Readings of Biblical Narratives.* Philadelphia: Fortress Press, 1984.

Tuckett, Christopher M. "Introduction to the Gospels," in James D. G. Dunn and John W. Rogerson, eds., *Eerdmans Commentary on the Bible.* Grand Rapids and Cambridge: Eerdmans, 2003, 989–99.

Vacek, Edward V. "The Eclipse of Love for God," *America* 174/8 (March 1996) 13–16; reprinted in Paul Jersild et al., eds., *Moral Issues and Christian Response.* 7th ed. New York: Harcourt Brace College Publications, 2002, 6–10.

Wainwright, Elaine M. *Women Healing/Healing Women: The Genderization of Healing in Early Christianity.* London, UK and Oakville, CT: Equinox, 2006.

Wright, David P., and Richard N. Jones. Art. "Leprosy," in David Noel Freedman et al., eds., *Anchor Bible Dictionary.* 6 vols. New York: Doubleday, 1992, 4:277–82.

Scripture Index

Modern Author Index

Subject Index

Note: **Bold** type indicates principal areas of definition and discussion